Prabodhacandrodaya of Kṛṣṇa Miśra

PRABODHACANDRODAYA
of Kṛṣṇa Miśra

(Sanskrit Text with English Translation, a Critical Introduction and Index)

DR. SITA K. NAMBIAR

MOTILAL BANARSIDASS PUBLISHERS
PRIVATE LIMITED • DELHI

Reprint : Delhi, 2012
Second Edition : Delhi, 1998
First Edition : Bombay 1936

ISBN: 978-81-208-1518-6

MOTILAL BANARSIDASS
41 U.A. Bungalow Road, Jawahar Nagar, Delhi 110 007
8 Mahalaxmi Chamber, 22 Bhulabhai Desai Road, Mumbai 400 026
203 Royapettah High Road, Mylapore, Chennai 600 004
236, 9th Main III Block, Jayanagar, Bangalore 560 011
Sanas Plaza, 1302 Baji Rao Road, Pune 411 002
8 Camac Street, Kolkata 700 017
Ashok Rajpath, Patna 800 004
Chowk, Varanasi 221 001

Printed in India

By Jainendra Prakash Jain at Shri Jainendra Press,
A-44 Naraina, Phase-I, New Delhi 110 028
and published by Narendra Prakash Jain for
Motilal Banarsidass Publishers Private Limited,
Bungalow Road, Delhi 110 007

PREFACE

When I was working for my thesis '*Prabodhacandrodaya-A Philosophical and Theological Analysis* under Prof. Paul Hacker at the university of Bonn, the only English translation of the drama available was that of J. Taylor published in 1898. I found this translation rather inadequate and began to toy with the idea of bringing out another translation. The idea could not materialize until sometime later when I returned home and tried to get my thesis published.

While in Delhi I approached Messrs Motilal Banarsidass, the Veteran publishers of Oriental Studies. Shri Sunder Lal Jain, the leading proprietor of the firm, agreed to publish the work but suggested that I should render the play into English and prefix my thesis as introduction to the text and translation. I welcomed the suggestion, undertook and completed the task within the shortest time possible.

The translation is based on the fairly reliable Sanskrit text published by Panduranga Javaji, Nirnayasagar Press, Bombay, 1935. But at certain places the text is defective and as a result it defies attempts for the correct translation. But such occasions are few and far between. In general I have kept close to the original and tried to preserve the spirit of the text without violating the English expression.

This stupendous task could not have been completed without the inspiring cooperation of Shri Sundarlal Jain. He, therefore, deserves my hearty thanks. I am also beholden to my friend and colleague Dr. (miss) Sheila Uttam Singh for her valuable suggestions. I owe special thanks to my young friend and colleague Mrs. Ranga Kapoor for going through the manuscript. I am specially grateful to Pandit Jagdishlal Shastri for correcting the proofs so thoroughly.

Finally I avail of this opportunity to state that I shall welcome any critical suggestion and advice for improvement and be glad to utilize the same in the next edition of this work.

Indraprastha College
Delhi
1.4.1971

Sita Krishna Nambiar

PUBLISHER'S NOTE TO SECOND EDITION

Prabodhacandrodaya is an important allegorical play. The first edition appeared as early as 1971 and the work then remained out of print for a number of years.

Now in view of a persistent demand by interested readers we are happy to issue a second edition with most of the printing errors detected in the first edition carefully corrected in the text.

CONTENTS

CHAPTER I

GENERAL

1. *The author and his play*

In the 19th century Kṛṣṇamiśra's Prabodhacandrodaya was widely read by European Indologists and as a result the work was translated into several European languages[1]. At least one scholar[2] to my knowledge has written a study on it, investigating it as a drama. But the philosophical contents of this play have not yet been specially treated. I am undertaking this work with the hope that it may contribute to tracing the history of the development of Indian philosophy.

This play can be dated with some precision from the author's references in the Prologue. It was produced at the instruction of one Gopāla in the presence of his friend Kīrtivarman, whom Gopāla had restored to his kingdom after defeating the Cedi king Karṇa[3]. Now the Deogarh inscription of the same Kīrtivarman of Jejakabhukti is dated 1098 A.D. According to the Mahoba inscription Kīrtivarman defeated Lakṣmīkarṇa, i.e. the Cedi king Karṇa of Tripuri, who is mentioned in an inscription dated 1042 A.D. In the Vikramāṅkadevacarita 1819[3] Karṇa is called Kālaḥ Kālāñjaragiripateḥ, "The Death of the (Candella) king of Kalāñjara", which corresponds to Kṛṣṇamiśra's statement[4]. Gopāla might have been an ally through whose valour Kīrtivarman defeated Karṇa, but the commentator Maheśvara says that he was the Commander-in-Chief (*senāpati*) of Kīrtivarman and was a Brāhmaṇa Most probably the play was written between 1042 and 1098[5], and it can be concluded that the author belonged to the second half of the 11th century, perhaps even to the beginning of the

1. Cp. Winternitz, *Geschichte der Indischen Litteratur*, Vol. 3 p. 252 n. 1
2. Boissevain. Cp. the Bibliography.
3. Cp. Hultzsch and Kielhorn, in: *Epigraphia Indica* I, pp. 217 ff., 325; V. A. Smith, in: *Indian Antiquary* XXXVII, 1908, p. 143.
4. Cp. Konow, *Drama*, p. 92, 103.
5. Levi, *Theatre*, p.232 ff.

12th century. According to a tradition[1], Kṛṣṇamiśra was an ascetic belonging to the Haṁsa order of the Advaita school and had many disciples. One of them was interested in *kāvya* but not in philosophy. Kṛṣṇamiśra is said to have written his drama in order to teach him the Advaita doctrine.

Prabodhacandrodaya is an allegorical drama. Kṛṣṇamiśra was not the first Indian poet to write an allegorical play, though not much is known about the earlier literature of this class. There are the fragments of a Buddhist allegory with Kīrti (Fame), Dhṛti (Firmness) and Buddhi (Wisdom) as characters, which was perhaps written by Aśvaghoṣa[2]. Then, there is an allegorical play called Āgamaḍambara, still in manuscript, written by Jayanta, the author of the Nyāyamañjarī, who lived in the 9th century A.D. After Kṛṣṇamiśra, however, quite a number of allegorical plays were composed[3].

The name *Prabodhacandrodaya* has been translated variously by various scholars. J. Taylor translated it as "Rise of the Moon of Intellect", Winternitz as "Erkenntnismondaufgang[4]", Macdonell as "Rise of the Moon of Knowledge[5]", S. K. De as "The Moonrise of True Knowledge[6]", and Dr. Boissevain as "Maansopgang der Ontwaking"[7]. The word *prabodha* requires some discussion. Taylor's translation of it as *intellect* is not satisfactory. Winternitz' and Macdonell's translation as *Erkenntnis* and *knowledge* is certainly nearer to the correct meaning. However, if we accept it, we have to render *vidyā* by some other term, but *vidyā* is properly knowledge. Boissevain's translation as "Ontwaking", i.e. Awakening, which is literal, seems to be the best rendering of the Sanskrit word. The awakening treated in the play is a sort of spiritual realization. Puruṣa (Man), who had forgotten his identity with the Supreme Being, Parameśvara, and had fallen as it were, into a deep slumber, is awakened by Vidyā or Knowledge to realize his identity.

1. Krishnamacharya-History p. 676.
2. See Winternitz, *Geschichte*, Vol. III, p. 181 f.
3. See Dasgupta, *History of Sanskrit Literature*, p. 480 ff.; Winternitz, *Geschichte*, Vol. III, p. 256 ff.
4. Winternitz, *Geschichte*, *Vol.* III, p. 252.
5. Macdonell, *History*, p. 366.
6. Dasgupta, *History*, p. 481.
7. Boissevain, *Prabodhacandrodaya*.

As for the question how the compound *prabodhacandrodaya* has to be split, there are two possibilities :

1. *prabodha eva candraḥ prabodhacandraḥ, tasya udayaḥ,* or
2. *candrasya udayaḥ candrodayaḥ, prabodha eva candrodayaḥ, prabodhacandrodayaḥ.*

In the first case, awakening is identified with the moon and in the second case with the moon-rise. Taylor and Macdonell follow the first, while De and Boissevain follow the second. Winternitz' translation is quite as ambiguous as the original. It can mean either *Erkenntnismond-Aufgang* or *Erkenntnis-Mond-aufgang*. What Kṛṣṇamiśra means, however, is clearly *prabodhacandrasya udayaḥ*, "the rise of the moon which is awakening". This can be proved by a passage of the play itself. In the first act[1] the compound *prabodhacandra* is used by Kāma: *Prabodhacandreṇa bhrātrā*......Therefore, I would translate *Prabodhacandrodaya* as "The Rise of the Moon of (spiritual) Awakening".

There are several editions of the play, which I have listed in the Bibliography. Though the text of the Nirṇayasāgar edition is not always the best, I have used this edition throughout and given references according to it. Where its readings seemed unacceptable, I have in a few places preferred those of the Trivandrum edition. The commentaries which accompany the text in the Nirṇayasāgar edition, *Candrikā* and *Prakāśa*, I found useful in several places. The commentary of the Trivandrum edition, *Nāṭakābharaṇa*, has also been consulted.

Before analysing the philosophical contents of the drama, I will first give a brief survey of the plot. In the analysis of the philosophical contents, a compromise seemed advisable between a systematic arrangement, necessary for a clear presentation of the doctrines, and an arrangement following the succession of events, corresponding to the process of gradual enlightenment represented in the play. Such matter of philosophical interest as could not find place under the compromise adopted, will be treated in a concluding chapter, which is arranged according to some important characters.

2. *The main characters and the plot*

The central character in the drama, though appearing on

1. Nirṇayasāgar edition, p. 34.

the stage only in the last act, is Puruṣa. *Puruṣa* primarily means *Man*, *Male Person*, but in this sense the word is used here only for the sake of the allegory. In some situations it can actually be interpreted as referring to a male person in general, a person, however, who represents the spiritual Puruṣa at the same time. The spiritual or philosophical sense of the word, to which the allegory points, is the true self of man as understood by monistic Vedānta, taken to be identical with the Supreme Self (Paramātman), the Supreme Lord (Parameśvara), or Brahman. Accordingly, the Puruṣa of the play is a supreme sovereign, excelling even the king in dignity.

Puruṣa's wife is Māyā, Illusion. Her son is Manas, Mind. Manas has two wives, Pravṛtti and Nivṛtti, Activity and Resignation. Pravṛtti gives birth to Moha or Delusion and Nivṛtti to Viveka or Discrimination.

Manas, accompanied by Ahaṃkāra or Egoism, has bound Puruṣa. Delusion and others have strengthened this bond. Under the influence of Ahaṃkāra, Puruṣa has fallen a victim to delusions. He dreams as if he were in sleep. Māyā deludes him by producing illusory things. He can be brought back to his real nature only by the rise of Vidyā or Knowledge and Prabodha or Spiritual Awakening. In order that this might be attained, Mind has to remain quiet and Discrimination has to be united with Upaniṣad or Sacred Lore with the assistance of Śānti (Peace) and others. In the meantime the strife continues between the forces of the two powerful sons of Mind born of his two wives, Activity and Resignation, respectively. These two sons, King Delusion and King Discrimination, are the leaders of the two hostile armies. The followers of Delusion are :

Cārvāka (Materialist)—his great friend,
Kāma (Concupiscence), Krodha (Anger), Lobha (Greed), Daṃbha (Deceit), Ahaṃkāra (Egoism)—his Ministers,
Mithyādṛṣṭi (Error)—his wife,
Vibhramāvatī (Confusion)—his wife's friend,
Rati (Pleasure)—Kāma's wife,
Hiṃsā (Violence)—the wife of Krodha,
Tṛṣṇā (Desire)—the wife of Lobha.

The followers of Viveka are:—

Mati (Reason)—his wife,
Saṃtoṣa (Contentment)—his friend,
Vastuvicāra (Investigation into Truth)—his servant,
Viṣṇubhakti (Devotion to Viṣṇu),
Śānti (Peace),
Śraddhā (Faith)—Śānti's mother,
Kṣamā (Patience),
Maitrī (Friendliness),
Karuṇā (Pity),
Upaniṣad (Sacred Lore), and others.

Daṃbha is ordered by Moha to go to Banaras and try to create obstacles for Śama (Tranquillity) and Dama (Self-restraint). There he meets his grandfather Ahaṃkāra. Daṃbha is the son of Lobha, Ahaṃkāra's son. Moha has made Banaras his capital. Cārvāka tells Moha about Viṣṇubhakti, in front of whom he cannot propagate his views. Moha orders Kāma, Krodha, Lobha, Mada, Mātsarya etc. to work against Viṣṇubhakti. Kāma is separately ordered to imprison Dharma (Righteousness). Śānti is to be killed by Krodha and Lobha. Moha, also thinks of another method to kill Śānti. Śānti is the daughter of Śraddhā who lives with Upaniṣad. If Śraddhā is some-how taken away from Upaniṣad, Śānti will die owing to the separation from her mother. In order to take away Śraddhā from Upaniṣad and deposit her with Pāṣaṇḍas (Heretics), Moha engages Mithyādṛṣṭi (False View).

Śānti has lost her mother Śraddhā. She searches for Śraddhā in the company of Karuṇā. But she comes across a false Śraddhā in the Digaṃbara (Jaina), Bauddha and Kāpālika.

The real Śraddhā is saved by Viṣṇubhakti from the grip of Mahābhairavī. Viṣṇubhakti knows that it is all due to Moha. So she decides to uproot Moha. She sends Śraddhā to Viveka with a message asking him to get ready to defeat Kāma, Krodha etc., the followers of Moha. Once Kāma, Krodha etc. are defeated, Vairāgya (Dispassionateness) will be born. Viṣṇubhakti herself will assist the party with Prāṇāyāma (Breath Control). Ṛtambharā (Bearer of Truth) etc. will bring about the birth of Prabodha, when Upaniṣad is united with Viveka, through the cleverness of Śānti etc.

Maitrī (Friendliness) along with her three sisters—Anukampā (Compassion), Muditā (Joy), and Upekṣā)Indifference)—is also ordered by Viṣṇubhakti to reside in the hearts of Mahātmans.

Viveka in the meanwhile is practising asceticism in the Cakratīrtha, on the banks of the Gaṅgā, in Rāḍha, along with Mati accompanied by Mīmāṁsā (Inquiry). He is with great difficulty somehow managing to live.

Kāma has to be defeated by Vastuvicāra (Investigation into Truth) and Krodha by Kṣamā. Krodha's defeat involves the destruction of other forces. Saṃtoṣa (Contentment) has to overcome Lobha.

King Viveka goes to Banaras with his army to fight against Moha. First he sends Naiyāyikadarśana, the System of Logic, to Moha as a messenger asking him to withdraw from the abodes of Viṣṇu, river banks, and the minds of pious people. Moha, however, sends the heretic religions and heretical logic to fight. Sarasvatī (Learning) appears in front of the army of Viveka. Religious and philosophical schools that are acknowledged to be in harmony with the Veda join her in the battle.

Cārvāka, whose view is opposed to both the Āstikas, who acknowledge the authority of the Veda, and the Nāstikas, who deny it, is destroyed in the battle. With his defeat, the other anti-Vedic schools, who are said to have their foundation in the Cārvāka system, are also ruined. The Saugatas or Buddhists flee to the Sindhu, Gāndhāra, Pārasika, Magadha, Āndhra, Hūṇa, Vaṅga, and Kaliṅga countries—i.e., as we may assume, to those regions where Buddhism was still in existence at Kṛṣṇamiśra's time. The Digambaras and Kāpālikas take refuge in Pāñcāla, Mālava, and Ābhīra, where they live hidden among the illiterate. The Logic of the anti-Vedic schools is defeated by Mīmāṃsā accompanied by Nyāya.

Now that the exterior opponents are destroyed, Puruṣa has to fight against his inner enemies. Vastuvicāra destroys Kāma, Kṣamā defeats Krodha, Pāruṣya (Harshness) and Hiṃsā, Saṃtoṣa subdues Lobha, Tṛṣṇā, Anṛta (Falsehood), Paiśunya (Slander), Steya (Theft), and others. Anasūyā (Non-Spite) prevails over Mātsarya (Spite). Mada (Arrogance) is killed by Parotkarṣasaṃbhāvanā (Respect for others' virtues) and Māna (Conceit) by Paraguṇādhikya (Excellence of others' qualities). At this stage Moha disappears with the obstructive elements.

Manas separated from Pravṛtti attempts to destroy himself owing to the grief caused by the loss of his sons and grandsons. Viṣṇubhakti, however, sends Sarasvatī to enlighten him. She has to inspire Vairāgya or Dispassionateness in him. She lectures to him about the transitory nature of beings. But Mamatāvāsanā (Feeling of mine-ness) creates Vyāmoha (Great Confusion); so it has to be destroyed. After Sarasvatī's teaching Manas becomes willing to take advice (upadeśasahiṣṇu). Vāirāgya or Dispassionateness is born in him and the bondage caused by the feeling of mine-ness (mamatā-pāśa) is broken. Through non-thinking (acintā) Manas gets rid of Śoka (Grief). From now onwards Nivṛtti becomes the favourite consort of Manas. Śama, Dama, Saṃtoṣa are his sons; Yama (Morality), Niyama (Obeservance) etc. his ministers.

Viveka, with the blessing of Manas, is united with Upaniṣad. Viṣṇubhakti along with the four sisters Maitrī etc. is honoured by Manas. When Manas is quiet, Puruṣa can attain his real nature. Viveka and Upaniṣad together make him realize that he is no other than Parameśvara (The Supreme Lord). Nididhyāsana (Meditation) enters Puruṣa, at the command of Viṣṇubhakti. At this moment Vidyā (Knowledge) comes out breaking the chest of Manas and disappears immediately devouring Moha and his followers and Prabodha comes to Puruṣa. Now Puruṣa awakens to his oneness with Viṣṇu.

3. LIST OF THE CHARACTERS

Anasūyā	—Nonspite
Anukampā	—Compassion
Anṛta	—Falsehood
Ahaṃkāra	—Egoism
Upaniṣad	—Sacred Lore
Upekṣā	—Indifference
Ṛtambharā	—Bearer of Truth
Karuṇā	—Pity, Compassion
Kāma	—Concupiscence

1. Arrangement according to the Sanskrit alphabet.

Krodha —Anger
Kṣamā —Patience
Cārvāka —Materialist
Tṛṣṇā —Desire
Dama —Self-restraint
Daṃbha —Deceit
Digaṃbara —Jaina
Dainya —Helplessness
Dharma —Righteousness
Nididhyāsana —Meditation
Niyama —Observance
Nivṛtti —Resignation

Paraguṇādhikya —Excess of superior qualities
Parameśvara —Supreme Lord
Parotkarṣasaṃbhāvanā —Respect of others' virtues
Pāruṣya —Harshness
Pāṣaṇḍa —Heretic
Puruṣa —Man
Paiśunyavāk —Slander
Prabodha —Spiritual Awakening
Pravṛtti —Activity
Prāṇāyāma —Control of breath
Mati —Reason
Mada —Arrogance
Manas —Mind
Mamatāvāsanā —Feeling of mine-ness
Mātsarya —Spite
Māna —Conceit
Māyā —Illusion
Mithyādṛṣṭi —False View, Error, Heresy
Mīmāṃsā —Inquiry
Muditā —Joy
Maitrī —Friendliness
Mokṣa —Liberation
Moha —Delusion
Yama —Morality
Rati —Pleasure

LIST OF THE CHARACTERS

Lobha	—Greed
Vastuvicāra	—Investigation into Truth
Vidyā	—Knowledge
Vibhramāvatī	—Confusion
Viveka	—Discrimination
Viṣṇubhakti	—Devotion to Viṣṇu
Vairāgya	—Dispassionateness
Śama	—Tranquillity
Śoka	—Grief
Śānti	—Peace
Śraddhā	—Faith
Saṅga	—Attachment
Saṇkalpa	—Determination or Intention
Saṃtoṣa	—Contentment
Sarasvatī	—Learning
Saugata	—Buddhist
Hiṃsā	—Injury or Violence

4. *Genealogy*

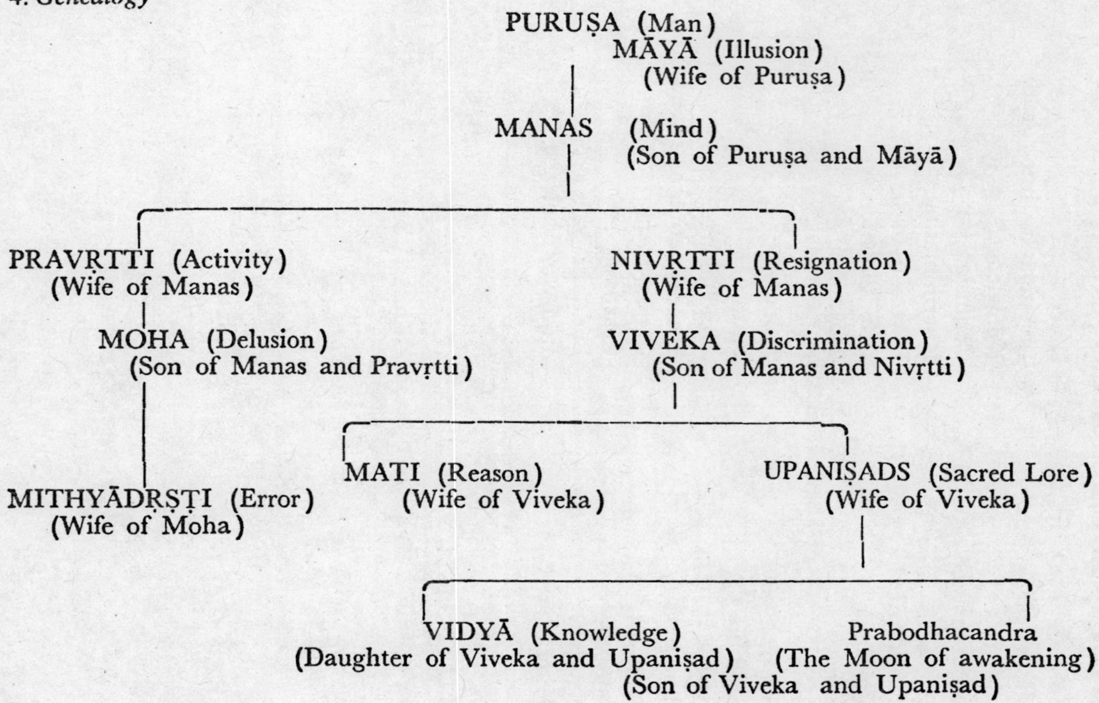
PURUṢA (Man)
MĀYĀ (Illusion)
(Wife of Puruṣa)
MANAS (Mind)
(Son of Puruṣa and Māyā)
PRAVṚTTI (Activity)
(Wife of Manas)
NIVṚTTI (Resignation)
(Wife of Manas)
MOHA (Delusion)
(Son of Manas and Pravṛtti)
VIVEKA (Discrimination)
(Son of Manas and Nivṛtti)
MITHYĀDṚṢṬI (Error)
(Wife of Moha)
MATI (Reason)
(Wife of Viveka)
UPANIṢADS (Sacred Lore)
(Wife of Viveka)
VIDYĀ (Knowledge)
(Daughter of Viveka and Upaniṣad)
Prabodhacandra
(The Moon of awakening)
(Son of Viveka and Upaniṣad)

CHAPTER II

The Vaiṣṇava Vedānta

1. *Puruṣa* and *Māyā*

The doctrine which Kṛṣṇamiśra wishes to establish in the play is Vaiṣṇava Vedānta. It is illusionistic and extremely monistic, but at the same time devotional. It falls more or less in the line of the Vedānta represented by the Paramārthasāra ascribed to Ādiśeṣa and by the Bhāgavatapurāṇa. A similar sort of Vedānta was later on followed by the Adhyātmavāmāyaṇa. All these texts identify Viṣṇu with Brahman[1]. Their Vaiṣṇavism is different from that of the Pāñcarātra texts, which is dualistic. It may perhaps be described as Bhāgavatism, though the term *bhāgavata* is not strictly confined to non-Pāñcarātra Vaiṣṇavism. It is only from the times of Yāmuna and Rāmānuja that Pāñcarātra Vaiṣṇavism becomes Vedic and tends towards qualified monism. Śaṅkara, who possibly comes in between the time of the Paramārthasāra[2] and the Bhāgavatapurāṇa, was apparently brought up in a Vaiṣṇava environment[3]; but in the works which are undoubtedly composed by him, there is no stress on Vaiṣṇavism or *bhakti*. After Śaṅkara, different schools, both devotional and monistic, seem to have developed, some identifying Viṣṇu, others identifying Śiva[4] with the Supreme Reality. We do not know whether Kṛṣṇamiśra was familiar

1. Paramārthasāra 74; Bhāgavata 10, 3, 24; Adhyātmarāmāyaṇa 1, 2, 7; Pra. Ca. VI v. 30.

2. According to S. S. Suryanarayana Sastri the Paramārthasāra seems to be earlier than even the Gauḍapādīya-Kārikās. Cp. Paramārthasāra, Introduction.

3. This is suggested by the fact that in Śaṅkara's genuine works there are allusions to elements of Vaiṣṇava religion whereas Śaivism is more or less ignored (oral communication of Prof. Hacker). In the works of Śaṅkara's disciple Sureśvara, Vaiṣṇava leanings are even more conspicuous than in the works of his master, and the initial *maṅgala* of Padmapāda's sub-commentary on Śaṅkara's Brahmasūtrabhāṣya bears indirect evidence of the fact that Śaṅkara was not, as later tradition would have it, a Śaiva. Cp. Paul Hacker, *Untersuchungen über Texte des frühen Advaitavāda*, Mainz 1950, pp. 14 and 24.

4. Abhinavagupta, Appayadīkṣita, and others.

with the Bhāgavatapurāṇa. In any case, he combines Māyāvāda with Viṣṇubhakti as the great Purāṇa does.

In the Paramārthasāra *bhakti* or devotion does not play any role. In the Prabodhacandrodaya, however, as in the Bhāgavatapurāṇa and later in the Adhyātmarāmāyaṇa, *bhakti* forms the most prominent subject of the teaching.[1] According to Kṛṣṇamiśra, worship of the Lord of the Universe is the seed from which the fruit of awakening grows.[2] It is through *bhakti* that man attains knowledge so that he can awaken to realize his identity with Viṣṇu.

Two verses in the play describe the universe as an illusion and also state the nature of Brahman. The first one is the opening verse of the play :

> "I adore that light which is dense bliss, pure, to be known as one's own self; through its ignorance the three worlds are manifested as ether, air, fire, water, and earth like a flow of water in the rays of the midday sun; their (the three worlds') reality disappears for the wise like the body of a snake in a garland.[3]"

This means that the universe is only an appearance. Its reality is like that of a mirage or a snake illusorily perceived in a garland. The verse gives the *svarūpa-lakṣaṇā* or definition by essential nature[4] as well as the *taṭastha-lakṣaṇā* or definition per accidens[5] of Brahman. The *svarūpa-lakṣaṇā* is expressed in the words light, dense bliss, one's own self. The *taṭasthalakṣaṇa* consists in the statement that the three worlds originate from Bhahman as the waterstreams that are seen in a mirage originate from the rays of the sun; they rest in Brahman and disappear in it, as the body of a snake that is by delusion seen in garland disappears in it once the reality is known. Both the

1. Pra. Ca. p. 240 : *sarvathā kṛtakṛtyo'smi bhagavatyā viṣṇubhakteḥ prasādāt.* Cp. Bh. pu. 2, 3, 10. : *akāmaḥ sarvakāmo vā mokṣakāma udāradhīḥ tīvreṇa bhaktiyogena yateta puruṣam param.* Adh. Rā. Bālakāṇḍa, 2. 21 : *saṃsārāmayataptānāṃ* bheṣajaṃ *bhaktir eva te.*

2. Pra. ca. IV, 7 : *viśveśvarārādhanabījajātāt tattvāvabodhāt...*

3. Pra. Ca. I v. 1. Cp. Paramārthasāra v. 22 : *mṛgatṛṣṇāyām udakaṃ śuktau rajataṃ bhujaṅgamo rajjvām taimirika-candrayugavad bhrāntaṃ nikhilam jagadrūpam.*

4. *svarūpam eva lakṣaṇam svarūpalakṣaṇaṃ* Ved. Pari. p. 114.

5. *taṭasthalakṣaṇaṃ nāma yāvallakṣyakālam anavasthitatve sati Ved. Pari.* p. 115.

waterstreams and the body of the snake originate from ignorance[1] (*ajñana*, *avidyā*), which is also called illusion (*māyā*) and which is believed to be the material out of which all appearances are made. The ignorance is Brahman's. This does not mean that Brahman is ignorant in the ordinary sense of the word. The ignorance mysteriously "belongs" to Brahman in the sense that Brahman is its ontological locus. It is the underlying reality of the pure spirit which makes illusory manifestations possible. These cannot subsist and exist apart from their substratum, which is Brahman.

Another translation of the verse is also possible :

> "I adore that light which is dense bliss, pure, to be known as one's own self; by whose ignorance the three worlds are manifested as ether, air, fire, water, and earth like a flow of water in the rays of the midday sun, which (the three worlds), similar to the body of a snake in a garland, again conceal truth from the wise."

If we accept this translation, the meaning is that Kṛṣṇamiśra wishes to describe the *vikṣepaśakti* or projecting power[2] and the *āvaraṇaśakti* or concealing nature[3] of *māyā* (illusion) or *ajñāna* (ignorance). Through the former the three worlds are produced, which in turn through the latter cover the Truth. Both the mirage and the body of the snake are products of the projecting power and they also cover the real nature of the sun's rays and of the garland, respectively, through the concealing power of ignorance.

A verse of similar contents is put in the mouth of Viveka in the 6th act :

"Just as the moon seen in water, as a city in the sky, as dreams, magic, and the like, the universe is an effect, it is an object of knowledge (*meya*), it is unreal, its is subject to origin, destruction, etc. It arises when self-luminous Hari is not known, like silver in a shell and a serpent in a garland, but disappears when the knowledge of truth arises[4] ."

1. This is an illusionistic interpretation of *Janmādy asya yataḥ*, Br. Sū. I. 1.2, and of *yato vā imāni bhūtānī jāyante......*, Taitt. Up. 3.1.

2. *vikṣepaśakti* produces the snake in the rope conditioned by ignorance. Cp. Sadānanda, *Vedāntasāra*, p. 36 f.

3. By the *āvaraṇaśakti* the small cloud covers the sun, which is far away from the eyes of the onlooker. Ibidem, p. 34.

4. Pra. Ca. VI v. 22.

The ultimate Reality, otherwise described as Brahman or the Highest Self, is here called *Hari*, i. e. *Viṣṇu*. His self-luminosity implies that he does not require the opposition of subject and object to be known or to be established as a reality. The underlying idea is that his absolute reality consists just in his self-luminosity. Consequently the world, which is an object of knowledge, lacks in reality, nay, it is simply unreal. Ultimate reality is further conceived as immutability and eternity. This again entails the conclusion that the world, whose constituents are subject to origin, change and destruction, depends on causes, is not real. It is comparable to things that have no real existence at all and disappear as soon as the reality is known. The comparison with the reflection of the moon in water also suggests that the plurality of things is not ultimately real. For the real moon is one, though its reflections are many. The illusory appearance of the universe disappears with the knowledge of Truth, *tattvāvabodha*. This knowledge does not include the opposition of subject and object. It is an awakening to one's own self, *svātmāvabodha*, which is *identical* with self-luminous Hari, who is known in this knowledge. The object of knowledge and the fact of knowledge become identical here. This idea is expressed by Kṛṣṇamiśra by using the same word, *avabodha*, to describe the self-luminous nature of Hari (*svātma-avabodha*) and the knowledge of the Reality (*tattva-avabodha*).

The illusionistic Vedānta explains the origin and existence of all things from an illusory association of the Universal Self with Māyā, the Principle of illusion, which is at the same time a sort of Primary Matter. Kṛṣṇamiśra makes Māyā the consort of Puruṣa, Man, and what in the philosophical system is represented to be products of Māyā appears as her progeny in the play. Though untouched by Puruṣa, who is free from attachments (*saṅgasamujjhita*), Māyā gives birth to Manas first and then to the worlds.[1]

The association of Māyā with Puruṣa is of a peculiar kind. Although she is called Puruṣa's house-wife (*gṛhiṇī*[2]), she behaves rather like a prostitute (*veśyā*[3]). Kṛṣṇamiśra depicts her

1. Pra. Ca. I v. 19.
2. Pra. Ca. I v. 19.
3. Pra. Ca. p. 41.

behaviour in terms which admit of a double interpretation, describing at the same time the manners of a wayward woman and the qualities of the Principle of Illusion as taught by the Vedānta. She is *avicārasiddhā*[1], i.e. accomplished in thoughtless folly; but the word is also a philosophical term, synonymous with the more usual *anirvacanīya*, which means that Māyā can be described neither as real nor as unreal. In this interpretation *avicārasiddha* is something whose existence is firmly established (*siddha*) *although* it cannot be accounted for or, more correctly, just *by the fact that* it defies logical approach and cannot be explained or demonstrated by reason, since it is the Principle of Illusion; so it is "established in its existence" (*siddha*) by "absence of logical thinking" (*a-vicāra*). Both meanings may be loosely combined in the translation "unaccountable." Māyā is an unaccountable, wayward woman and, as the Principle of Illusion, indefinable as to her state of reality. The same idea, again characterizing Māyā the prostitute as well as Māyā the Principle of Illusion, is also expressed by the sentence, spoken by the king : "Māyā acts without regard to ends (*prayojana*) or reasons (*kāraṇa*)[2]"

Māyā "makes appear" or "displays" or "affects" (*upadarśayanti*) "states of mind" or "feelings" (*bhāva*) which she does not really experience, which are therefore "spurious" or "unreal" (*asat*)[3]. This is peculiar to her as a prostitute. But the same phrase has also a philosophical meaning, viz., the Principle of Illusion "makes appear" (*upadarśayantī*) "things" (*bhāva*) which are not really existent and the product of Māyā according to the Vedānta system. By her indecent, depraved[4] behaviour, Māyā the prostitute "deceives" (*vañcayanti*[5]) her husband—just as Māyā the Principle of Illusion superimposes illusory appearances on the pure spirit of the self. The deception is depicted in two stanzas, both spoken by the King conversing with Mati (Reason). The first stanza, (I. 26) is more philosophical. In it the King says that Puruṣa, although he

1. Pra. Ca. P. 41.
2. Pra. Ca. p. 43.
3. Pra. Ca. p. 41 : *Māyā asato 'pi bhāvān upadarśāyantī....*
4. *anāryā* p. 42; *durācārā* p. 43.
5. Pra. Ca. p. 41.

is immutable (*avikriya*) and effulgent like a crystal (*spaṭika-maṇivad bhāsvān*), is by Māyā seemingly subjected to changes or deformations (*vikṛti*), but in spite of Māyā's "embrace" (*upaśleṣa*) by which she creates a certain unsteadiness (*adhīratā*) in him, his radiance or beauty (*ruci*) does not vanish. This means philosophically, that the association of the self-luminous self with the Principle of Illusion (which is also the stuff of everything material) is itself illusory, so that in reality the self remains unaffected by it. Just as the sun is not really obscured by a streak of darkness covering it, so the effulgent self is never really overwhelmed by Māyā[1]. The second stanza (1.27) describes the deception in terms which primarily refer to the action of prostitutes. They enter the tender hearts of men, delude them, intoxicate them, ridicule them, rebuke them, please them, and finally make them languid and dejected[2].

2. *Mind and its activity*

The first outcome of the illusory association of Illusion with Puruṣa is the rise of Mind, called *manas,* sometimes also *citta*[3] or *antarātman*[4]. Owing to its proximity to Puruṣa, Manas acts as if it—or he, as we shall henceforth say—were the Supreme Lord himself[5]. Māyā herself has placed him in the position of the Sovereign—acting like a queen who instals her favourite son in the position of the king, as the commentary Candrikā remarks.

The fact that Manas is here the first-born son of Māyā points to a special form of Vedānta, similar to the Sāṅkhya, according to the classical form of which the first products of cosmogony are successively Egoism (*ahaṃkāra*), Intellect (*buddhi*), and Mind (*manas*).

Manas in his turn constructs the "towns with nine doors[6]", i.e. the bodies. The nine doors are the two eyes, the two ears, the two nostrils, the mouth, and the organs of excretion and

1. Pra. Ca. p. 41.
2. Pra. Ca. p. 43.
3. Pra. Ca. p. 45.
4. Pra. Ca. IV v. 5.
5. Pra. Ca. p. 44.
6. Pra. Ca. p. 44. Cp. Kaṭha-Up. VI. 1; Śvet. Up. III. 18; Bh. Gī. V. 13. In the Kaṭha-Up. 11 doors are mentioned, the two additionsl ones being the navel and the *brahmarandhra*.

generation. After the creation of the bodies, the one self, Puruṣa, is made manifold and put in the bodies—similar to a king who, after being dethroned by his son who is aided by the queen, is confined in a fortress. Manas imposes his actions on Puruṣa—acting like a prince who, after stealthily ousting his father, still represents his actions as his father's.

Mind's actions are reflected in Puruṣa "as in a crystal[1]." This means that the functions of the mind are made conscious only by the light of the self-luminous self, but as a thing which is reflected in a crystal is not really in it, so the actions of Manas are in Puruṣa only by illusory superimposition[2].

The position given by Kṛṣṇamiśra to Manas in the process of cosmogony implies an identification of Mind and Īśvara, the personal God. Here Kṛṣṇamiśra deviates from common Advaita teaching and his view stands in close proximity to Purāṇic Sāṅkhya. For to most Advaitins Iśvara is Brahman in its association with Māyā, whereas Kṛṣṇamiśra's doctrine implies that Iśvara, the creator of the bodies, is the outcome of that association and the first product of cosmogony, similar to the *Mahat* which is identified with *Manas* and *Īśvara* in some Purāṇas[3]. An important difference between the Prabodhacandrodaya and the Purāṇas consists in the illusionism of the drama, which is foreign to the older pieces of the Purāṇas.

The first-born son of Manas is Ahaṃkāra or Egoism. He goes to embrace his grandfather.[4] This means that the concept of "I" arises to strengthen the bondage of the self. The result is that Puruṣa now has ideas like: "I am born," "This is my father", "This is my mother", etc., i.e. he brings his own body as well as things and persons of his environment into a relationship to himself. But all these relations are, as Kṛṣnamiśra says, nothing but dreams. Puruṣa, though by nature "knowing" (*vidvān*), has fallen into "the sleep of nescience" (*avidyāmayīm nidrām etya*), and in his dreams "he experiences the fabrications of Mind's vibrations"[5].

1. Pra. Ca. I. v. 28.
2. The reading *nidadhāti* in I. 28 of the Trivandrum edition seems to be preferable to *vidadhāti* of the Nirṇayasāgar edition.
3. Cp. W. Kirfel, *Purāṇa Pañcalakṣaṇa*, p. 47, vv 15 ff. Information from Prof. Hacker.
4. Pra. Ca. p. 45.
5. Pra. Ca. I v. 29.

Mind's activity is inevitably bound up with delusion; only when its activity ceases, does discrimination of true and false become possible. This is why in the play Pravṛtti or Activity and Nivṛtti or Resignation or Repose are said to be the wives of Manas. Manas is able to produce two sorts of ideas, wrong and correct. Moha or Delusion and Viveka or Discrimination are said to be his sons. At first, Manas is attached to Activity. The specific character of his functions is represented by Saṃkalpa, i.e. Intention, who, as a male person, enters along with Manas in the fifth Act. All activity in man dpends on Manas. In the wakeful state (*jāgrad—avasthā*), the body is active in consequence of Mind's activity. In the dream state (*svapnāvasthā*), although the body is inactive, the mind continues to be active. In deep sleep (*suṣupti*), where there is no activity, Manas is as if he were dead[1]. But he continues to exist and therefore Puruṣa remains bound.

3. *Moral preparation*

The psychological process of man's gradual awakening to the monistic experience forms the main part of the contents of the drama. Puruṣa, deluded by Māyā and kept in bondage by Manas and Ahaṃkāra, becomes subject to arrogance, anger, greed, desire etc. He is attracted towards materialism. The discriminating power in him along with reasoning—in the play Discrimination and Reason are husband and wife—has to struggle hard to get rid of this deluding power and error. Devotion to Viṣṇu, Faith (Śraddhā), Peace (Śānti), etc. help Puruṣa to get rid of the delusion. It is difficult to discriminate the right faith from the false one by which heretical Dharma, heretical Liberation etc. attract Man. However, he does not find any peace in the heretical religions (Act III). But in spite of his devotion to Viṣṇu, Delusion is very active. As long as Delusion is there, Man cannot attain realization

To uproot Delusion, the first step is to destroy Concupiscence, Anger, etc. Then only can Dispanssionateness be aroused in Man. Friendliness, Compassion, Joy, and Indifference have to be cultivated. In dealing with a happy person, the soul or the mind (*antarātman*) should realize friendliness, in

1. Pra. Ca. VI v. 13.

association with an unhappy one, compassion, to good actions he should respond with joy, and to bad thoughts with indifference. Thus the soul or mind, though still tainted by attachment, greed, spite, etc., attains sedateness.[1]

King Discrimination in his reflexions comes to the conclusion that Ignorance (*abodha*) is the root cause of Delusion which propels the wheel of Saṃsāra.[2] Though immersed in the immortal ocean of intelligence and bliss, which is quiet, of endless greatness and free from rows of waves, Man does not take even a sip from it. Instead, he seeks refreshment by drinking the essenceless water of the sea of a mirage, bathes in it, enjoys it, and plunges into it again and again.[3] To uproot the tree of *saṃsāra* grown from ignorance, there is no other means than realization born of the seed of worship of the Lord of the Universe[4].

Investigation into Truth (Vastuvicāra) destroys Concupiscence in Man. The means to reach this end are : refraining from looking at women or thinking of them; consideration of the repulsive features of woman's body and of sexual intercourse; retiring to lonely places, as banks of rivers, mountains, or forests; listening to the soothing words of Vyāsa, i. e. the Brahmasūtras and the Mahābhārata, especially the Bhagvadgītā, and perhaps also select Purāṇas; contact with wise men[5].

Patience (Kṣamā) is the force that fights Anger (Krodha). Her methods are the following : In dealing with an angry man, disregard him with a smiling face; if he is possessed (with wrath), composure is the right course; if he abuses you, ask him about his health; if he beats you, it is a happy occasion for you to destroy your own evil *karma*. For him who thinks : 'Fie upon him who has no self-restraint, for it will be difficult for him to ward off great calamity caused by fate', and whose mind is soft with the juice of kindness, there is no rise of anger[6]."

When anger is destroyed, Injury, Harshness, Conceit, Spite, etc. are automatically overcome as they are nothing but

1. Pra. Ca. IV v. 5.
2. Pra. Ca. p. 140.
3. Pra. Ca. IV v. 6.
4. Pra. Ca. IV v. 7.
5. Pra. Ca. pp. 146-147.
6. Pra. Ca. IV v. 18.

the outcome of Anger. But Greed still remains alive. Contentment (Saṃtoṣa) is the remedy for it. His teaching is : "Death dances constantly on your head, old age like a frightful serpent swallows you, the world is swallowed by the vultures which are your family. Wash off with the water of knowledge that dust (*rajas*, the second of the three constituents of matter) which is born of Greed and consists mainly of ignorance. He who is immersed (even) a little in the water of the nectar-ocean of Contenntment, lives happy[1]."

4. *Anti-Vedic doctrines warded off*

After he is freed of the affections by Discrimination, Puruṣa is prepared for the struggle against Delusion. Now that the moral obstacles are removed, the first step towards intellectual enlightenment can be undertaken. At this stage all those schools and sects who are acknowledged as Vedic, are Man's allies. With their assistance, Man has to convince himself that the non-Vedic schools do not bring him final emancipation. During this struggle Viṣṇubhakti remains in the background. Peace also retires with her. Viṣṇubhakti goes away from Banaras as she does not want to see the battle in which there is so much injury.[2] It is very natural that devotion to Viṣṇu does not play any part here. For though Man has got rid of Concupiscence, Anger and Greed, Delusion is still there and he does not know which religion or philosophy to adopt. There are the Cārvāka, the Buddhist, the Jaina, the Śaiva, the Kāpālika, and others. He cannot of course worship Viṣṇu before he is convinced that all these schools are false. Faith, however, remains with his discrimination throughout the struggle. Through Nyāya or logic he tries to find out the right course. But Delusion counteracts with heretical logic (*pāṣaṇḍa-tarkaśāstra*). The struggle becomes more and more violent.

Learning comes to Man's rescue. He takes refuge with all the brahmanical schools in order to escape the claims of the heterodox schools. That is why it is said in the play that the Vaiṣṇavas, Sauras and Śaivas join Sarasvatī, the Goddess of Learning, when she appears in front of the army of Discrimina-

1. Pra. Ca. IV v. 23.
2. Pra. Ca. p. 166 : *hiṃsāprāyasamaradarśanaparāṅmukhī.*

tion. The philosophies that are acknowledged to be in harmony with the Vedas also join her. Mīmāṃsā who has the three Vedas as her eyes, whose beautiful face is the moon of Dharma, appears accompanied by Sāṅkhya, Nyāya, Vaiśeṣika, Mahābhāṣya and others, with her hands pointing towards a thousand rules (dealing with *karman* and Brahman). Faith says that good comes out of it when the schools that have their origin in the Vedas join together to overthrow the common enemy, the materialist, eventhough they are mutually opposed[1]. She believes that those who reflect on the truth of the Śāstras do not really contradict each other[2]. She says : "The tranquil, endless, indivisible, unborn Light is variously praised as Brahmā, Acyuta (Viṣṇu), Umāpati (Śiva) according to the predominance of qualities. Thus, the Lord of the Universe can be attained through various good systems which are based on the Vedas and have taken diverse paths, just as the ocean is reached by streams of water[3]." Now Man is convinced that Materialism will not lead to final emancipation. Buddhism, Jainism and the Kāpālika sect, which too are non-Vedic, are also refuted through proper arguments from the Vedas. Heretical logic is defeated by Mīmāṃsā accompanied by Nyāya.

Now Man's external enemies, i.e. the heretical schools, are all destroyed. For the time being he is free from Delusion. But as he has not yet acquired positive knowledge, Delusion may reappear at any moment. Moha keeps himself hidden, as Śraddhā says[4].

3. *The rise of dispassionateness*

After the removal of the external and internal obstacles, Dispassionateness has to be aroused in Man's mind. Devotion to Viṣṇu appears again and it is she who sends to Mind, Sarasvatī, the Goddess of Learning. She helps Mind to attain tranquillity. But the whole process is not so easy. Though Mind is himself an outcome of Illusion, he has to work out Man's liberation from Illusion. To this end, Mind has to be prepared

1. Pra. Ca. V v. 8.
2. Pra. Ca. p. 174 : *āgamānāṃ ca tattvaṃ vicārayatām avirodha eva.*
3. Pra. Ca. V v. 9.
4. Pra. Ca. p. 178.

for renunciation and tranquillity. This forms the subject of a special interlude.

Mind is utterly dejected because he has been deprived of all affections, like Passion, Hatred, etc., which were his children, and even Activity (Pravṛtti) has perished. Mind wishes to destroy himself. At that moment, the Goddess of Learning appears to enlighten him (*prabodhana*). She reminds him of epical and mythological stories which are known to him and which illustrate the transitoriness of all beings. She calls upon him to realize that the whole cosmos with all its gods and other superhuman beings has already perished more than ten millions of times; in comparison with it, however, the body of an individual being which on dying dissolves into the five elements of which it is composed, is nothing but foam on the sea; so it is great folly to grieve at its loss[1]. "He who sees the eternal and the non-eternal does not see the flurry of grief.[2] "Brahman is eternal, truth and one only. All else is imaginary. What delusion or what grief can there be for him who sees the Oneness[3]."

But Mind cannot discriminate the eternal from the non-eternal before he is freed from his grief. Sarasvati teaches him that the cause of such sorrow is the attachment (*sneha*) to related persons. She denounces this feeling by vividly depicting the dangers and losses into which Man is thrown by indulging in it. Mind objects that to part from one's own offspring is as painful as to give up one's own life. The goddess explains that at the bottom of attachment or affection there is simply the feeling "This is mine" (*mamatā*), which is an illusion. People remove insects which (as Kṛṣṇamiśra thinks) arise out of their own body, without thinking that they are theirs. What arises from one's body is not really one's own. So it is an illusion to give the name of "children" to what has sprung from one's body and to grieve at their loss.[4]

1. Pra. Ca. V. v. 14.

2. Pra. Ca. p. 183. The reading *nittyānityavastudarśanaḥ* seems to be preferable to *nityam anityavastudarśanah.*

3. Pra. Ca. V v. 15. The second half of this verse is verbatim-repeated from Iśopaniṣad 7.

4. Pra. Ca. V v. 21.

These teachings prepare Mind to understand the message of Dispassionateness (Vairāgya), who enters to continue and support Sarasvatī's instruction by describing the body as loathsome, enjoyment as resulting in disgust, wealth as perilous, and association with parents, children, relatives and wives as extrinsic and accidental.[1] As a means of getting rid of the "fetter of mineness" i. e. the feeling "This is mine", Sarasvatī recommends meditation on the transitoriness of beings, inviting Mind to consider that a person now living had innumerable millions of parents and wives and children and relatives in his countless previous existences.[2] This meditation relieves Mind of his infatuation (*vyāmoha*). The cure for the grief which still harrasses Mind, is "not-thinking" or "absence of anxiety" (*acintā*), and to become free from the "trains of thought" (*cintā-saṃtāna*) which are still overwhelming him, Mind is called upon to concentrate attention on one "peaceful object" (*śānto viṣayaḥ*), either on god Viṣṇu, "who is dark-blue as a cloud and wears splendid ornaments : a necklace, bracelets, ear-rings, and a diadem", or on the neuter Absolute, Brahman, "which is free from grief and like a cool pond in summer[3]."

This means, in the terminology of Vedānta spirituality, that Mind may practise either *saguṇa* or *nirguṇa* worship, i. e. he may meditate on the Supreme either as possessed of the mythological attributes of god Viṣṇu or as qualityless Spirit.

Mind follows Sarasvatī's advice and everything that had previously delighted him is now regarded by him as a mirage.[4] He is now ripe for renunciation. But as he by nature belongs to the order (*āśrama*) of married men, he should now, after having lost his wife Activity (Pravṛtti), live with Resignation (Nivṛtti) as his spouse. His sons Tranquillity, Self-restraint, Contentment (Śama, Dama, Saṃtoṣa) and others shall serve him; Morality, Observance[5] (Yama, Niyama) and others shall be his ministers or advisers. Discrimination (Viveka)

1. Pra. Ca. V vv. 23. 24. 25.
2. Pra. Ca. V vv. 26. 27.
3. Pra. Ca. V vv. 28-31.
4. Pra. Ca. V v. 32.
5. These translations are only approximations. *yama* according to Yogasūtra II. 30 comprises non-violence, truthfulness, chastity, abstention from theft and from appropriating objects; *niyama* comprises purity, contentment, asceticism, recital and devotion to God according to Yogasūtra II. 31.

shall have the post of heir-apparent, with Sacred Lore (Upaniṣad) as his consort. The four sisters Friendliness, Joy, Compassion and Reason (Maitrī, Prīti, Karuṇā, Mati) are sent by Viṣṇubhakti to calm and please Mind.[1]

Thus Mind recovers his "health" or "natural state" (*svāsthya*), and this gives Puruṣa (here called *kṣetrajña*, i. e. the spiritual Person) the opportunity of also attaining his "real nature" (*prakṛti*). Therefore, Sarasvatī says to Mind : "It is due to the association with thee that the one eternal God (i. e. Puruṣa), overwhelmed by the clouds of affection, appears in a manifested form, as if he were many, in the functions of the intellect, as the (one) sun (appears as many) in the waves of the ocean. If thou, my dear, remainest quiet, somehow withdrawing thy extended functions, then his self will shine forth with his innate dense bliss like the sun (reflected) in a clear mirror.[2]"

Thus, "after the sons (of Mind) have perished, after Delusion has vanished, after Mind associated with Dispassionateness has become tranquil and the five troubles (*kleśa*[3]) have disappeared simultaneously Man extends his desire towards the awakening of Truth[4])." Man has now all prerequisites for liberation. "His beloved is Inquiry into eternal and noneternal things, his only friend is Dispassionateness, his truthful allies are Morality etc., Tranquillity, Self-restraint etc. are his attendants, Friendliness and others his servants, Desire for liberation is always his companion. The enemies like Delusion, Feeling of mineness, Volition, (Intention, Saṃkalpa), Attachment (Prasaṅga) etc. are to be forcibly uprooted[5]." But he does not yet know what Truth is. That can be known only through the study of the Upaniṣads with discrimination. Illusion has to be destroyed. Man will enjoy sovereignty when he inquires into himself.[6]

1. Pra Ca. p. 196.
2. Pra. Ca. V v. 33.
3. They are, according to Yogasūtra II. 3 : *avidyā* (Ignorance), *asmitā* (feeling of "I am"), *rāga* (attachment), *dveṣa* (hatred), and *abhiniveśa* (clinging to life).
4. Pra. Ca. VI v. 1.
5. Pra. Ca. VI v. 3.
6. Pra. Ca. p. 201 : *yathātmānam anusaṃdhatte tato deva eva svarāt sāmrāṭ ca bhavati.*

6. *The problem of ritualism*

At this stage, a very important question arises, viz. whether Man should practise religious observances (*dharma*) or not. It seems that Kṛṣṇamiśra does not think *dharma* to be reconcilable with the highest stage. From the time he attains dispassionateness, Man becomes indifferent to *dharma*. He has no interest in the fruits of his good actions, which are pleasures in this or in the other world. "He is afraid of the perishing fruits of meritorious actions as much as he is afraid of hell, which is the fruit of sin. Thus having given up mental concern with objects desired, he observes holy rites to some extent[1]." "But Dharma, considering the master's inclination towards the inner self, has himself become void of actions, thinking that he has done his duty[2]."

The "holy rites" referred to in the quotation are daily (*nitya*) and occasional (*naimittika*) rites. The meaning is that Man confines himself to these ceremonies to the exclusion of rites which aim at the fulfilment of desires. Kṛṣṇamiśra thinks that such practice leads to self-exhaustion of Dharma, because the aim of all religious action, viz. the purification of the mind and the "inclination towards the inner self", has been attained.

7. *The temptation of yogie powers*

However, Mahāmoha (Grand Delusion) uses one final trick to divert Man from reaching his goal. While remaining hidden himself, he sends forth Madhumatī Vidyā (Honey—Wisdom[3]) with the Upasargas (Portentous Phenomena[4]) to

1. Pra. Ca. VI. v. 4. There are two possible interpretations cf this verse. The phrase *kathaṃcana manyate* can be split up in two ways: (i) *kathaṃca na manyate* and (ii) *kathaṃcana manyate*. The first means: "He somehow observes holy actions". I have accepted the second interpretation, because the word "but" (*kiṃtu*) at the beginning of the following sentence seems to call for it, the meaning being: Though Man still performs some rites, *dharma*, which is the performance of rites, has eventually rendered iteslf superfluous.

2. Pra. Ca. p. 203.

3. The commentary Candrikā explains this as the magical visdom taught in the madhukāṇḍa of the Bṛhadāraṇyaka-Upaniṣad, but this explanations seems un-acceptable. The commentary Prakāśa says that Madhumatī is a certain "magical power" (*siddhi*).

4. What the Upasargas are, is clear from the context. They are also mentioned on p. 178 (Act V, after v. 10): *mahāmoho, pi yogopasargaiḥ saha.* The Candrikā, the Prakāśa, and also the Nāṭakābharaṇa explain the word at that passage as meaning "obstacles of yoga", but that seems unacceptable.

(*Contd. on page 26*)

seduce Man. Honey-Wisdom is magic craft and the Portentous Phenomena are magic faculties. These forces teach Man how to hear distant sounds, to perceive passages from sacred and profane and philosophical literature, to compose works of science and poetry, and to roam in the region of Mount Meru, where Vidyādhara women seek to allure him.[1] All these are magic accomplishments, *siddhis*, which are supposed to be attainable to yogins. It is interesting that Kṛṣṇamiśra regards them as unreal, as delusions, as deviations from the path that leads to liberation, as temptations which divert Man and prevent Discrimination from thinking of the upaniṣads. Reasoning (Tarka) warns Man, pointing out that he is misusing Yoga : "You who have recently boarded the boat of Yoga to cross the ocean of Saṃsāra, how can you now be so mad as to give up that (boat) and plunge into a river of fire[2]." Man realises his mistake and is no longer attracted by Madhumatī vidyā. Discrimination is led to him by Faith, and Sacred Lore (Upaniṣad) by Peace

By the grace of Viṣṇubhakti Man is saved from all temptations. Now he is almost at the other shore of the ocean of Saṃsāra. "The billows of misery have been crossed, the whirlpools (or delusions) of the feeling "This is mine" have been avoided, the clutches of the sharks and crocodiles which are friends, wife and relatives have been loosened, the submarine fire of anger has been removed, the spreading creepers of desire have been torn asunder; now the other shore of the ocean of Saṃsāra has almost been reached.[3]"

8. *Non-Vedāntic systems discarded*

Man's next problem is to know which of the philosophical systems is the right one. In the preparatory stages, as long as gross errors and diversions had to be overcome, the philosophical systems that are commonly acknowledged as not being opposed to the Veda, i. e. Mīmāṃsā, Nyāya and others, were welcome

In Act VI, p. 204 (after v. 4), the Candrikā explains *upasargā mohakā dharmāḥ*, "Upasargas are deluding qualities", which seems better. The Upasargas are aberrations of Yoga caused by Mahāmoha or Grand Delusion.

1. Pra. Ca. VI vv. 5-6; pp. 203 -205.
2. Pra. Ca. VI v. 7.
3. Pra. Ca. VI v. 8.

allies of king Discrimination, who fought for the cause of Man. But from the time Discrimination is anew associated with his lawful wife Upaniṣad, the position of those systems becomes different. They were allies of Discrimination only so long as this king was severed from Upaniṣad. Upaniṣad, however, reveals that they are intrinsically hostile to her. This implies that, in Kṛṣṇamiśra's opinion as in the opinion of Vedāntists generally, the idea of a unity of all the Hindu systems, which was professed in a previous act, has only a relative value and is only relatively true. It is upheld as long as common opponents are to be repelled, but abandoned as soon as the specifically Vedāntic path, which is enunciated in the upaniṣads and which Vedāntists of course believe to be the only right path, is taken up. The non-Vedāntic Hindu systems afford valuable weapons for reason to ward off the allurements of such philosophies and ways of life as are totally incompatible with the path of Vedānta, but their views on the ultimate goal have to be discarded by him who believes in the upaniṣads. Therefore, it is upaniṣad personified who in the play makes it clear to Man and to Discrimination that the teaching cannot ultimately co-exist with that of any other system. She relates the misfortunes which happened to her during the time of her severance from her husband Discrimination :

"I spent my days in retreats of Saṃnyāsins, in public places and empty temples in the company of talkative fools, who interpret my words by arbitrary conjunctures without understanding their meaning, as if they were spoken by a Draviḍa woman[1]."

This means that Upaniṣad cannot be understood when she is severed from Discrimination. Her own doctrine or profession is summarized by her in the verse[2]. "I adore that Puruṣa out of whom the universe arises, in whom it exists with joy (*ramate*) and into whom it is absorbed again,[3] by whose lustre the world shines[4] (i. e. becomes manifest); the light that is

1. Pra. Ca. VI v. 12.
2. Pra. Ca. VI v. 14.
3. Cp. Br. Sū. I. 1.22 : *janmādy asya yataḥ*, "Whence the birth etc. of this (world are). Cp. also Taitt. Up. 3. 1 : *yato vā imāni bhūtāni jāyante, yena jātāni jīvanti, yaṃ praviśyābhisaṃviśanti*, "From whom these beings are born, by whom the born things live, entering whom they are reabsorbed."
4. Cp. Mu. Up. 2. 2. 10 and Kaṭh Up. 5. 15 : *Tasya bhāsā sarvam idam vibhāti*, "By his light this universe shines" Śvet. Up. 6. 14 : *tam eva bhāntam anubhāti sarvam*, when he shines, everything shines after him."

effulgent with its natural bliss; the Lord of all beings who is tranquil, eternal, and without actions; to whom holy men go after having dispelled the darkness of duality, not to come back again[1]."

But this doctrine is not appreciated by any of the other systems. Speaking to Discrimination and Man, Upaniṣad gives an account of how each of those systems in turn has disavowed her teaching, some of them even maltreating her[2]. This account helps Discrimination to discriminate between the doctrine of Vedānta and the tenets of other schools. After each item of Upaniṣad's report of her adventures, Discrimination gives comments of his own, showing that he is gradually realizing the falseness of the non-Vedāntic philosophy, and Man, while listening intently to Upaniṣad's narration as well as to Discrimination's explanations, is progressing towards enlightenment.

The philosophical import of this scene may be described as Man's search for truth by the study of the upaniṣads and the critical examination of the philosophies of non-upaniṣadic schools.

First, Man examines Yajñavidyā, the Science of Sacrifice or Ritualism. "Yajñavidyā is surrounded by deer-skins, fire, sacrificial fuel, clarified butter, sacrificial vessels like the ladles called *juhu*, *sruva* etc. and with sacrifices, among which oblations (*iṣṭi*), animal-sacrifices and *soma*-sacrifices are prominent and the performance of which is described in all ritual texts (*karmakāṇḍa*)[3]." "This school thinks : "How can a Puruṣa who is not an agent (as Upaniṣad teaches) be the Supreme Lord ? Action alone destroys Saṃsāra, not the knowledge of truth. Only a man destroying Saṃsāra by performing actions can desire to live for a hundred years with a tranquil mind[4]." Thanks to Discrimination, however, Man realizes that this is a false argument. In reality Brahman is not an agent. It is only Illusion (Māyā) that creates the world. "As iron, though motionless by nature and non-sentient, is

1. Cp. Bh. GĪ XV. 6 : *yad gatvā na nivartante tad dhāma paramam mama*, "Having gone where there is no return, that is my supreme abode."

2. Upaniṣad's account is analysed below, p. 55

3. Pra. Ca. VI v. 13.

4. Pra. Ca. VI v. 15. Cp. Īśopaniṣad 2 : *kurvann eveha karmāṇi jijīviṣec chataṃ samāḥ*, "By doing actions alone one should desire here to live for a hundred years."

forced to move in the proximity of a magnet, in the same way Illusion is prompted to spread out the worlds by the (mere) looking-on of the Spectator of the Universe (*viśvekṣitṛ*). This is what constitutes the Lord's quality of being the Lord[1]."

The argument implies that the Absolute not by its nature a creator or Lord or ruler, but it is only its association with Māyā or Cosmic Illusion which makes the Absolute appear as "the Lord". "Consequently," the Candrikā remarks, "the qualities of being the creator of the world and the lord are illusory[2]."

Saṃsāra, which is caused by ignorance, cannot be annihilated by actions which are themselves a result of ignorance. One cannot destroy pitch darkness through darkness[3]. Knowledge and not action is the means of attaining freedom from worldly existence, from *bhava* or *saṃsāra*. "Knowling him who illumines the seven worlds which are of a perishable nature and full of darkness, the wise man transcends death. There is no other path leading to freedom from existence[4]."

In the text analysed above, the relation of the Absolute is once described as spectatorship or looking-on, once as illumination. Both descriptions belong to the ancient stock of the teaching of Vedānta as well as of Sāṅkhya.

After Yajñavidyā has been disposed of, Man inquires into Mīmāṃsā, which is "attended by the means of knowledge (*pramāṇa*) like *śruti* etc.[5], dividing the rituals according to qualifications (*adhikāra*[6]), and join them with various auxiliaries (*aṅga*[7]) according to the available injunctions (*upa-*

1. Pra. Ca. VI v. 16. The example of the iron and the magnet is a favourite one in Sāṅkhya to prove that matter (*pradhāna*) is non-sentient and moves by the existence and proximity of Puruṣa. The Māṭharavṛtti says : "Proximity and existence of a magnet is the cause of the action of iron. This itself is therefore the cause of action of insentient matter" (p. 9). The Advaitin puts illusion in the place of matter, which is a reality according to the Sāṅkhya but not according to the Vedānta. Cp. also Paramārthasāra v. 12.

2. Pra. Ca. p. 219 : *ato jagatkartṛtvam Īśvaratvaṃ māyikam eva.*

3. Pra. Ca. p. 219.

4. Pra. Ca. VI v. 17 Cp. Śvet. Up. III. 9, VI. 15.

5. *śruti* (direct assertion), *liṅga* (indication), *vākya* (syntactical connection), *prakaraṇa* (context), *sthāna* (position), and *samākhyā* (designation). Mī. pari. p. 23.

6. i. e. statements about what kind of aspirant is qualified for performing a particular rite.

7. They are twofold, viz. those which are componently (*saṃnipatya*) helpful (*upakāraka*) and those which are directly (*ārāt*) so. Mī. pari. p. 31.

deśa[1]) and rules for extended application (*atideśa*[2])[3]."

According to Mīmāṃsā, the soul (*puruṣa*) is the immortal doer and enjoyer of actions. As Upaniṣad teaches a *puruṣa* different from the body, personified Mīmāṃsā in the play says that Upaniṣad's teaching would be a useful supplement to the ritual doctrines if only she were ready to accept ritual action as the means of salvation. This view is approved by one of Mīmāṃsā's disciples. The commentary Candrikā says that the disciple meant here is Prabhākara, who accepts the Upaniṣads as supplementary to, and commendatory of, ritual injunctions. The commentary Nāṭakābharaṇa thinks that the disciple follows Śabarasvāmin's explanation of the Mīmāṃsāsūtras. Kumārila, however, the renowned master of Mīmāṃsā, is of a different opinion. Kṛṣṇamiśra makes him say: "She (Upaniṣad) does not bring a *puruṣa* fit for action but a Lord who is neither a doer nor an enjoyer. This Lord cannot be used for action.[4]"

Another question is raised then, namely whether there is a Lord who is other than the soul living in the world (*laukikah puruṣah*). To this Kumārila replies: "There is one who beholds the actions of the creatures, while the other's intellect is blinded by delusion; one desires the fruits of actions while the other gives them to the seeker; one engages himself in actions while the other is a deity, the protector, as it were, of the embodied ones; how can this *puruṣa*, who is not attached to actions, be considered to be an agent[5]?" Thus, according to Kṛṣṇamiśra, Mīmāṃsā or at least one group of this school does recognise the Lord as well as the individual soul, though the soul according to this teaching is the agent of actions and not, as Vedānta holds, ultimately identical with the Lord of the Universe who is inactive.

Discrimination approves Kumārila's words by almost literally quoting a famous verse from an upaniṣad: "Two birds with beautiful feathers, inseparable friends, cling to one and the same tree; one of them eats the ripe fruit while the other

1. *ittham kartavyam ity upadeśah* Pra. Ca. Candrikā p. 222.
2. *tadvad idam kartavyam ity atideśaḥ* Pra. Ça. Çandrikā p. 222,
3. Pra. Ca. VI v. 18.
4. Pra. Ca. p. 224.
5. Pra. Ca. VI v. 19.

looks on without eating[1]." The two birds are the individual soul and the supreme soul or the Lord. The tree to which both of them cling is the body, according to the commentators of the Prabodhacandrodaya. The soul "eats the fruit", i.e. enjoys the result, of its previous actions, whereas the Lord remains inactive. The dualistic simile can of course be accepted by the monist and illusionist only as a preliminary statement, describing as it does the nature of the illusion-bound individual soul as active and distinct from the inactive Supreme Soul. But at this moment Man's Discrimination has not yet reached the stage of absolute monism. So he can applaud to Kumārila's statement.

After Mīmāṃsā, Rational Philosophy (Tarkavidyā) is taken up for investigation by Man. Nyāya, Vaiśeṣika, and Sāṅkhya are placed in the same class of Tarkavidyā by Kṛṣṇamiśra. "One (of the schools of Tarkavidyā, viz. Vaiśeṣika) is engaged in establishing the differentiae (*viśeṣa*) of the universe; another (viz. Nyāya) deals with disputation (*jalpa*), discussion (*vāda*), and polemics (*vitaṇḍa*) by arguments containing good tricks (*chala*), futile answers (*jāti*), and faulty syllogisms (*nigraha*)[2]; yet another (viz. Sāṅkhya), stating the difference between matter (*prakṛti*) and soul (*puruṣa*) after separating them, is engaged in enumerating the principles, *mahat*, *ahṃkāra*, etc., in the order of cosmogony[3]." According to the Nyāya and Vaiśeṣika schools, the universe originates from atoms. God is only an efficient cause[4]. A Sāṅkhya philosopher, apparently alluding to the view of early Vedānta that Brahman is the material cause of the world, reproaches Upaniṣad : "You wicked one ! How can you make the Lord subject to change and teach that he has perishable properties ! Does not the world arise from Primary Matter (*pradhāna*), you foolish one ?[5]" This argument contends that the doctrine of the Lord being the material cause is contradictory to the *idea* of God, but it does not imply that the Sāṅkhya philosopher speaking here admits the existence of a Supreme God.

1. Pra. Ca. VI v. 20. Cp. Muṇḍ. Up. III. 1. 1 and Śvet. Up. IV. 6.
2. Cp. Nyāyasūtra 1. 1. 1., 2. 2-3, 10.
3. Pra. Ca. VI v. 21.
4. Pra. Ca. p. 228.
5. ibidem.

9. *The teaching of illusionism*

King Discrimination cannot accept the view of any of the Tarkavidyā systems. He has a different view about the material cause of the world. According to him, neither the atoms not primary matter is the cause, nor is it Brahman or the Lord directly. He says: "Everything which is an object of knowledge is an effect like a pot. Therefore (the ideas of) the atoms or primary matter being the material cause of the world are to be discarded[1]. For "just as the moon seen in water, just as a city in the sky, just as dreams and magic, so also the universe is an effect, an object of knowledge, unreal, subject to origin, destruction, etc. It arises when Viṣṇu, who is self-awakening (self-luminous), is unknown, like silver in a shell and a serpent in a garland, but disappears when the knowledge of truth has arisen[2]."

Thus the problem of the material cause of the world is solved by the theory of illusionism. Everything which is subject to origin, to change and ruin, everything which is an effect and an object of knowledge, is on the same level with illusions of vision and nothing but an outcome of the soul not having realized its identity with the Absolute, which is here given the name of god Viṣṇu (Hari). A shell may be mistaken for silver and in a garland one may erroneously see a serpent, but the silver and the serpent vanish into the shell and the garland, respectively, once the real thing is discerned. As the shell and the garland may be described as the material cause of the illusion superimposed on it, in this way only is the Absolute the material cause of the world. Therefore, the apprehension that the Absolute or God might become mutable by being the material cause of the world, is quite inept: "How can that tranquil Light, which is beginningless bliss, eternally luminous, partless and stainless, be subject to changes when the universe originates? In the same way, what kind of change happens to the sky when rows of clouds shining like the petals of a blue lotus appear[3]?" The clouds do not in any way change the sky. If one thinks on seeing them that the sky is blue or limited, it

1. Pra. Ca. p. 228.
2. Pra. Ca. VI v. 22.
3. Pra. Ca. VI v. 23.

is due to ignorance. In the same way Brahman is not affected by the appearance of the universe. If it appears so it is an illusion[1].

10. *The realization of monism*

By now Man has realized the doctrine of illusionism, but the monism which teaches the identity of the individual soul and the supreme soul is still unintelligible to him. He asks: "who is he who is called 'the Lord' ?" Upaniṣad angrily retorts : "Who can give a reply to one who does not know his own self ?" Man asks : "How can myself be the Supreme Lord ?" Upaniṣad replies : "That eternal Puruṣa is no other than you, and you are not different from that Lord, the Supreme Puruṣa. Through beginningless Illusion he is separate from you, like the reflection of the sun in water (which is seemingly separate from the sun itself)[2]." Still Man finds it difficult to accept that he who is different from God, limited, and subject to old age and death, is identical with Reality, Bliss and Intelligence.[3] This doubt arises because he has not comprehended the sentence *tat tvam asi*, "Thou art that", for he does not know what is meant by the words *tat* and tvam[4]. The meaning of these words has therefore to be contemplated.

Discrimination explains : "(In the conception) 'This I am' (the idea of the pure spiritual essence of the self) is mixed up with (the idea of) the mind. When (the purely spiritual self) has been discriminated (from the mind) with the aid of (the upaniṣad saying) 'it is not this'[5]; when the gross elements have been dissolved (i. e. reduced to their primary, unevolved state by thinking that they are in reality nothing but this state); when, then, the meaning of 'thou' (in the upaniṣad saying 'Thou art that') is known to be the spiritual self : then, on hearing "Thou art that", (the self) becomes effulgent with

1. Cp. Paramārthasāra v. 33 :
jvalanād dhūmodgatibhir vividhākṛtir ambare yathā bhāti
tadvad viṣṇau sṛṣṭiḥ svamāyayā dvaitavistarā bhāti.

2. Pra. Ca. pp. 232 ff.; VI v. 25. The readings adopted here for the preceding prose portions, translated above, are those of the Trivandrum edition (p. 201 f.).

3. Pra. Ca. VI v. 26.

4. Pra. Ca. p. 234.

5. Bṛ. Up. III. 9. 26.

bliss internally abounding : the self-luminous, tranquil, infinite light, from which the darkness of Saṃsāra has been removed."[1] This shows that, in order to understand the sentence *tat tvam asi* as meaning: 'Thou art' pure spirit and as such identical with 'that', viz. with the Absolute which is pure spirit, one has to discriminate the self from the mind. In the worldly state the self identifies itself with the mind or inner organ. But in reality the mind is an outcome of the gross elements and an object. With the aid of the Great Saying "Not this, not this" (*neti neti*) one has to discriminate the self from all that is elemental and objective, even from the mind. When this is done, the gross things vanish into nothingness. Then it is easy to know what is meant by the word "thou" and to identify the spiritual "thou" with the spiritual "that". In this way monism is realized.

Knowledge is imparted to Man through the discriminative study of the upaniṣads. It is only a means of spiritual awakening. Its purpose is to destroy ignorance. When this has been done and awakening has arisen, knowledge destorys itself. "Knowledge comes out breaking the chest of Mind and disappears suddenly devouring Delusion along with his followers. And Rise of Spiritual Awakening goes to the One Puruṣa[2]." Knowledge presupposes a subject and an object ; so as long as it exists there is duality. That is why in the real state there is no place for knowledge. This state is only awakening. Rise of Awakening (Prabodhodaya) gives utterance to the experience of monism in the words : "I am that Rise of Awakening by whose rising the three worlds, burst by (my) natural splendour, cease to be the object of arguments such as whether they are attached or lost, born or removed, woven together or dissolved, or whether they are a thing or nothing.[3]"

As soon as the awakening dawns, Man realises his identity with the Absolute: "After shaking off the darkness of delusion, after throwing off the sleep of error, a cool ray of awakening has been born. I am that Viṣṇu who becomes manifest as the Universal Self through faith, discrimination, reason, peace, self-restraint, etc[4]."

1. Pra Ca. VI. v. 27.
2. Pra. Ca. VI v. 28.
3. Pra. Ca. VI. v. 29.
4. Pra. Ca. VI v. 30.

Kṛṣṇamiśra accepts liberation in the embodied state (*jīvanmukti*). Man has awakened to his identity with Brahman but is not yet freed from the body. The body, however, does not limit him in any way. He says: "I shall soon be a sage (*muni*) who is in a house only at night, who is not attached to anything, who does not ask for anything, who wanders in any direction without aiming at any fruit; tranquil; free from fear, sorrow, impurities, and delusion.[1]"

Man's awakening is "due to the grace of Viṣṇubhakti[2]". Even at the *jīvanmukti* stage Viṣṇubhakti remains with him. This shows that Kṛṣṇamiśra combines strict theism with his monistic views.

1. Pra. Ca. VI v. 31. I prefer the reading *sāyaṃgṛho* ("who is in a house only at night"), which is given as a varia lectio in the Nirṇayasāgar edition, to the *svāyaṃbhuvo* of the text. The text of the Trivandrum edition has *sāyaṃ gṛhe*.

2. Pra. Ca. p. 240.

CHAPTER III

Other Vedic schools and sects

Among the philosophical systems which are non-Vedāntic but supposed to be in harmony with the Vedas, Mīmāṃsā, Nyāya, Vaiśeṣika, and Sāṅkhya are mentioned by Kṛṣṇamiśra. The main doctrines of these systems and of the Science of Sacrifice, as far as included in Upaniṣad's report, have been analysed above. Among the teachers referred to are Guru, Kumārila, Vācaspati, Sārika, and Mahodadhi[1]. Guru, i. e. Prabhākara, and Kumārila are the well-known founders of the two schools of Mīmāṃsā. Vācaspati evidently is the great scholar that commented on works of different systems[2]. Sārika, or, as the Trivandrum edition reads, Śālika, is Śālikanātha according to the explanations of all the three commentaries which I used. He was a Mīmāṃsaka of the Prābhākara school. Mahodadhi also was an author of this school according to the Candrikā.

In the same context where these five names of teachers are mentioned, there is the passage *mahāvratī nekṣitā sūkṣmā vastuvicāraṇā*, "the subtle investigation into truth of Mahāvrata is not looked at". Here *māhāvratī* is the feminine of an adjective derived from *mahāvrata*. The question is what the meaning of *mahāvrata* is. The commentaries give different answers. According to the Candrikā the word refers to Mahāvrata, whom this commentary describes as an author of the Bhāṭṭa school of Mīmāṃsā and an opponent of Mahodadhi. As all the other names mentioned in the same context are those of Mīmāṃsā teachers or authors—since Vācaspati also wrote works on mīmāṃsā—, this explanation seems acceptable. But *mahāvrata* is also the

1. Pra. Ca. III v. 3.

2. J. H. Woods and L. Suali have placed him in the 9th century A.D. See also S. N. Dasgupta, *History*, Vol. I, p. 307. But according to Prof. Hacker, Vācaspati lived after Jayanta in the second half of the 10th century. See P. Hacker, *Jayantabhaṭṭa und Vācaspatimiśra*, ihre Zeit......., in : Studien zur indischen Philologie und Altertumskunde (Schubring-Festschrift, Hamburg, 1951, pp. 160 ff.

name of a Śaiva sect; so the Nāṭakābharaṇa, in one of its three explanations of *māhāvratī*, says that the word may denote a certain Śaiva sect (*śaivāgamabheda*), and the Prakāśa identifies the Mahāvrata with the Pāsupata sect[1]. The two other interpretations offered by the Nāṭakābharaṇa explain the word as denoting "the old school of Mīmāṃsā" or a collection of certain vows[2]. However, Śaiva sects are mentioned in the same context later. Egoism, who speaks of the general ignorance and hypocrisy of all the schools, first refers to Mīmāṃsakas, then to the Vedānta, then to other schools and sects, among which he expressly mentions the Śaivas (and) Pāśupatas. It does not, therefore, seem probable that the word māhāvratī, occuring between the references to Mīmāṃsā and Vedānta, should denote a Śaiva sect.

It is important to note that Kṛṣṇamiśra does not regard Yoga as a separate school of philosophy. But throughout the drama Yoga elements play a very important role. Yoga is not a rival system but a way to the final non-dualistic realization.[3] The second verse in the play is in praise of Śiva in his Yogic posture. The eight constituents of Yoga—Yama (consisting in moral precepts), Niyama (consisting in rules of self-control), Āsana (bodily posture), Prāṇāyāma (breath control), Pratyāhāra (withdrawal of the senses), Dhāraṇā (fixation of attention), Dhyāna (contemplation), and Samādhi[4] (absorptive concentration)—are treated as ministers of King Discrimination. Viṣṇubhakti is said to bless the army of Discrimination by enlivening the constituents of Yoga, Prāṇāyāma and the rest, at the appropriate time.[5] This means that Yoga is here

1. Others identify the Mahāvrata sect with that of the Kāpālikas or classify it as independent. See Bhandarkar, *Vaiṣṇavism* etc., p. 128; Karmarkar, *Religions*, Vol. I, p. 220; Dasgupta, *History*, Vol. V. p. 2.

2. *bhadradīpapratiṣṭhādiprajāpativratavíśeṣāṇām samāhārah*, T. S. S. edition p. 45. For the *prajāpativrata* mentioned here see P. V. Kane, *History of Dharmaśāstra*, vol. V. Poona, 1958, p. 349, where, however, the "varieties" (*viśeṣāh*) alluded to in the *Nāṭakābharaṇa* are not mentioned. These varieties consist in the "installation of an auspicious lamp" (*bhadradīpratiṣṭhā* and other observances; cp. Kane, op. cit., p. 314, s. v. *dīpapratṣṭhāvrata*.

3. Cp. Frauwallner, *Geschichte der indischen Philosophie*, vol. I, p. 408: "Der Yoga ist Kein System, sondern ein Weg, die Erlösung zu finden, und konnte als solcher mit den verschiedensten philosophischen Lehren verbunden werden."

4. Yogasūtra II. 29.

5. Pra Ca. p. 137.

regarded as an expression of devotion; devotion is the force that impels acts of Yoga. Another Yoga term which is found in the play is *ṛtaṃbharā*[1], i.e. Bearer of Truth. This means a state of consciousness attained in yogic concentration and said "to bear truth and nothing else; in it there is not even a trace of misconception[2]." Ṛtambharā co-operates in bringing about the awakening of Puruṣa when Discrimination is united with Upaniṣad through the activity of Peace and other forces.

Apart from the eight constituent parts of Yoga, there are four other practices recommended in the Yogasūtras as a means to attain tranquillity of mind. They are *maitrī* (friendliness), *karuṇā* (compassion), *muditā* (joy), and *upekṣā* (indifference[3]) These practices, only with a change in one of the names (*anukampā* instead of *karuṇā*), are personified in the play as four sisters who help Discrimination. What Vyāsa says in prose in his commentary on Yogasutra I. 33, Kṛṣṇamiśra expresses in a verse: "Towards a happy person, have thoughts of this (i. e. friendliness), towards an unhappy one, thoughts of compassion, towards good actions, of joy, and towards malice, of indifference. Thus the inner self (i.e. the mind), though tainted by attachment, greed, spite, etc., attains clarity.[4]"

Another term typical of the Yoga system is *kleśa*, occurring in the compound *kleśamahormayaḥ*[5], "the great waves of troubles." By this word the five mental afflictions *avidyā* (ignorance), *asmitā* (I-am ness), *rāga* (attachment to worldy objects), *dveṣa* (hatred), and *abhiniveśa*[6] (clinging to life) are meant. In the end it is only through *nididhyāsana* or meditation that knowledge is born and along with it Puruṣa awakens to his oneness with the Supreme Reality.

1. Pra Ca. p. 137. Cp. Yogasūtra I. 48 : *ṛtaṃbharā tatra prajñā.*
2. Vyāsa's commentary on Yogasūtra I. 48.
3. Yogasūtra I. 33 : *maitrīkaruṇamuditopekṣāṇām sukhaduḥkhapuṇyāpuṇyaviṣayāṇāṃ bhāvanātas cittaprasādanam.*
4. Pra Ca. IV v. 5 :
   dhyāyann imām sukhini duḥkhini cānukampām
   puṇyakriyāsu muditām kumatāv upekṣām
   evaṃ prasādam upayāti hi rāgalobha-dveṣādidoṣakaluṣo 'py ayam antarātma.

   Vyāsa on Yogasūtra I. 33 : *tatra sarvaprāṇiṣu sukhasaṃbhogāpanneṣu maitrīṃ bhāvayet, duḥkhiteṣu karuṇāṃ, puṇyātmakeṣu muditām, apuṇyaśileṣūpekṣām. evam asya bhāvayataḥ śuklo dharma upajāyate. tatas ca cittaṃ prasīdati.*
5. Pra. Ca. VI v. 8.
6. Yogasutra II. 3.

Perhaps it is due to the presence of these Yoga elements that Kṛṣṇamiśra's devotion is rational rather than emotional.

Apart from the philosophical schools, Kṛṣṇamiśra also mentions religious sects: Vaiṣṇavas, Śaivas, Sauras, and Pāśupatas. But we cannot gather much information about them from the drama.

The Vaiṣṇavas are mentioned only once, along with the Śaivas and Sauras[1], among the allies of King Discrimination. Kṛṣṇamiśra's attitude as to the difference of Ṣaivism and Vaiṣṇavism is rather complex. It is obvious from the whole play that he is a Vaiṣṇava and his Vedānta may even be described as a spiritualized form of Vaiṣṇavism. Viṣṇubhkti, Devotion to Viṣṇu, is represented by him as the force that guides Man on his path to emancipation, and she stays with him even in the state of emancipation. In the play Viṣṇu is worshipped even at a place like Banaras where, as is well known, the presiding deity is Śiva.[2] But Kṛṣṇamiśra's Vaiṣṇavism is a liberal one. It is true that he identifies the Supreme Reality with Viṣṇu; that he classifies the Śaiva sect of the Kāplikas among the abject heresies; that he describes Mahābhairavī, who after all is nobody else than Śiva's consort Kālī, as a demoniac being who had overwhelmed Faith and from whose grip Faith had to be rescued by Devotion to Viṣṇu[3]. But all this does not imply that he is hostile to Śiva. As a matter of fact, he worships Śiva in the opening section of the play, following a general practice based on the belief that Śiva is the patron of drama. Speaking of Śaivas in general, he classifies them, along with the Vaiṣṇavas, among the groups helpful in the preliminary stages of Man's liberation. Fundamentally, for Kṛṣṇamiśra, there is no difference between Śiva and Viṣṇu. In the fifth act, where all Vedic schools and sects join their forces, Faith says: "The tranquil, endless, indivisible, unborn Light is variously praised as Brahmā, Acyuta (i. e. Viṣṇu), and Umāpati (i. e. Śiva) according to the emergence of various qualities.[4]" Viṣṇu is said to be dear to Śiva.[5] This may imply that he is higher than

1. Pra. Ca. p. 172.
2. Pra. Ca. pp. 161 ff.
3. Pra. Ca. IV vv. 1-4, pp. 132-136.
4. Pra. Ca. V v. 9.
5. Pra. Ca. p. 164.

Śiva or that both are equal. Viṣṇu's avatāras are also accepted.[1] Viṣṇu is the inner self of all; he is sung by the wise as the soul of the body (kṣetrasyātmā).[2] Ultimately, he is the only Reality, the whole universe being only an illusion.[3]

The Sauras are mentioned only once[4]. They form a small sect in central and southern India whose special object of worship is the Sun, Sūrya.[5] Little is known about this sect except for a few stray references and anecdotes. One such anecdote is given by Ānandagiri in his Śaṅkaradigvijaya.[6]

There is a phrase in the Prabodhacandrodaya referring to the Śaivas, Pāśupatas, etc. : *Śaivapāśupatādayo durabhyastākṣapādamatāḥ.*[7] By the compound *Śaivapāśupatādayaḥ* the author perhaps means the Śaivas, Pāśupatas, and other schools. But the commentary Candrikā gives another interpretation. According to it, there are two kinds of Pāśupatas, Saivapāśupatas and Śāktapāśupatas, and the word *ādayaḥ* is meant to include the Śāktapāśupatas.

The compound *durabhyastākṣapādamatāḥ* shows that the Śaivas (in general) took great pains in learning the doctrines of Akṣapāda, who is the same as Gautama, the author of the Nyāyasūtras.[8] This confirms the view of Rājaśekhara (about 1350 A. D.) that the Naiyāyikas were regarded as Śaivas. In his Ṣaḍdarśanasaṃhitā he mentions the names of

1. Pra. Ca. p. 20 and pp. 162-164. Paraśūrāma is expressly mentioned (p. 20), while Vāmana, Kṛṣṇa, Nṛsiṃha, and Kūrma are alluded to. According to the commentary Candrikā (p. 163 f.), Buddha and Balarāma are also referred to.

2. Pra. Ca. IV v. 30.

3. Cp. Pra. Ca. VI v. 22.

4. Pra. Ca. p. 172.

5. Cp. *Encyclopedia of Religion and Ethics*, Vol. XI, s. v. Saura; Bhandarkar, *Vaiṣṇavism* etc., p. 152 f.

6. Prakaraṇa 13.

7. Pra. Ca. p. 55.

8. Here, I think, the Southern schools of Śaivism are meant. The other school, known as Kāṣmīr Śaivism which developed in the beginning of the 9th or perhaps towards the end of the 8th century of the Christian era, does not seem to have taken special interest in Nyāya.

Śaiva teachers who were particularly revered. One among them is Akṣapāda.[1] Both the Naiyāyikas and the Śaivas held that God was only the efficient cause of the universe. Both schools believed in *duḥkhānta* (end of all sorrow) as liberation.[2]

1. See Dasgupta, *History of Indian Philosophy*, vol. V, pp. 6, 8-9.

2. For the doctrines of the old school of Pāśupata Śaivism, cp. the thesis of Friedrich A. Schultz : *Die philosophisch-theologischen Lehren des Pāśupata-Systems...*, Bonn, 1958.

Chapter IV

Non-Vedic Schools

1. *The Cārvāka or Lokāyata*

Kṛṣṇamiśra deals with this school at great length. Lokāyata is the system founded by Vācaspati, also known as Bṛhaspati, who handed it over to Cārvāka, who in turn spread it in the world through his disciples.[1] The word *lokāyata* means "what prevails among men." The Lokāyata or Cārvāka system is materialistic. It is the foremost enemy of all religious and philosophical schools based on the Vedas. According to Kṛṣṇamiśra, Buddhism, Jainism, and the Kāpālika sect are based on the Lokāyata system.[2] Therefore, once this system is overthrown, the schools and sects derived from it are also ruined. All the Vedic schools in the play join together to defeat the Cārvāka system.

As to the question whether there is a soul separate from the body, we get the answer in the following verse, put in the mouth of Delusion who is depicted in the play as the great friend of Cārvāka : "(The view) that there is a soul separate from the body, which on reaching the other world enjoys rewards, is (like) the hope to get tasty fruits from the big flower of a tree in the sky.[3]" The opinion that after the death of the body no soul remains is expressed in the following : "The many talkative believers (*āstikas*) who jabber in vain that a thing which does not exist, exists, condemn the truth-speaking non-believers (*nāstikas*)[4]. Oh, look,has anyone in reality seen a soul separate from the body, which has formed the intelligence as a transformation (of itself)[5]."

1. Pra. Ca. p. 71. The word Cārvāka means "sweet-tongued." (*cāru-vāka*). It is also supposed to have derived from *carv*, to eat.
2. Pra. Ca. V p. 176 f.
3. Pra. Ca. II. 16. *ākāśataroḥ prasūnam*, more commonly *khapuṣpa*, is an example given usually for a thing which does not and can never exist.
4. The words *āstika* and *nāstika* specifically denote those who accept, and those who do not accept, the authority of the Vedas.
5. Pra. Ca. II v. 17. Cp. S. D. S. p. 2 : *caitanyaviśiṣṭa eva ātmā.* The reading *varṣmaṇām* in the *Nirṇayasāgar* edition is a misprint for *varṣmaṇo.*

The materialist does not believe in the caste system (*varṇa-bheda*). He does not recognise moral precepts. He teaches : "If the bodies are alike in their different parts, the mouth, etc, how can there be a hierarchy of castes ? We do not accept any difference between a woman or wealth belonging (to us or) to somebody else. Only those who are devoid of manliness consider whether an act should be done or not, when it entails injury, approaching women at one's pleasure and seizing the wealth of others.[1]"

According to the Cārvāka, the only means of knowledge is perception.[2] The elements are earth, water, fire, and air. Wealth and pleasure[3] are the sole aims of man The elements move through original impulse. There is no other world. Emancipation is death. Knowledge consists only on statecraft. *Vārtā* or the science of agriculture and trade is included in this.[4] The three Vedas are incoherent talk of cheats.[5] If their teachings about sacrifices lead to heaven, then processes similar to sacrifices must lead to the same result : "If sacrifices obtain heaven by the destruction of the sacrificial matter through the action of the officiating (priest), then the trees burnt by the forest fire will bear ample fruit.[6]" The teachings of the Veda are nothing but nonsense: "If it is assumed that an animal slain (in sacrifice) goes to heaven, why does not the sacrificer forthwith im-

1. Pra. Ca. II v. 18.

2. There is a work of the materialist school called *Tattvopaplavasiṃha*, by Jayarāśi Bhaṭṭa (8th century) (published in Gaekwad's Oriental Series, 1940), which does not accept any *pramāṇa*, not even *pratyakṣa*. This shows that the Cārvākas were divided among themselves, some accepting perception and some accepting no valid means of knowledge at all.

3. *artha* and *kāma*. *dharma* and *mokṣa* are dismissed.

4. Pra. Ca. p. 71 : *daṇḍanītir eva vidyā. atraiva vārtāntarbhavati.* Cp. Kauṭīlyā, Arthaśāstra: *anvikṣikī trayī vārtā daṇḍanītiś ceti vidyāh* (I. 2. 1); *vārtā daṇḍanītiś ceti bārhaspatyāḥ* (I. 2. 4); *daṇḍanītir eva vidyety auśanāsaḥ* (I. 2. 6); *tasyām hi sarvavidyārambhāh pratibaddhā iti* (I. 2. 7); *kṛṣipaśupālye vāṇijyā ca vārtā* (I. 4. 1); Bṛhaspatisūtra 1. 3.: *daṇḍanītir eva vidyā.* It is to be noted that whereas the Bṛhaspati of Kauṭilya accepts *vārtā* and *daṇḍanīti* the author of the Bṛhaspatisūtras, who is obviously a theist, accepts only *daṇḍanīti*, like the Cārvāka of Kṛṣṇamiśra and Kauṭilya's Auśanasa. Cp. also Frauwallner, *Philosophie* II p. 296 : "...die enge Verbindung des Materialismus mit der politischen Theorie." Also cp. Ruben, *Materialismus*.

5. Cp. S. D. S. p. 3 : *dhūrtapralāpas trayī.*

6. Pra. Ca. II. v. 19. This verse is quoted verbatim in the Sarva-matasaṃgraha.

molate his own father[1] ?" "If *śrāddha* (offering of rice-balls to a dead person) produces gratifications to beings who are dead, then oil may rear the flame of an extinguished light[2]." "It is the reasoning of fools that the pleasure which arises to men from contact with sensible objects is to be relinquished as accompanied by pain. What man seeking his true interest would fling away the berries of paddy, rich with the finest white grains, because they are covered with husks and dust ?[3]" "Bṛhaspati says that the oblation in the fire, the three Vedas, the carrying of three sticks tied together, and smearing oneself with ashes are the means of livelihood of those who are devoid of intelligence and manliness.[4]"

The Cārvāka classifies the Vedāntins along with the Buddhists : "If the Vedantas (i. e. the upaniṣads), which accept things contradictory to what is established through the means of knowledge, sense perception etc., are authoritative scriptures (śāstra), then what wrong are the Buddhists doing[5] ?" The Vedāntin says that the world which he knows through the means of knowledge is unreal. That implies a contradiction. The Buddhist, on the other hand, says that everything has only momentary existence, which is just as contradictory to experience as the Vedāntin's view.

2. *The Jaina*

The Jaina is called Digaṃbara[6] and Kṣapaṇaka in our text. He speaks Māgadhī Prākṛt whereas the Buddhist and Kāpālika speak Sanskrit. This means that he is assigned to a

1. Pra. Ca. II v. 20. Cp. S. D. S. p. 6.

2. Pra. Ca. II v. 21. Cp. S. D. S. p. 6, where the second line of the verse is different.

3. Pra. Ca. II v. 23. Cp. S. D. S. p. 3.

4. Pra. Ca. II v. 26. Cp. S. D. S. p. 3 and Śrīharṣa, *Naiṣadhīyacarita* 17. 39. The verse also occurs in the Sarvamatasaṃgraha and in the Sarvasiddhāntasaṃgraha attributed to Śaṅkara. All these works must have quoted from a work of Bṛhaspati which must have been extant as late as the 12th century, in which both Śrīharṣa and Mādhava, the author of S. D. S., lived.

5. Pra. Ca. II v. 4. This verse too is quoted in the Sarvamatasaṃgraha.

6. There are two sects of Jainas, followers of the Jina, the Digambaras and the Śvetāmbaras. The Digambaras are also known as Vivasanas, Muktavasanas, and Muktāmbaras, all these words meaning "without clothing." The Śvetāmbaras, "clad in white", are of modern origin and less strict.

low class of society. He is dirty to look at, the hair of his head has been plucked out[1] and he wears no clothes. He carries in his hand a peacock feather. He has no manliness about him (*nirvīrya.*)

Very little of the doctrines of the Jaina system is mentioned in the drama. Kṛṣṇamiśra's main object in bringing a Jaina on the stage is to depict this sect as an abject heresy, detestable and comical at the same time, quarrelling with the other non-Vedic sects. Unlike the Buddhist, the Jaina believes in the eternal nature of the self; so he opposes the Buddhist who holds that the self has only a momentary existence. That is why he asks the Buddhist : "For whose sake do you, who perish in a moment, keep this observance ?[2]" This means: If there is no continuity of the self, who then is the being who will be emancipated, according to the Buddhists belief, as a result of observing the rules of Buddhism ? The Jaina teaches : "The self shines like a lamp in the middle of the town with nine gates[3]." The intrinsic nature or the self of soul (*ātman, jīva*) is purity[4], whereas the body is a lump of impure matter[5]. The self is to be known through the service of sages: "From a distance one should prostrate oneself at the feet (of sages) and should welcome them and give them sweet food. One should not pollute oneself with jealousy when the sages are enjoying their wives."[6] The Jaina believes that the founder of his religion was omniscient because he knew, and gave information of, the mysteries of astronomy and astrology.[7] This implies that the Jaina's soul had attained "absolute knowledge". The Buddhist, however, contends that the assumption of a soul being omniscient is incompatible with the doctrine, which he implicitly attributes to the Jaina, that the soul is confined to the body. So he says: "Tell me how the soul, limited by the body, without association with anything else, can know the three worlds. Can a lamp,

1. The word *ulluñcitacikura* alludes to the practice of eradicating the hair of the head or body by way of mortification.

2. Pra. Ca. p. 107.

3. Pra. Ca. p. 100. The "town with nine gates" is the body.

4. *appā vimala-sahāo* Pra. Ca. p. 101.

5. *mala-maa-puggala-pinda* p. 101. *puggala,* Sanskrit *pudgala,* is the Jaina term for "matter".

6. Pra. Ca. III v. 6.

7. Pra. Ca. p. 110. There are many variant readings of this passage.

though having a bright flame, but placed in a jar, illuminate the things inside a house ?"[1]

3. *The Buddhist*

Like Jainism, Buddhism is not dealt with much in detail by Kṛṣṇamiśra. The Buddhist religion like that of the Jaina's is described as *tāmasika*, i.e., an outcome of darkness. The Buddhist monk is depicted as indulging in worldly pleasures.[2] That may point to a certain degeneration of Indian Buddhism at Kṛṣṇamiśra's time but most probably it is simply meant as a means to represent the non-Brāhminical religion of the Buddhist as detestable.

The philosophy of the Buddhist is outlined in a very condensed form: "All elements of existence are momentary and devoid of self. They appear as if they were outside (had objective existence), (but are only) super-imposed on the chain or flux of consciousness which shines without any object-tinge, when all the Vāsanās[3] are dropped[4]." Lord Buddha says "I see with a divine eye how people rise and fall (in transmigration). All conformations[5] are momentary. There is no lasting self.[6] "Somebody characterised by pure consciousness who has fallen into the chain or flux of (consciousness which is) my person, will attain liberation, when he is freed from all *vāsanās*[7]."

The doctrine which is summarised here points to the final stage of development of Buddhist philosophy. The Sarvāstivāda of the Hīnayāna, i. e. the school that believed that "everything exists", had developed, as its basic tenet, the doctrine that all elements of existence (*bhāva*, *dharma*) have an instantaneous being only, that there is no real connection between them and that they are devoid of self. This doctrine is alluded to in the first line of verse III 8, quoted above. But it is combined, in the Pra. Ca., with the tenet of Buddhist idealism (*vijñānavāda*)

1. Pra. Ca. III v. 11. By "something else" he perhaps here means *citta*, intelligence.
2. Pra. Ca. III v. 9.
3. Explained later.
4. Pra. Ca. III v. 8.
5. This translation of '*saṃskāra*' is taken from Dasgupta, *Phil.* Vol. I p. 86.
6. Pra. Ca. p. 106.
7. Pra. Ca. p. 107.

which denies the reality of the external world[1], and explains the external world to be only an appearance, superimposed on the flux of consciousness. This combination roughly corresponds to the stage of development represented by Asaṅga and Vasubandhu, who tried to integrate the theory of momentariness with their idealism, or even to the final stage reached in the logical school by Diṅgnāga and Dharmakīrti[2].

Some of the expressions in the passages quoted above need explanation. In explaining them I shall depend on both Sarvāstivāda and Vijñānavāda sources.

The word *bhāva* (element of existence) in Pra. Ca. III v. 8 corresponds to the *dharma* commonly used in Buddhistic texts. In the Sarvāstivāda, *dharma* (element), *vastu* (reality), *bhāva* (existence), *dravya* (thing) are convertible terms[3]. The elements of existence are momentary appearances. According to the Sarvāstivādin[4] every element is affected simultaneously by four different forces called *saṃskāras*, the forces of origination (*utpāda*), decay (*jarā*), maintenance (*sthiti*) and destruction (*ani tyatā*). The elements when affected by these forces are called manifested elements (*saṃskṛta-dharma*). The term *saṃskṛta* is therefore synonymous with *kṣaṇika* i. e. "impermanent" or "momentary."

Saṃskāra (force) and *Cetanā* (will) are the same.[5] The Buddhists converted all the elements of existence into forces subtle to some degree. The subtler the element, the more it was given the character of a force. The Buddhists used the word *saṃskāra* (force) and *saṃskṛta* (the element influenced by the force) for one and the same. Yaśomitra[6] remarks that the name *saṃskṛta* is given in anticipation, since an element will become *saṃskṛta* only when the forces (*saṃskāras*) have exercised their efficiency.

So when Kṛṣṇamiśra says *kṣaṇikāḥ sarve saṃskārah*

1. This is the view of Asaṅga and his followers and also of Vasubandhu, the author of Vijñaptimātratāsiddhi. The logical school of Buddhism did not accept this theory completely.

2. Cp. Stch., *Logic* I p. 108 ff.

3. Stch. *Logic* I, p. 507.

4. Abhidharmakośa, II 46. See Stch., *The Central Conception*, p. 39.

5. Stch., *The Central Conception*, p. 20.

6. Commentary to Abhi. Ko. 1, 15. See Stch., *The Central Conception*, p. 22, footnote.

(all conformations are instantaneous), the word *saṃskāra* stands for *saṃskṛta-dharma*.

Another important word is *Vāsanā*, literally "perfume". It is something which remains like a perfume after an action has been done. Suzuki translates it as "habit energy", and explains it as "a kind of super-sensuous energy mysteriously emanating from every thought, every feeling or every deed one has done, or does, which lives latently in the store house called *ālayavijñāna*."[1] With the idealistic Buddhist, this perfoms the function of explaining the origination of phenomenal plurality out of transcendental unity. It is similar to the *Karma* or *Cetanā* of the early Buddhists, the *māyā* of the Mādhyamikas, the *bhāvanā* of the Mīmāṃsakas, the *adṛṣṭa*, *apūrva*, *adhyāsa* and *saṃskāra* of all schools[2].

Next, the word '*vijñāna*' requires explanation. The Buddhists classify the elements of existence into five *skandhas*; *rūpa* (matter), *vedanā* (feelings) *samjñā* (ideas), *saṃskarās* (volition and other faculties) and *vijñāna* (pure sensation or general consciousness). The mind according to Buddhist philosophy is divided into two chief parts, one subjective and one objective. "The subjective part, or mind viewed as a receptive faculty, is represented by one element called, indiscriminately, *citta*, *vijñāna* or *manas*. It represents pure consciousness, or pure sensation, without any content. Its content is placed in the objective part, which contains the definite sensation (*sparśa*), feelings (*vedanā*), ideas (*saṃjña*),volitions (*cetanā*) and various other mental phenomena upto the number of forty-six separate elements."[3] Kṛṣṇamiśra uses the words *dhī* and *vijñāna* as synonyms. *Vijñāna* (consciousness) and *vijñānasaṃtati* (chain or flux of consciousness) are the same. "Consciousness is a conventional name for a chain of conscious moments[4]." Kṛṣṇamiśra terms this *dhīsaṃtati*. The self or *ātman* is a conventional term applied to what is only a flux of elements. When the *vāsanās* are freed, this self becomes *vijñānalakṣaṇa*, pure consciousness. That is liberation (*mokṣa*). As everything is momentary the person who observes religious practices and the one

1. Suzuki, *Studies*, quoted in : Thomas, *Buddhist Thought*, p. 235.
2. Stch., *Logic* II, p. 367 f. (footnote).
3. Stch., *The Central Conceptions*, p. 15.
4. Ibid. p. 57.

who attains liberation are not the same. "Liberation is attained by somebody characterised by pure consciousness who has fallen into the chain or flux of (consciousness which is) my person, when he is freed from all *vāsanās*[1]."

4. *The Kāpālika*

The Kāpālika sect is in the Prabodhacandrodaya referred to as the *Somasiddhānta*, *Parameśvarasiddhānta*, and *Bhairavaśāsana*. The words *Kapālin*, *Soma* (*sa-Umā*, *Umayā sahitaḥ*), *Parameśvara* and *Bhairava*, from which these names are derived, all mean Śiva. The sect seems to have originally been spread over various parts of India. But if we may take Kṛṣṇamiśra's remark as a historical statement, "the Digaṃbaras, the Kāpālikas and other heretical sects secretly retired to the countries, rich in vulgar people, of the Pāñcālas, the Mālavas, the Ābhīras, the Ānartas, to places on the sea-shore.[2]" The specification "places on the sea-shore" can refer only to the two last-mentioned countries, that of the Ābhīras, which is the south-eastern part of modern Gujarat, and that of the Ānartas, which is Saurāṣṭra or modern Kathiawar. The country of the Mālavas had Ujjain as its capital; the Pāñcāla country is the Gangetic Doab, between the Gangā and the Yamunā. The sect is referred to in different works of Sanskrit Literature.[3] The Prabodhacandrodaya furnishes a good account of the Kāpālikas and throws some light on their philosophy and way of life.

The Kāpālika who appears on the scene in the drama is adorned with a garland of human bones. He lives in a cremation ground and eats out of a human skull. He professes : "With an eye purified by the ointment of *yoga*, I see the world having differences within itself but being non-different from

1. Pra. Ca. p. 107.

2. Pra. Ca. p. 177. There are different readings of this passage. My translation follows the text of the Trivandrum edition (p. 152).

3. See Karmarkar, *Religions*, Vol. I pp. 220 and 239 ff. To the references given there the following may be added. The sect is mentioned by Vasubandhu, *Abhbidharmakośa*. Adhy. 3, Kārikā 28; in the subcommentaries of Vācaspatimiśra and Govindānanda on Śaṅkara's *Brahmasūtrabhāṣya* II. 2. 37; in Rāmānuja's Bhāṣya on the same *sūtra*. Cp. also Dasgupta, *History*, vol. V, p. 2.

God.[1]" His philosophy, therefore, is a sort of monism of the *Bhedābheda* type, teaching diffcrence included in non-difference. The commentary Prakāśa illustrates this view by comparing the way in which the world is related to God with the relation existing between seal-rings, bangles, etc., and gold : the things made of gold are different from each other but not diffeernt from gold[2]. The religious practice of the Kāpālika consists in offering oblations into the fire in the form of human flesh steeped in brains, entrails and marrow. His *pāraṇā* (eating or drinking after a fast) consists of alcohol kept in the skull of a Brāhmaṇa. He teaches: "God Mahābhairava (a form of Śiva) has to be worshipped with human offerings, lustrous with streams of blood flowing from the hard throat which is freshly cut[3]...Bhavānīpati (i. e. Śiva), whose dignity is that of the doctrine established in the Vedānta, is the creater, sustainer and destroyer of the fourteen worlds[4]. Let me now show you the greaterness of this religion. I can bring here Hari and Hara (i.e. Viṣṇu and Śiva), who are the senior and superior gods (and aslo) the (other) gods; I can obstruct the course of the stars moving in the sky; I can flood with water this earth with its mountains and towns and, think of this, drink up all that water again in a moment[5]". The Kāpālika also worships Śiva's wife, Bhavānī or Mahābhairavī: "I please the wife of Bharga (Śiva) with blood springing out in thick foamy streams of bubbles from the throat which is cut with this frightful sword accompanied by hosts of ghosts called by the booming sound of the *damaru*[6]."

The Kāpālika, like the Cārvāka, maintains that a state of liberation with no sense of pleasure is not worthy of being aimed at. "Nowhere is happiness seen without objects of pleasure. If liberation is a state of the self without the experience of pleasure, how can a state equal to that of a stone be desired? Mṛḍānī-

1. Pra. Ca. III v. 12. The commentary Candrikā reads *mithobhinnam* as *mitho' bhinnam*, which would mean "non different within itself", but this interpretation does not seem acceptable. What is meant is evidently a form of *bhedābheda*.
2. Pra. Ca. p. 112.
3. Pra. Ca. III v. 13.
4. Pra. Ca. p. 114. This shows that the Kāpālikas were not anti-Vedic on principle as, e.g. Rāmānuja describes them. They only interpret the vedānta to suit their own views.
5. Pra. Ca. III. v. 14.
6. Pra. Ca. III v. 15. *damaru* is a small drum which the Kāpālika holds in his hand.

pati (i. e. Śiva) has said that the liberated one, having a body (equal to that of Śiva, whose body is decorated) with the crest-ornament of the moon, enjoys the pleasant embrace of his beloved, who is an image of Pārvatī.[1]" Alcohol is the means to attain this kind of Liberation: "Drink this pure nectar (alcohol which is the medicine for worldly existence; Bhairva has said that this is the instrument to remove the bondage (*pāśa*) of the soul (*paśu*).[2]" A liberated person has all the eight *siddhis* (perfections[3]) and is all-powerful: "Here (in our belief), even without giving up attachment towards the objects of (the senses), the eyes etc., the eight great *siddhis* are attained by the desirous, and their excellent results are near at hand. The primitive *siddhis* (*prākṛta-siddhayaḥ*), however, like subjection, attraction, causing bewilderment, subduing, exciting and causing to quit, are obstacles of *yoga* for the wise.[4]"

Kāpālika's Faith personified (*Kāpālinīrūpadhāriṇī Śraddhā*) also appears on the stage in the Prabodhacandrodaya. She is described by Compassion as "the daughter of passion" (*rajasaḥ sutā*[5]. She embraces the Jaina and Buddhist monks and entices them to drink intoxicating liquor. This feature is of course primarily meant to mark the contrast between the abject heretics and pure Vedic schools, but it may also imply that Kṛṣṇamiśra saw a certain connection or similarity between degraded forms of Buddhism and Jainism and the Kāpālika sect or even a certain influence from this sect on those schools.

1. Pra. Ca. III v. 16.
2. Pra. Ca. III v. 20.
3. They are, according to the Candrikā; the faculty of becoming small (*aṇiman*), big (*mahiman*), heavy (*gariman*) light (*laghiman*), the faculty of attainment (*prāpti*) and of doing what one desires (*prākāmya*), lordship over all beings (*iśitva*) and the power of controlling the senses (*vaśitva*).
4. Pra. Ca. III v. 22. Even to-day there is an South India a sect of people called "Kuḍu Kuḍu pāṇḍis", who with *damarus* in their hands beg from door to door and are believed to practise the primitive *siddhis* mentioned above.
5. Pra. Ca. p. 118.

Chapter V

Supplementary remarks on some characters of the play.

1. *Puruṣa*

Puruṣa himself makes his appearance only in the last act of the drama. With the help of Viveka (Discrimination) he discards the non-Vedāntic brahmanical schools and adopts the teaching of Upaniṣad that he is identical with the Supreme Being. But this instructional knowledge does not bring about realisation immediately. Now comes Nididhyāsana, i. e. Meditation.[1] She helps Puruṣa to proceed from knowledge to intuition, which brings along with it awakening. Thus Puruṣa realizes that he is one with Viṣṇu.[2] Devotion to Viṣṇu alone remains with him in the end. As he is identical with Viṣṇu, devotion to Viṣṇu at this stage means devotion to himself although this is not expressly said in the play.

The fact that indirect or instructional knowledge is by Kṛṣṇamiśra distinguished from direct or intuitional knowledge, marks a difference of this type of Vedāntā from that of the Śāṅkara school, in which meditation or *nididhyāsana* or *parisaṃkhyāna* is not a means to *create* intuition, but only to *strengthen* it.[3] Among the great masters of Vedāntā, it is Maṇḍanamiśra who taught *prasaṃkhyāna*, i. e. meditation, as a means to bring about the transition from indirect to direct knowledge. But he had no leanings towards Vaiṣṇavism as Kṛṣṇamiśra had; on the contrary, some passages in his Brahmasiddhi seem to suggest that he lived in a Śaiva environment.[4]

2. *Discrimination, Reasoning, and Upaniṣad.*

Reasoning is represented in the play as the wife of king Discrimination for it is only through reasoning that one can

1. Pra. Ca. p. 235.
2. Pra. Ca. VI v. 30.
3. Cp. Śaṅkara, *Upadeśasahasrī*, Gadyaprabandha, part 3.
4. Information from Prof. Hacker,

discriminate good from bad. In the first act Discrimination along with Reasoning discovers that the bondage of Puruṣa is due to Māyā. It is Reasoning who wants to find out the cause of Māyā's deluding Puruṣa; it is Reasoning again who discerns that Māyā covers or overwhelms the Lord, i. e. Puruṣa, who is the luminous ocean of great light, like a streak of darkness which covers the thousand-rayed Sun.[1]

Discrimination originates from sacred knowledge, from instruction in the *śāstras*. The *śāstras* specially meant here are the upaniṣads. Therefore, if Puruṣa is to be freed, Discrimination has to be united with Upaniṣad personified. In order to achieve this, the help of Śānti or Peace is needed. For only when one is peaceful, can one study the upaniṣads with discrimination. Reasoning, however, is not required at this stage[2]. This is why Reasoning personified does not appear again on the scene after Discrimination has been united with Upaniṣad.

3. *Faith, Peace and Upaniṣad.*

Śraddhā or Faith is represented by Kṛṣṇamiśra as three fold : *Sāttvikī*, i. e. of the nature of purity; *rājasī*, of the nature of passion; and *tāmasī*, of the nature of darkness. Sāttviki Śraddhā is associated with Devotion to Viṣṇu, Righteousness, and Peace. Rājasī Śraddhā is the faith proper to the Kāpālika, and Tāmasī Śraddhā, pertains to the non-Vedic schools.

Peace (Śānti) is treated as the daughter of Sāttvikī Faith. The Yoga view that faith and peace pervade each other is expressed in the lines : "Without me (i. e. without Peace) Faith cannot live even for a moment," and : "Without Faith the life of Peace even for a moment is a ridicule.[3]" As Peace and Faith are inseparable, Peace perishes automatically when Faith is ruined. Peace is the enemy of Delusion[4]. Faith is dependent on Upaniṣad[5]. That is why Delusion, in order to overcome her, seeks the help of Error.

1. Pra. Ca. p. 41.
2. Cp. Pra. Ca. I v. 30.
3. Pra. Ca. p. 96.
4. Pra. Ca. p. 85.
5. ibidem.

Faith has a prominent place in Vaiṣṇavism[1] and also a definite place among the prelimaries of Vedānta.[2] Accordingly, many important teachings are put in the mouth of Faith personified by Kṛṣṇamiśra. It is also significant that, when Peace expresses doubts as to the possibility of uniting schools and sects that are mutually contradictory in the struggle against the common enemy, it is Faith who replies : "When the opposite schools, all having the same source, join together on being attacked by enemies, good ensues from it[3]"; it is Faith again who states that "those who reflect on the truth of the traditional schools (*āgamānāṃ tattvam*) do not contradict each other[4]."

The parts played by Upaniṣad, Faith, and Peace in the sixth act are particularly instructive as to Kṛṣṇamiśra's conception of the process of spiritual enlightenment. Upaniṣad is here brought to King Discrimination, at his command, by Peace. On her way to find Upaniṣad, Peace meets her mother Faith, who in her turn is directed to lead Discrimination to Man. Peace and Faith have a conversation about the state of affairs, Faith relating what has happened to Man recently. This means that in the development of spiritual enlightenment Faith operates as an initiating, assisting and supervising power, antecedent to reason and productive of that state of tranquillity which is required for any further progress.

Upaniṣad, on making her appearance, complains of Discrimination, who for a long time neglected her though she is his legitimate consort. This period of abandonment she spent in various places and in the company of various persons, who were lacking in discrimination and understanding and therefore arbitrarily misinterpreted her sayings. This means that in Kṛṣṇamiśra's opinion the upaniṣads are misused unless they are

1. Cp. the following passages of Bh. Gī. : *yo yacchraddaaḥ sa eva saḥ*, "What his faith is that he is" (17. 3); *yo yo yāṃ yāṃ tanuṃ bhaktaḥ śraddhayārcitum icchati tasya tasyācalaṃ śraddhāṃ tām eva vidadhāmy aham*, "Whenever any devotee wishes to worship any form, I make his faith steady" (7.21); *yepy anyadevatābhaktā yajante śraddhayānvitāḥ te'pi mām eva Kaunteya yajanty avidhipūrvakam*, "Even the devotees of other deities, who worship them with faith, they also sacrifice to me alone, though in an unlawful manner" (9.23).

2. Cp. Paul Hacker, *Über den glauben in der Religionsphilosophie des Hinduismus*, in: Zeitschrift für Missionswissenchaft und Religionswissenschaft (Münster), 1954, pp. 56 ff.

3. Pra. Ca. V v. 8.

4. Pra. Ca. p. 174.

studied with proper use of reason and for the purpose of enlightenment.

No school of philosophy can pay Upaniṣad the honour that is due to her. Having been abandoned by Discrimination, she seeks refuge with Yajñavidyā (science of Sacrifice), but as she refuses to admit the principle of deliverance by ritual work, Yajñavidyā politely requests her to depart. In the school of Mīmāṃsā, to whom Upaniṣad then resorts, her doctrine meets with a sympathetic response, but as the masters of this school want to subordinate her teaching to their purposes, she feels she cannot stay in their company. She then meets Rationalistic Philosophy (Tarkavidyā), i. e. a school in which the systems of Vaiśeṣika, Nyāya, and Sāṅkhya are united.

It is surprising to find Sāṅkhya mentioned here as pertaining to one and the same school with Nyāya and Vaiśeṣika. Probably Sāṅkhya was no longer a living school at Kṛṣṇamiśra's time, and its classification in the Prabodhacandrodaya may be a mere reflex of the Vedāntins' habit of placing Sāṅkhya, along with Nyāya and Vaiśeṣika, in the class of "rationalistic philosophy". This only meant that the three systems depended on reason as the ultimate authority, not that there was any real companionship between the respective schools[1].

In her report Upaniṣad says that Tarkavidyā has many followers. This may be an indication of a particularly flourishing state of the combined school of Nyāya and Vaiśeṣika at Kṛṣṇamiśra's time and in his environment.

The rationalists revile Upaniṣad for holding nihilistic views. They drive her away and maltreat her brutally, until she finds refuge in the home (*āśrama*) of her daughter (Bhagvad-) Gītā. Upaniṣad's account seems to imply that Gītā's *āśrama* is near a temple of Viṣṇu. For immediately before she seeks refuge there with her daughter, some men rush out from a temple of Viṣṇu and repel her rationalistic assailants. This dramatic event may point to real enmity having existed between Vedānta and Nyāya-Vaiśeṣika; it may also be an indication of a rivalry between Vaiṣṇava and Śaiva sects, for the adherents of Nyāya-Vaiśeṣika, who are known to have been generally Śaivas, are here attacked by men coming from a temple of Viṣṇu[2].

1. Suggestion of Prof. Hacker.
2. Suggestion of Prof. Hacker.

The mention of Gītā as Upaniṣad's daughter, occurring here as in some other passages of the drama, shows that the famous religious poem was held in high respect as embodying teachings derived from the upaniṣads. Gītā does, not, however, appear on the scene, not does she take any direct part in the enlightenment of Man. It is Upaniṣad alone who enunciates the doctrines which are then approved by Discrimination and thus brought home to Man.

Upaniṣad holds the position of a mother as it is due to her care that Puruṣa attains knowledge. But there is a difference between the way a mother blesses and the way Upaniṣad does. While a mother tightens the bondage, Upaniṣad cuts it asunder[1]. Once Puruṣa has found that he is one wih the Supreme Being, Upaniṣad retires.

4. *Devotion to Viṣṇu*

Eventhough Viṣṇubhakti as a character appears very seldom on the scene, she plays a central role throughout. Kṛṣṇamiśra says that though in the Kali era devotion to Viṣṇu is less popular, still it is very powerful. The materialists cannot even cast a glance at those who are blessed by Devotion to Viṣṇu[2]. Viṣṇubhakti personified is by nature the enemy of Moha or Delusion. Faith and Peace join her in combating him[3]. Faith is her constant companion. She directs Faith to Discrimination to destroy the evil affections, Anger, Concupiscence, etc. It is she who saves Faith from Mahābhairavī who had overwhelmed Faith. She realizes that Delusion is the root cause of all the trouble of Man. It is she who, along with Prāṇāyāma (Breath Control) etc., blesses Discrimination's army. During the battle she retires to a place called Śāligrāma for she is averse to see so much injury. It is she who ensures Discrimination's victory[4] and by whose blessing Peace reaches the hearts of sages[5]. When Faith narrates that after the battle, Delusion along with the obstructions of Yoga have disappeared, Devotion to Viṣṇu realizes that the evil is not yet

1. Pra. Ca. VI v. 11.
2. Pra. Ca. pp. 76 f.
3. Pra. Ca. p. 81.
4. Pra. Ca. p. 167.
5. Pra. Ca. p. 168.

removed[1]. She knows that Mind has to be eradicated if Puruṣa is to attain the supreme state. It is not enough when Delusion is destroyed. Mind, who is the source of Delusion as well as of Discrimination, should also be uprooted in the final state. As Faith says, this can be achieved once Devotion to Viṣṇu has determined to do so[2]. Even after Puruṣa's awakening, Viṣṇubhakti remains with him.

5. *Delusion, Error, and Confusion.*

Cārvāka, the Materialist, is the friend of Delusion, Moha. Error is Delusion's wife and Confusion (Vibhramāvatī) his maid. This means that it is due to delusion one is attracted to materialism and the materialist's words become pleasant to the ear[3]. Delusion is possessed by Concupiscence, Anger, Greed, etc., for all these are said to be his friends. When he is united with Error (Mithyādṛṣṭi), whatever faith one has is destroyed. Therefore it is said in the play that Error alone is capable of overcoming Faith[4]. Error cannot exist without Delusion; she is like a painted doll on the heart-wall of Delusion[5]. Pleasure, Violence, and Desire are Error's friends as they are not happy even for a moment without her[6]. Faith can be removed when Error succeeds in teaching that there is nothing like *dharma* (sacred precepts), *mokṣa* (final emancipation), Vedic religion and reward in heaven and that the doctrines of the śāstras are only obstructions to happiness[7]. Every time Delusion embraces Error, he gains new youth[8]. This means that whenever an error is committed new delusion is produced. The rise of Dispassionateness does not imply the destruction of Delusion, who does not die when the battle is lost but disappears only. Only when Knowledge appears bursting the heart of Mind is Delusion annihilated. Knowledge (Vidyā) devours Delusion along with his followers[9].

1. Pra. Ca. p. 178.
2. Pra. Ca. p. 179.
3. Pra. Ca. p. 74.
4. Pra. Ca. p. 85.
5. Pra. Ca. II v. 37.
6. Pra. Ca. p. 88.
7. Pra. Ca. p. 93.
8. Pra. Ca. p. 90.
9. Pra. Ca. VI v. 28.

6. *Concupiscence, Pleasure, and Investigation into Truth.*

As usual in Indian literature, in the Prabodhacandrodaya too Rati or Pleasure is treated as the wife of Kāma or Concupiscence. Both of them belong to the party of King Delusion (Moha). Kāma is Moha's foremost warrior[1]. It is significant tha they are the first characters to appear on the scene after the Stage-Director (*sūtradhāra*). In this way it is suggested that Puruṣa is indulging in concupiscence and pleasure and this is an outcome of his bondage. As long as concupiscence is in existence there is no possibility of knowledge (*vidyā*) arising[2]. It is Kāma who is asked by Moha to destroy Dharma or Righteousness[3]. Only Investigation into Truth (Vastuvicāra) can kill Concupiscence. It is Vastuvicāra who realizes that the universe is deceived by Kāma[4]. Kāma agitates people without being perceptible himself[5]. His main weapon is woman. When woman is defeated, Kāma along with his friends too are conquered[6]. It is Kāma who prevents Man from studying the upaniṣads with discrimination.

1. Pra. Ca. p. 145.
2. Pra. Ca. p. 33.
3. Pra. Ca. p. 80.
4. Pra. Ca. p. 142.
5. Pra. Ca. p. 144.
6. Pra. Ca. p. 147.

ABBREVIATIONS AND BIBLIOGRAPHY

Abbreviation	*Bibliography*
Adh. Rā.	Adhyātmarāmāyaṇam, Nirṇayasāgar Press Bombay, 1933.
Paramārthasāra	Ādiśeṣa: Paramārthasāra. Ed. by S. S. Suryanarayana Sastri, Karnatak Publishing House, Bombay, 1941.
	Ānandagiri : Śaṃkaravijaya. Ed. by Jayanarayana Tarkapanchanan Calcutta, 1868.
Bh. Gī.	Bhagavadgītā. Gita Press, Gorakhpur, Saṃvat 2008.
Vaiṣṇavism etc.	Bhandarkar, R. G.: Vaiṣṇavism, Śaivism and minor religious systems, (Encyclopedia of Indo Aryan Research III, 6.) Trübner, Strassburg, 1913.
Bh. Pu.	Bhāgavatapurāṇam, Gita Press, Gorakhpur, Saṃvat 2008.
	Bhavabhūti: Mālatīmādhavam, Ed. by R. G. Bhandarkar, Bombay Sanskrit series, No. XV, Bombay 1. 1876.
	Boissevain, J. W.: Prabodhacandrodaya, Amsterdam, (without year).
	Boissevain, Maasopgang der Ontwaking, Servive, Den Haag, 1951.
Br. Sū.	Brahmasūtras.
Bṛ. Up.	Bṛhadāraṇyakopaṇiṣad. Ed. by Roer. Bibliotheca Indica Vol.2 Calcu tta, 1849.
	Bṛhaspati Sūtra. Ed. by F. W. Thomas, Lahore, 1921.
Colebroke	Colebrooke, H. T.: Life and Essays Vol. II, Trübner, London 1873.
Dasgupta: Philosophy.	Dasgupta Surendranath: A history of Indian Philosophy Vols. I and V, University Press, Cambridge, 1951 and 1955 respectively.

Abbreviation	*Bibliography*
Dasgupta History	Dasgupta Surendranath: A history of Sanskrit Literature, Calcutta 1947.
Ved. Pari.	Dharmarāja Adhvarin: Vedānta Paribhāṣā, Ed. with an English Translation by S. S. Suryanarayana Sastri, Adyar, 1942.
E.B.C. & A.E.G.	E. B. Cowell and A. E. Gough: Transl. Sarvadarśansaṃgraha, Trübner, London 1882.
	Encyclopaedia of Religion and Ethics Vol. XI. Ed. James Hastings. Edinburgh and New York, 1920.)
Frauwallner, Philosophie	Frauwallner, E.: Geschichte der indischen Philosophie, Vol. I and II., Müller, Salzburg, 1953 & 1956 resp.
	Frauwallner, E.: On the date of the Buddhist master of the Law, Vasubandhu (serie Orientale Roma, 1951.
	Hacker Paul: Untersuchungen über Texte des frühen Advaitavāda, Mainz 1950.
	Hacker Paul: Über den Glauben in der Religionsphilosophie des Hinduisms. (Zeitschrift für Missionwissenschaft und Religionswissenschaft, Münster, 1954).
	Harṣa: Naiṣadhīyacaritam, Trans. Krishnakanta Handiqui, Motilal Banarasi Dass, Lahore, 1934.
Hiriyanna	Hiriyanna, M.: Outlines of Indian Philosophy, George Allen and Unwin Ltd., London, 3. 1956.
Īśa. Up.	Iśopaniṣad—Daśopaniṣads Vol. I, Ed. by C. Kunhan Raja. Adyar Library series 15, Adyar, 1935.
	Jayarāśibhaṭṭa: Tattvopaplavasiṃha, Oriental Institute, Baroda 1940.
Kaṭh. Up.	Kaṭhopaniṣad—Daśopaniṣads Vol. I, Ed. by C. Kunhan Raja. Adyar Library series 15, Adyar, 1935.

Abbreviation	*Bibliography*
Karmarkar Religions	Karmarkar, A. P.: The Religions of India, Vol. I, The Vratya or Dravidian systems, Mira Publishing House, Lonavla. 1950.
	Kaunḍinya- Pañcārthabhāṣya on the Pāśupatasūtras, Ed. by R. Anantha-krishna Sastri, Trivandrum Sanskrit series 143, Trivandrum 1940.
Kauṭilya.	Kauṭilya: Arthaśāstra. Ed. by J. Jolly and R. Schmidt, Lahore 1923.
Konow, Drama.	Konow, Sten: Das indische Drama, (Encyclopaedia of Indo-Aryan Research, II, 2.) Berlin, Leipzig, 1920.
Krishmamacharya History.	Krishnamacharya: History of classical Sanskrit Literature, Tirumalai Tirupati Devasthanam Press, Madras 1937.
Pra. Ca.	Kṛṣṇamiśra: Prabodhacandrodayam with the commentaries Candrikā and Prakāśa, Nirnayasagara Press, Bombay, 1935.
	Kṛṣṇamiśra: Prabodhacandrodayam with the commentary Nāṭakābharaṇa, Ed. by K. Sambasiva Sastri, Trivandrum Sanskrit series LXXII, Trivandrum, 1936.
	Kṛṣṇamiśra: Prabodhacandrodaya, Ed. by F. A. Brockhaus, Lipsiae, 1845.
Mī. Pari.	Kṛṣṇa Yajvin: Mīmāṃsāparibhāṣā, Translated and annotated by Swami Madhavananda, The Ramakrisṇna Mission, Howrah, 1948.
Lévi, Theatre.	Lévi, Sylvain: Le théâtre indian, Paris, 1890.
Macdonnell History	Macdonell: A history of Sanskrit Literature, William Heinemann, London, 1905
S. D. S.	Mādhava, Sāyaṇa: Sarvadarśnasaṃgraha, Calcutta 1908.
	Māṭharavṛtti, Ed. by Vishnuprasad Sarma, Chowkhamba Sanskrit series No. 296, Benares, 1922.

Abbreviation	*Bibliography*
Mu. Up.	Muṇḍakopaniṣad, Daśopanishads, Vol. I, Ed. by C. Kunhan Raja, Adyar Library series 15, Adyar 1935.
	Nāradīyamahāpurāṇam, Bombay 1928.
Yogasūtra.	Patañjali: Yogasūtra with Vyāsabhāṣya Ānandāśrama Sanskrit series, Poona 1904.
Raychaudhuri: Materials.	Ray Chaudhuri, Materials for the study of the Early History of the Vaiṣṇava sects, Calcutta, 1920.
Ruben, Materialismus	Ruben, Walter: Materialismus in Leben des alten Indin, I, II. Acta Orientalia, Vol. XIII, 1935.
Vedā Sāra.	Sadānanda: Vedāntasāra, Bengali edition, Calcutta, San. 1328.
Br. Bh.	Śaṃkara: Brahmasūtrabhāṣya, with the commentaries Ratnaprabhā of Śrīgovindānanda, Bhāmatī of Vācaspatimiśra, and Nyāyanirṇaya of Ānandagiri, Nirṇayasagara Press, Bombay, 1909.
	Śaṃkara: Upadeśasahasrī, Translated by Swami Jagadananda, Madras, 1949.
	Sarvamatasaṃgraha,Ed. by T.Ganapathi Sastri, Trivandrum Sanskrit series 62, 1918.
	Sarvasiddhāntsaṃgraha attributed to Śaṃkara, Edited, translated and annotated by Prem Sunder Bose, Calcutta, 1929.
	Schulz Friedrich A.: Die philosophisch-theologischen Lehren des Pāśupata Systems, Bonn, 1958.
Stcherbatsky, The Central Conception,	Stcherbatsky, Th.: The central conception of Buddhism and the meaning of the word "Dharma", Royal Asiatic Society, London, 1923. Stcherbatsky, Th.: The soul theory of the Buddhists, Bulletin de l'Academie des sciences de Russie, 1919.

Abbreviation	*Bibliography*
Stch. Logic.	Stcherbatsky, Buddhist Logic I & II, Reprint 1958.
	Stcherbatsky: The Conception of Buddhist Nirvana Leningrad 1927.
	Sṭrauss Otto: Indische Philosophie, Munchen 1925.
Śveta. Up.	Svetāśvataropaniṣad, Ed. by Roer, Bibliotheca Indica Vol. VI, Calcutta 1850.
	Suzuki, D. T. : The Laṅkāvatārasūtra, George Routeledge...., London, 1932.
	Takakusu : Essentials of Buddhist Philosophy, Asia Publishing House, Bombay, 1956.
Taitt. Up.	Taittirīyopaniṣad, Daśopaniṣads, Vol. I, Ed. by....C. Kunhan Raja, Adyar Library series, Adyar, 1935.
	Taylor, J. : Prabodhacandrodaya or Rise of the Moon of Intellect, Tookaram Tatya, Bombay, 2. 1893.
Thomas : Buddhist Thought.	Thomas, E. T.: The history of Buddhist Thought, Routeledge and Kegan Paul, London, 1953.
TSS.	Trivandrum Sanskrit Series.
Abhi. Ko.	Vasubandhu: Abhidharmakośa Ed. by Louis de La Vallee Poussin, Societe Belge D'Etudes Orientales, Paris, 1923.
Winternitz Geschichte.	Winternitz, Moritz : Geschichte der indischen Litteratur Amelangs Verlag, Leipzig, Vol. I, 1909; Vol. II, 1913; Vol. III, 1922.

प्रबोधचन्द्रोदयम्

प्रथमोऽङ्कः

मध्याह्नार्कमरीचिकास्विव पयःपूरो यदज्ञानतः
खं वायुर्ज्वलनो जलं क्षितिरिति त्रैलोक्यमुन्मीलति ।
यत्तत्त्वं विदुषां निमीलति पुनः स्रग्भोगिभोगोपमं
सान्द्रानन्दमुपास्महे तदमलं स्वात्मावबोधं महः ॥१॥

अपिच

अन्तर्नाडीनियमितमरुल्लङ्घितब्रह्मरन्ध्रं
स्वान्ते शान्तिप्रणयिनि समुन्मीलदानन्दसान्द्रम् ।
प्रत्यग्ज्योतिर्जयति यमिनः स्पष्टलालाटनेत्र-
व्याजव्यक्तीकृतमिव जगद्व्यापि चन्द्रार्धमौलेः ॥२॥

(नान्द्यन्ते सूत्रधारः ।)

सूत्रधारः : अलमतिविस्तरेण । आदिष्टोऽस्मि सकलसामन्तचक्रचूडामणिमरीचिमञ्जरीनीराजितचरणकमलेन बलवदरिनिवहवक्षस्तटकपाटपाटनप्रकटितनृसिंहरूपेण प्रबलतरनरपतिकुलप्रलयमहार्णवनिमग्नमेदिनीसमुद्धरणमहावराहरूपेण सकलदिग्विलासिनीकर्णपूरीकृतकीर्तिलतापल्लवेन समस्ताशास्तम्बेरमकर्णतालास्फालनबहलपवनसंपातनर्तितप्रतापानलेन श्रीमता गोपालेन । यथा खल्वस्य सहजसुहृदो राज्ञः कीर्तिवर्मदेवस्य दिग्विजयव्यापारान्तरितपरब्रह्मानन्दरसैरस्माभिः समुन्मीलितविविधविषयरसास्वादवूषिता इवातिवाहिता दिवसाः । इदानीं तु कृतकृत्या वयम् ।

Act I

I adore that light which is intense bliss, pure, to be known as one's own self; through its ignorance the three worlds are manifested as ether, air, fire, water and earth like a flow of water in the rays of the midday sun; their (the three worlds') reality disappears for the wise like the body of a snake in a garland or (which (the three worlds) similar to the body of a snake in a garland, again conceal truth from the wise). (1). Moreover,

I adore the inward light of the one crowned with the Half-moon (Śiva) the one who has restrained his passions, the light which has entered Brahmā's crevice by making the air stop in the inner vein, the light which is identical with the unfolded happiness, which manifests itself in the inner self seeking peace, and which pervades the Universe, as if it has been manifested through the distinctly visible eye in the forehead. (2).

(*At the end of the prayer to the deities—Stage Manager.*)

S. M. : No more of prolixity. The celebrated Gopāla whose lotus-feet are illumined by the cluster of rays emanating from the tiaras of all the tributary kings, who revealed himself in the form of Nṛsiṁha by tearing open the doors of the breasts of the group of his strong opponents, who like the Great Boar raises up the earth submerged under strong Kings as under the deluge of the great ocean; he whose fame spreads in all directions like the tender leaves of the creeper adoring the ears of damsels, whose fire-like valour is kindled by the strong wind caused by the flapping of the ears of all the guardian elephants of the directions, has commanded me thus : "We whose enjoyment of the Supreme Brahman was obstructed by the activities of our friend from birth, King Kīrtivarmadeva (*engaged*) in conquering the world, spent the days polluted by the enjoyments of various sensual pleasures. But now we have fulfilled our purpose.

यतः

नीताः क्षयं क्षितिभुजो नृपतेर्विपक्षा
रक्षावती क्षितिरभूत्प्रथितैरमात्यैः ।
साम्राज्यमस्य विहितं क्षितिपालमौलि-
मालार्चितं भुवि पयोनिधिमेखलायाम् ॥३॥

तद्वयं शान्तरसप्रयोगाभिनयेनात्मानं विनोदयितुमिच्छामः। ततो यत्पूर्वमस्मद्गुरुभिस्तत्रभवद्भिः श्रीकृष्णमिश्रैः प्रबोधचन्द्रोदयं नाम नाटकं निर्माय भवतः समर्पितमासीत् तदद्य राज्ञः श्रीकीर्तिवर्मणः पुरस्तादभिनेतव्यं भवता। अस्ति चास्य भूपतेः सपरिषदस्तदवलोकने कुतूहलमिति। तद्भवतु। गृहं गत्वा गृहिणीमाहूय संगीतकमनुतिष्ठामि (परिक्रम्य, नेपथ्याभिमुखमवलोक्य।) आर्ये, इतस्तावत्।

(प्रविश्य नटी।)

नटी : एसम्हि। आणवेदु अय्यउत्तो को णिओओ अणुचिट्ठियदुत्ति।

[एषास्मि। आज्ञापयत्वार्यपुत्रः को नियोगोऽनुष्ठीयतामिति।]

सूत्रधारः : आर्ये, विदितमेव भवत्याः।

अस्ति प्रत्यर्थिपृथ्वीपतिविपुलबलारण्यमूर्च्छत्प्रताप-
ज्योतिर्ज्वालावलीशत्रिभुवनविवरो विश्वविश्रान्तकीर्तिः।
गोपालो भूमिपालान्प्रसभमसिलतामात्रमित्रेण जित्वा
साम्राज्ये कीर्तिवर्मा नरपतितिलको येन भूयोऽभ्यषेचि ॥४॥

अपि च

अद्याप्युन्मदयातुधानतरुणीचञ्चत्करास्फालन-
व्यावल्गन्नृकपालतालरणितैर्नृत्यत्पिशाचाङ्गनाः।
उद्गायन्ति यशांसि यस्य विततैर्नादैः प्रचण्डानिल-
प्रक्षुभ्यत्करिकुम्भकूटकुहरव्यक्तै रणक्षोणयः ॥५॥

तेन च शान्तपथप्रस्थितेनात्मनो विनोदार्थं प्रबोधचन्द्रोदयाभिधानं नाटकमभिनेतुमादिष्टोऽस्मि। तदाविश्यन्तां भरता वर्णिकापरिग्रहाय।

For

The king's enemies are destroyed, the earth is protected by well known ministers; his sovereignty which is adored by the garlands of the heads of the kings,[1] is established on the earth encompassed by the ocean. (3).

Now we want to entertain ourselves by the enacting of the sentiment of peace. Therefore you have now to produce in the presence of king Śrīkīrtivarman the play named Prabodhacandrodaya, which was written and given to you earlier by our revered teacher Śrī Kṛṣṇamiśra. The king along with his courtiers is curious to see it." Be it so. I shall go home and call my wife and then get the music ready (*turns around, looks at the back stage*). Lady please come here.

(*Enter Actress*)

Actress : Here I am. Command me, my Lord, what is to be done.

S. M. : Revered Lady. It is known to you that there is Gopāla whose valour like the flames of light fills in all the crevices of the three worlds, which blazes in the forest of the great armies of the enemy kings, and whose fame has spread throughout the universe, who by the aid of his sword alone defeated the kings, has again crowned Kīrtivarman the best of kings as the sovereign. (4).

Moreover,

Even today the battlefields where the Piśāca women dance to the sound of the cymbals made out of human skulls, which are beaten by the beautiful hands of the Rākṣasa women, proclaim his fame through the loud sound produced by the strong wind blowing through the lofty skulls of elephants (killed in the battle). (5).

I am commanded by him who now has entered the path of peace to produce the play named Prabodhacandrodaya to entertain himself.

1. The tributary kings whose heads are adorned with flower garlands bend their heads at the feet of the Sovereign king out of respect.

नटी : (सविस्मयम् ।) अज्जउत्त, अच्चरियं अच्चरियं । जेण तधाविहणिअभुअबलविक्कमेक्कणिब्भच्छिदसअलराअमण्डलेण आयण्णाकिट्ठकठिणकोअण्डदण्डबहलवरिसन्तसरणिअरजज्जरिदतुरंअतरंअमालं णिरन्तरणिवडन्ततिक्खविशिखनिक्खित्तमहस्सपल्लत्थतुरङ्गमाअङ्गमहामहीहरसहस्सं भमन्तभुअदण्डमन्दराहिहाघुमन्तसअलपत्तिसलिलसंघादं कण्णसेणासाअरं णिम्महिअ महुमहणेणेव खीरसमुद्दं आसादिदा समरविजअलच्छी । तस्स संपदं सअलमुणिअणसलाणिज्जओ कहं एरिसो उवसमो संवुत्तो ।

[आर्यपुत्र, आश्चर्यमाश्चर्यम् । येन तथाविधनिजभुजबलविक्रमैकनिर्भर्त्सितसकलराजमण्डलेन आकर्णाकृष्टकठिनकोदण्डबहुलवर्षच्छरनिकरजर्जरिततुरङ्गतरङ्गमालम्, निरन्तरनिपतत्तीक्ष्णविशिखनिक्षिप्तमहास्त्रपर्यस्तोत्तुङ्गमातङ्गमहामहीधरसहस्रम्, भ्रमद्भुजदण्डमन्दराभिघातघूर्णमानसकलपत्तिसलिलसंघातम्, कर्णसेनासागरं निर्मथ्य मधुमथनेनेव क्षीरसमुद्रमासादिता समरविजयलक्ष्मीः । तस्य सांप्रतं सकलमुनिजनश्लाघनीयः कथमीदृश उपशमः संवृत्तः ।]

सूत्रधारः : आर्ये, निसर्गसौम्यमेव ब्राह्मं ज्योतिः कुतोऽपि कारणात्प्राप्तिविकारमपि पुनः स्वभावमेवावतिष्ठते । यतः सकलभूपालकुलप्रलयकालाग्निरुद्रेण चेदिपतिना समुन्मूलितं चन्द्रान्वयपार्थिवानां पृथिव्यामाधिपत्यं स्थिरीकर्तुमयमस्य संरम्भः । पश्य तदा

कल्पान्तवातसंक्षोभलङ्घिताशेषभूभृतः ।
स्थैर्यप्रसादमर्यादास्ता एव हि महोदधेः ।।६।।

अपि च । भगवन्नारायणांशसंभूता भूतहिताय तथाविधाः पौरुषभूषणाः पुरुषाः क्षितिमवतीर्य निष्पादितकृत्याः पुनः शान्तिमेव प्रपद्यन्ते । यथा परशुराममेवाकलयतु भवती तावत् ।

येन त्रिःसप्तकृत्वो नृपबहुलवसामांसमस्तिष्कपङ्क-
प्राग्भारेऽकारि भूरिच्युतरुधिरसरिद्वारिपूरेऽभिषेकः ।
यस्य स्त्रीबालवृद्धावधिनिधनविधौ निर्दयो विश्रुतोऽसौ
राजन्योच्चांसकूटक्रथनपटुरटद्घोरधारः कुठारः ।।७।।

Actress : (*with surprise*) My Lord, it is a wonder, he who has put to shame the entire host of kings by the strength of his arms alone, has like Kṛṣṇa obtained prosperity by the victory in the battles by churning the ocean in the form of the army of Karṇa, where the chain of waves were horses shattered by the host of arrows showered from the staff like strong bow drawn till his ear, where the big mountains are the lofty elephants which were killed by innumerable sharp weapons which fell incessantly all over, where the waters were the foot-soldiers crushed by the revolving Mandara mountain in the form of his staff-like arm. How is it that he now has attained tranquillity which is to be commended by the sages?

S. M. : Revered Lady. The lustre belonging to Brahman which is by nature tranquil, by some reason having changed, again goes back to its own nature. It was aroused only to re-establish the sovereignty of the kings of the Lunar race on this earth which was uprooted by the Cedi king who was like the cruel fire at the time of the deluge of the kings of earth. See then,

The ocean which enraged by the wind at the end of the kalpa overthrew all the mountains, (now) possesses the same old virtues of calmness, clarity and does not cross the limits any more. (6).

Moreover, those men whose ornament is valour who have sprung from a portion of the divine Nārāyaṇa for the welfare of the beings, having come down on the earth to complete their mission, return to a state of tranquillity. Think my lady of Paraśurāma himself. Thrice seven times did he bathe himself in the great river of blood flowing in plenty which was filled with the mud in the form of the abundant marrow, flesh and heads of kings, whose merciless axe is well known in killing all except women, children, and old people, with cruel blade that is an expert in breaking the lofty shoulders of the kings making a sound. (7).

सोऽपि स्ववीर्यादवतार्य भारं भूमेः समुत्खाय कुलं नृपाणाम् ।
प्रशान्तकोपज्वलनस्तपोभिः श्रीमान्मुनिः शाम्यति जामदग्न्यः ॥८॥

तथायमपि कृतकर्तव्यः संप्रति परमामुपशमनिष्ठां प्राप्तः ।

येन च

विवेकेनेव निर्जित्य कर्णं मोहमिवोर्जितम् ।
श्रीकीर्तिवर्मनृपतेर्बोधस्येवोदयः कृतः ॥९॥

(नेपथ्ये ।)

आः पाप शैलूषाधम, कथमस्मासु जीवत्सु स्वामिनो महामोहस्य विवेकसकाशात्पराजयमुदाहरसि ।

सूत्रधारः : (ससंभ्रमं विलोक्य ।) आर्ये, इतस्तावत् ।

उत्तुङ्गपीवरकुचद्वयपीडिताङ्ग-
मालिङ्गितः पुलकितेन भुजेन रत्या ।
श्रीमाञ्जगन्ति मदयन्नयनाभिरामः
कामोऽयमेति मदघूर्णितनेत्रपद्मः ॥१०॥

मद्वचनाच्चायमुपजातक्रोध इव लक्ष्यते । तदपसरणमेवास्माकमितः श्रेयः । (इति निष्क्रान्तौ ।)

प्रस्तावना ।

(ततः प्रविशति यथानिर्दिष्टः कामो रतिश्च ।)

कामः : (सक्रोधम् । आः पापेति पुनः पुनः पठित्वा ।) ननु रे भरताधम,

प्रभवति मनसि विवेको विदुषामपि शास्त्रसंभवस्तावत् ।
निपतन्ति दृष्टिविशिखा यावन्नेन्दीवराक्षीणाम् ॥११॥

अपिच

रम्यं हर्म्यतलं नवाः सुनयना गुञ्जद्द्विरेफा लताः
प्रोन्मीलन्नवमल्लिकाः सुरभयो वाताः सचन्द्राः क्षपाः ।
यद्येतानि जयन्ति हन्त परितः शस्त्राण्यमोघानि मे
तद्भोः कीदृगसौ विवेकविभवः कीदृक्प्रबोधोदयः ॥१२॥

Even he the son of Jamadagni (Parśurāma) having reduced the weight of earth by uprooting the family of kings, his fire of anger being pacified calms down through austerities. (8).

Thus he (*Gopāla*) also having fulfilled his purposes has now attained absolute tranquillity. Like Discrimination's conquest of strong Delusion bringing forth the awakening of knowledge, he has vanquished the strong Karṇa and has caused the rise of Kīrtivarman. (9).

(*Behind the curtain*)

Thou meanest of actors, while we live how can you speak of the defeat of our Lord Delusion at the hand of Discrimination?

S. M. : (*Looking in agitation*). My Lady, please come over here.

Here comes with Pleasure the handsome Concupiscence deluding the people with his lotus-like eyes blurred through drunkenness, whose body is pressed by the full-swelling breasts (of Pleasure) which has caused the hair to stand on his arms. (10).

He seems to be offended by my words. Therefore it is better for us to get away from this place. (*They go out*). Prologue.

(*Then enter Concupiscence and Pleasure as described.*)

Concu : (*Wrathfully*) *Repeating "Thou meanest of actors...*)
Oh! thou meanest of actors!
Discrimination originating from the scriptures remains in the minds of learned men only until the arrow-like glances from the eyes of lotus-eyed women, fall on them. (11).

Moreover.

A delightful house, young girls with beautiful eyes, creepers with the buzzing bees, the newly blossomed mallikās, the fragrant breeze, moonlit nights, if these my fruitful weapons around me are victorious then where is the success of this Discrimination and where is the birth of Spiritual awakening. (12).

रतिः : अज्जउत्त, गुरुओ क्खु महाराअमहामोहस्स पडिवक्खो विवेओ त्ति तक्केमि ।

[आर्यपुत्र, गुरुः खलु महाराजमहामोहस्य प्रतिपक्षो विवेक इति तर्कयामि ।]

कामः : प्रिये, कुतस्तवेदं स्त्रीस्वभावसुलभं विवेकाद्भयमुत्पन्नम् । पश्य ।

अपि यदि विशिखाः शरासनं वा कुसुममयं ससुरासुरं तथापि ।
मम जगदखिलं वरोरु नाज्ञामिदमतिलङ्घ्य धृतिं मुहूर्तमेति ॥१३॥

तथाहि—

अहल्यायै जारः सुरपतिरभूदात्मतनयां
प्रजानाथोऽयासीदभजत गुरोरिन्दुरबलाम् ।
इति प्रायः को वा न पदमपथेऽकार्यत मया
श्रमो मद्बाणानां क इव भुवनोन्माथविधिषु ॥१४॥

रतिः : अज्जउत्त, एव्वं णेदं । तहवि महासहाअसंपण्णो संकिदव्वो अरादी । जदो अस्स जमणिअमप्पमुहा अमच्चा महाबला सुणीअन्दि ।

[आर्यपुत्र, एवं नैतत् । तथापि महासहायसंपन्नः शङ्कितव्योऽरातिः । यतोऽस्य यमनियमप्रमुखा अमात्या महाबलाः श्रूयन्ते ।]

कामः : प्रिये, यानेतान्राज्ञो विवेकस्य बलवतो यमादीनष्टावमात्यान्पश्यसि त एते नियतमस्माभिरभियुक्तमात्रात्प्रागेव विघटिष्यन्ते ।

तथाहि—

अहिंसा कैव कोपस्य ब्रह्मचर्यादयो मम ।
लोभस्य पुरतः केऽमी सत्याऽस्तेयापरिग्रहाः ॥१५॥

यमनियमासनप्राणायामप्रत्याहारध्यानधारणासमाधयस्तु निर्विकारचित्तैकसाध्यत्वादीषत्करसमुन्मूलना एव । अपि च स्त्रिय एवामीषां कृत्यास्तेनैतेऽस्मद्गोचरा एव वर्तन्ते । यतः—

Pleasure : My Lord, I think that this Discrimination who is the enemy of our great king Delusion is a mighty person.

Concu : My dear one, how does Discrimination cause in you fear which is natural to women. See,

Oh beautiful thighed one! Even though my bow and arrows are made of flowers, this entire Universe consisting of gods and demons can dare not remain even for a moment against my command. (13).

For:—

The lord of gods, Indra, became the paramour of Ahalyā; the Lord of beings, Brahmā, courted his own daughter; and the Moon loved his teacher's wife; thus almost everyone is made to tread the forbidden path by me. What exertion is there for my arrows in misleading the people.? (14).

Pleasure : My Lord, it may not be so. Even then the enemy having great help should be feared. For his ministers Morality, Observance and others are said to be men of great strength.

Concu : My dear, Morality etc. whom you consider as the eight strong ministers of king Discrimination will be surely separated from him (*Discrimination*) even before he is attacked by us. For,

Where is Non-injury in front of Anger, where is Celibacy etc. in front of me (*Concupiscence*), where are Truth, Non-stealing and Non-possession in front of Greed? (15).

Morality, Observance, Bodily Posture, Breath Control, Withdrawal of the Senses, Contemplation, Fixation of Attention and Absorptive Concentration can be easily uprooted as they can be attained only through an inflexible mind. Moreover, women alone can work their ruin. Therefore they are under my control. For,

सन्तु विलोकनभाषणविलासपरिहासकेलिपरिरम्भाः ।
स्मरणमपि कामिनीनामलमिह मनसो विकाराय ।।१६।।

विशेषतश्चैते मदमात्सर्यदम्भलोभादिभिरस्मत्स्वामिवल्लभैरभियुज्यमाना नरपतिमन्त्रिणोऽधर्ममेवाश्रयिष्यन्ते ।

रतिः : अज्जउत्त, सुदं मए तुम्हाणं विवेअसमदमप्पहुदीणं च एक्कं उप्पत्तित्थाणं ति ।

[आर्यपुत्र, श्रुतं मया युष्माकं विवेकशमदमप्रभृतीनां चैकमुत्पत्तिस्थानमिति ।]

कामः : आः प्रिये, किमुच्यत एकमुत्पत्तिस्थानमिति । ननु जनक एवास्माकमभिन्नः । तथाहि—

संभूतः प्रथममहेश्वरस्य सङ्गान्मायायां मन इति विश्रुतस्तनूजः ।
त्रैलोक्यं सकलमिदं विसृज्य भूयस्तेनाथो जनितमिदं कुलद्वयं नः ।।१७।।

तस्य च प्रवृत्तिनिवृत्ती द्वे धर्मपत्न्यौ । तयोः प्रवृत्त्यां समुत्पन्नं महामोहप्रधानमेकं कुलम् । निवृत्त्यां च द्वितीयं विवेकप्रधानमिति ।

रतिः : अज्जउत्त, जइ एव्वं ता किंणिमित्तं तुम्हाणं सोअराणंवि परोप्परं एआरिसं वैरम् ।

[आर्यपुत्र, यद्येवं तत्किनिमित्तं युष्माकं सोदराणामपि परस्परमेतादृशं वैरम् ।]

कामः : प्रिये

एकामिषप्रभवमेव सहोदराणा-
मुज्जृम्भते जगति वैरमिति प्रसिद्धम् ।
पृथ्वीनिमित्तमभवत्कुरुपाण्डवानां
तीव्रस्तथा हि भुवनक्षयकृद्विरोधः ।।१८।।

सर्वमेवैतज्जगदस्माकं पित्रोपार्जितं तच्चास्माभिस्तातवल्लभतया सर्वमेवाक्रान्तम् । तेषां तु विरलः प्रचारः । तेनैते पापाः सांप्रतं पितरमस्मांश्चोन्मूलयितुमुद्यताः ।

The mere remembrance of looks, talks, sports, jokes, amorous sports, embraces of women are sufficient to disturb the mind. (16).

Moreover, these ministers when they have to fight against Arrogance, Spite, Deceit, Greed etc. who are dear to my master, they will certainly depend upon Non-righteousness.

Pleasure : My Lord, I have heard that you and Discrimination, Tranquillity, Self-restraint etc. are born out of the same source.

Concu : Oh ! dear, do you say that we have the same source? Well, only our father is not different. For

The well known mind is the first born as the son of Māyā's coming in contact with the great Lord. By the union of Māyā with the Supreme Lord, Mind was born first as their son who after creating the three worlds created again these two families of ours. (17).

He had two wives named Activity, Resignation. Of these two, the family which is headed by Grand Delusion is born out of Activity. Of Resignation is born the family led by Discrimination.

Pleasure : My Lord, if so, what is the cause for this kind of enmity between the brothers?

Concu : Dear,

It is well known in the world that enmity is seen among brothers for the sake of the same object. The vehement enmity between Kurus and Pāṇḍavas which brought about the ruin of the world was for the sake of the earth. (18).

The entire Universe is acquired by our father and because we are dear to our father we have taken possession of it. They (*Discrimination etc.*) are not at all known. Therefore those sinners are now attempting to uproot us as well as our father.

रतिः : सान्तं पावं । अज्जउत्त, किं एरिसं पावं विद्देसनमत्तेण तेहिं आरद्धं । होदु । अस्स उवाओ कोवि मन्तिदो ?

[शान्तं पापम् । आर्यपुत्र, किं तादृशं पापं विद्वेषणमात्रेण तैरारब्धम् । भवतु । अस्योपायः को वा मन्त्रितः ? ।]

कामः : प्रिये, अस्त्यत्र किंचिन्निगूढं बीजम् ।

रतिः : अज्जउत्त, ता किं ण उग्घाडीअदि ? ।

[आर्यपुत्र, तत्किं नोद्धाटयते ? ।]

कामः : प्रिये, भवती स्त्रीस्वभावाद्भीरुरिति न दारुणकर्म पापीयसामुदाह्रियते ।

रतिः : (सभयम् ।) अज्जउत्त, केरिसं तम् ? ।

[आर्यपुत्र, कीदृशं तत् ? ।]

कामः : प्रिये, न भेतव्यं न भेतव्यम् । हताशानामाशामात्रमेवैतत् । अस्ति किलैषा किंवदन्ती । अत्रास्माकं कुले कालरात्रिकल्पा विद्यानाम राक्षसी समुत्पत्स्यत इति ।

रतिः : (सभयम् ।) हद्धी हद्धी । कधं अम्हाणं कुले रक्खसीति वेवदि मे हिअअम् ।

[हा धिक् हा धिक् । कथमस्माकं कुले राक्षसीति वेपते म हृदयम् ।]

कामः : प्रिये, न भेतव्यं न भेतव्यम् । किंवदन्तीमात्रमेवैतत् ।

रतिः : अध ताए रक्खसीए किं कादव्वम् ।

[अथ तया राक्षस्या किं कर्तव्यम् ।]

कामः : प्रिये, अस्ति किलैषा प्राजापत्या सरस्वती—

पुंसः सङ्गसमुज्झितस्य गृहिणी मायेति तेनाप्यसा-
वस्पृष्टापि मनः प्रसूय तनयं लोकानसूत क्रमात् ।
तस्मादेव जनिष्यते पुनरसौ विद्येति कन्या यया
तातस्ते च सहोदराश्च जननी सर्वं च भक्ष्यं कुलम् ॥१९॥

रतिः : (सत्रासोत्कम्पम् ।) अज्जउत्त, परित्ताहि परित्ताहि ।

*आर्यपुत्र, परित्राहि परित्राहि ।

(इति भर्तारमालिङ्गति ।)

Pleasure : God forbid ! how have they started such sinful act merely because of jealousy. Have they thought of any means. ?

Concu : My dear, there is a hidden seed (*of a plot*).

Pleasure : My Lord, why don't you reveal it to me.

Concu : My dear, Being a woman as you are, timid by nature, you are not told the frightful acts of those sinners.

Pleasure : My Lord, what kind of action is that?

Concu : My dear, do not be alarmed, do not be alarmed. These are only the hopes of those in despair. There is a hearsay that a demoness who is like the Goddess of Destruction called Knowledge will be born in our family.

Pleasure : (*Fearfully*). Horrible ! Oh dear, Oh dear, My heart trembles that a Rākṣasī can be born in our family.

Concu : My dear, fear not—fear not, it is merely a rumour.

Pleasure : Then what is this Demoness going to do?

Concu : Dear, there is this teaching of Prajāpati.

Man who has given up all attachments has a wife called Illusion. Untouched by him she gave birth to a son called Mind, then in succession she gave birth to the worlds. From him (*mind*) alone again a daughter called Knowledge will be born who will devour your father, brothers, mother and the entire family. (19).

Pleasure : My Lord, protect me—protect me. (*She embraces her husband*).

कामः : (स्पर्शसुखमभिनीय । स्वगतम् ।)

स्फुरद्रोमोद्भेदस्तरलतरताराकुलदृशो
भयोत्कम्पोत्तुङ्गस्तनयुगभरासङ्गसुभगः ।
अधीराक्ष्या गुञ्जन्मणिवलयदोर्वल्लिरचितः
परीरम्भो मोदं जनयति च संमोहयति च ॥२०॥

(प्रकाशम् । दृढं परिष्वज्य ।) प्रिये, न भेतव्यं न भेतव्यम् । अस्मासु जीवत्सु कुतो विद्योत्पत्तिः ।

रतिः : अध किं ता एव रक्खस्सीए उप्पत्ती तुम्हाणं पडिवक्खाणं संमदा ?

[अथ किं तस्या एव राक्षस्या उत्पत्तिर्युष्माकं प्रतिपक्षाणां संमता ?]

कामः : बाढम्, सा खलु विवेकेनोपनिषद्देव्यां प्रबोधचन्द्रेण भ्रात्रा समं जनयितव्या । तत्र सर्वं एते शमदमादयः प्रतिपन्नोद्योगाः ।

रतिः : अज्जउत्त, कहं एदेहिं अप्पणो विनासकारिणीए विज्जाए उप्पत्ती एदेहिं दुव्विणीदेहिं सलाहिज्जदि ? ।

[आर्यपुत्र, कथमेतैरात्मनो विनाशकारिण्या विद्याया उत्पत्तिरेतैर्दुर्विनीतैः श्लाघ्यते ?]

कामः : प्रिये, कुलक्षयप्रवृत्तानां पापकारिणां कुतः स्वपरप्रत्यवायगणना । पश्य पश्य—

सहजमलिनवक्रभावभाजां
भवति भवः प्रभवात्मनाशहेतुः ।
जलधरपदवीमवाप्य धूमो
ज्वलनविनाशमनु प्रयाति नाशम् ॥२१॥

(नेपथ्ये ।) आः पाप दुरात्मन्, कथमस्मानेव पापकारिण इत्याक्षिपसि । ननु रे

Concu. : (*Enacting the pleasure derived out of her touch to himself*). The embrace of the woman possessing eyes with tremulous pupils, the embrace which makes the hair stand on the body and which is pleasing because of coming in contact with the prominent breasts trembling out of fear, the embrace with her creeper-like arms on which the bangles of precious gems make a pleasing sound. (20).

(*Aloud, embracing her ardently*) My dear, fear not, fear not, how can Knowledge be born while we are alive ?

Pleasure : And is the birth of this Demoness acceptable to your enemies ?

Concu. : Yes. She is to be begotten together with her brother, Moon of (*spiritual*) Awakening on Sacred Lore by Discrimination. Tranquillity, Self-restraint etc. are working towards it.

Pleasure : My Lord, how do these people rejoice at the birth of Knowledge who is their own destroyer ?

Concu. : My dear, where is the feeling of one's own and others' in the case of people who are bent upon annihilating the family ?

See.

The birth of those who are by nature tainted and crooked becomes the cause of destruction to those who gave them birth and themselves. Thus smoke having become the cloud after destroying the fire is itself destroyed. (21).

(*Behind the curtain*) Oh Sinful and depraved soul ! you call us sinners? Well,

गुरोरप्यवलिप्तस्य कार्याकार्यमजानतः ।
उत्पथप्रतिपन्नस्य परित्यागो विधीयते ॥२२॥

इति पौराणिकीं गाथां पुराणविद उदाहरन्ति । अनेन चास्माकं जनकेनाहंकारानुवर्तिना जगत्पतिः पितैव तावद्बद्धः । मोहादिभिश्च स एव बन्धः सुदृढतां नीतः ।

कामः : (विलोक्य ।) प्रिये, अयमस्माकं कुले ज्यायान् मत्या देव्या सह विवेक इत एवाभिवर्तते । य एषः--

रागादिभिः सरसचारिभिरात्तकान्ति-
निर्भर्त्स्यमान इव मानधनः कृशाङ्गः ।
मत्या नितान्तकलुषीकृतया शशाङ्कः
कान्त्येव सान्द्रतुहिनान्तरितो विभाति ॥२३॥

तन्न युक्तमिहास्माकमवस्थातुम् ।

(इति निष्क्रान्तौ ।)

विष्कम्भः ।

(ततः प्रविशति राजा विवेको मतिश्च ।)

राजा : (विचिन्त्य ।) प्रिये, श्रुतं त्वयास्य दुर्विनीतस्य कामबटोर्मदविस्फूर्जितं वचो यदस्मानेव पापकारिण इत्याक्षिपति ।

मतिः : अज्जउत्त, किं अप्पणो दोसं लोगो विआणादि ?
[आर्यपुत्र, किमात्मनो दोषं लोको विजानाति ?]

राजा : पश्य ।

असावहंकारपरैर्दुरात्मभि-
र्निबध्य तैः पापशठैर्मदादिभिः ।
चिरं चिदानन्दमयो निरञ्जनो
जगत्प्रभुर्दीनदशामनीयत ॥२४॥

त एते पुण्यकारिणो वयं तु तन्मुक्तये प्रवृत्ताः पापकारिण इत्यहो जितं दुरात्मभिः ।

"A person who is proud and does not discriminate right from wrong and who follows the wrong path, even if he is a teacher should be shunned." (22).

so the knowers of Purāṇas quote the Purāṇa saying. Even the Lord of the world Father is bound by our father accompanied by Egoism. The same bondage was tightened by Delusion etc.

Concu : (*Looking*) My dear, here comes Discrimination, the elder one in the family, along with Lady Reason. As if being reproached by Attachment etc. who follow their own impulses, he whose body is slender and whose wealth consists in his pride appears with Reason his lustre taken away from him like the Moon hidden in the dense dew with its lustre extremely obscured. (23).

It is not proper for us to remain here.

Exit.

Interlude.

(*Enter King, Discrimination and Reason*)

King : (*Musing*) Beloved, did you hear the proud swelling words of that immodest Concupiscence calling us evil-doers.

Reason : My Lord, do people realise their own faults?

King : See.

The wicked followers of Egoism and sinful Arrogance etc. have bound the Lord of the world who is stainless and is of the nature of consciousness and bliss, and brought Him to this condition since long. (24).

They are the virtuous people and we who are engaged in freeing Him are the sinners. Thus the wicked are victorious.

मतिः : अज्जउत्त, जदो सो सहजआणन्दसुन्दलसहाओ णिच्चप्पआसो पप्फुरन्तसअलतिहुअणप्पआरो परमेस्सरो सुणीअदि । ता कहं एदेहिं दुव्विणीदेहिं वधिअ महामोहसाअरे णिक्खित्तो ?

[आर्यपुत्र, यतोऽसौ सहजानन्दसुन्दरस्वभावो नित्यप्रकाशः प्रस्फुरत्सकलत्रिभुवनप्रचारः परमेश्वरः श्रूयते । तत्कथमेतैर्दुर्विनीतैर्बद्ध्वा महामोहसागरे निक्षिप्तः ?]

राजा : प्रिये,

सततधृतिरप्युच्चैः शान्तोऽप्यवाप्तमहोदयो-
ऽप्यधिगतनयोऽप्यन्तःस्वच्छोऽप्युदीरितधीरपि ।
त्यजति सहजं धैर्यं स्त्रीभिः प्रतारितमानसः
स्वयमपि यतो मायासङ्गात्पुमानिति विश्रुतः ॥२५॥

मतिः : अज्जउत्त, णं खु अन्धकारलेहाए सहस्सरस्सिणो तिरक्कारो जधा तधा माआए स्फुरन्तमहाप्पआससाअरस्स देवस्स वि अहिहवो ।

[आर्यपुत्र, नूनमन्धकारलेखया सहस्ररश्मेस्तिरस्कारो यथा तथा मायया स्फुरन्महाप्रकाशसागरस्य देवस्याप्यभिभवः ।]

राजा : प्रिये, अविचारसिद्धेयं वेश्याविलासिनीव माया असतोऽपि भावानुपदर्शयन्ती परपुरुषं वञ्चयति । पश्य—

स्फटिकमणिवद्भास्वान्देवः प्रगाढमनार्यया
विकृतिमनया नीतः कामप्यसंगतविक्रियः ।
न खलु तदुपश्लेषादस्य व्यपैति रुचिर्मनाक्
प्रभवति तथाऽप्येषा पुंसो विधातुमधीरताम् ॥२६॥

मतिः : अज्जउत्त, किं पुणो कारणं जेण सा तधा उदारचरिदं दुव्विदग्धा प्रतारेदि ?

[आर्यपुत्र, किं पुनः कारणं येन सा तथोदारचरितं दुर्विदग्धा प्रतारयति ?]

राजा : न खलु प्रयोजनं कारणं वा विलोक्य माया प्रवर्तते । स्वभावः खल्वसौ स्त्रीपिशाचीनाम् । पश्य—

संमोहयन्ति मदयन्ति विडम्बयन्ति
निर्भर्त्सयन्ति रमयन्ति विषादयन्ति ।
एताः प्रविश्य सदयं हृदयं नराणां
किं नाम वामनयना न समाचरन्ति ॥२७॥

Reason : My Lord, I have heard that the Supreme Lord is of the nature of innate bliss and beauty, eternally luminous, and pervades all the three worlds. Then how is He bound by the wicked ones, and thrown into the ocean of great delusion.

King : Dear! A man of unceasing fortitude who is mighty and calm, who has attained great success, who is prudent, pure within, and of well praised intelligence gives up his natural courage being deceived by women. It is well known that Man himself did so by his association with Illusion. (25).

Reason : My Lord, the overpowering of the Lord who is like the lustrous ocean of great light by Illusion is certainly like the obscuring of the thousand-rayed Sun by a streak of darkness.

King : Beloved, Illusion accomplished in thoughtless folly like a prostitute deceived the Supreme Man by displaying spurious, unreal states of mind.

See.

Man, who is immutable and effulgent like a crystal is certainly subjected to a certain change by Illusion but her embrace does not remove His radiance, but creates a certain unsteadiness in Him. (26).

Reason : My Lord, what is the cause by which this unclever person deceives the great Man?

King : Illusion does not act with any purpose or cause. This is the nature of the female evil spirits.

See.

They enter the tender hearts of men, delude them, intoxicate them, ridicule them, rebuke them, please them and finally make them dejected. Is there anything which these women do not do? (27).

अस्ति चापरमपि कारणम् ।

मतिः : अज्जउत्त, किं णाम तक्कारणम् ? ।

[आर्यपुत्र, किं नाम तत्कारणम् ?]

राजा : एवमनया दुराचारया विचिन्तितं यदहं तावद्गतयौवना वर्षीयसी । अयं पुराणपुरुषः स्वभावादेव विषयरसविमुखः । ततः स्वतनयमेव पारमेश्वरे पदे निवेशयामीति तमेव मातुरभिप्रायमासाद्य नितान्ततत्प्रत्यासन्नतया तद्रूपतामिवापन्नेन मनसा नवद्वाराणि पुराणि रचयित्वा

एकोऽपि बहुधा तेषु विच्छिद्येव निवेशितः ।
स्वचेष्टितमथो तस्मिन्विदधाति मणाविव ॥२८॥

मतिः : (विचिन्त्य ।) अज्जउत्त, जादिसी मादा पुत्तको वि तादिसो जेव्व जादो ।

[आर्यपुत्र, यादृशी माता पुत्रोऽपि तादृश एव जातः ।]

राजा : ततोऽसावहंकारेण चित्तस्य ज्येष्ठपुत्रेण नप्त्रा परिष्वक्तः । ततश्चासावीश्वरः ।

जातोऽहं जनको ममैष जननी क्षेत्रं कलत्रं कुलं
पुत्रा मित्रमरातयो वसु बलं विद्याः सुहृद्बान्धवाः ।
चित्तस्पन्दितकल्पनामनुभवन्विद्वानविद्यामयीं
निद्रामेत्य विघूर्णितो बहुविधान्स्वप्नानिमान्पश्यति ॥२९॥

मतिः : अज्जउत्त, एवं दीहतरणिद्दाविद्दविअप्पओहे पलमेस्सले कहं प्पवोहोप्पत्ती भविस्सदि ?

[आर्यपुत्र, एवं दीर्घतरनिद्राविद्रावितप्रबोधे परमेश्वरे कथं प्रबोधोत्पत्तिर्भविष्यति ?]

राजा : (सलज्जमधोमुखस्तिष्ठति ।)

मतिः : अज्जउत्त, किंति गुरुअरलज्जाभरणमिदसेहरो तूण्हींभूदोऽसि न प्पतिभणसि ?

[आर्यपुत्र, किमिति गुरुतरलज्जाभरनमितशेखरस्तूष्णीभूतोऽसि न प्रतिभणसि?]

राजा : प्रिये, सेर्ष्यं प्रायेण योषितां भवति हृदयम् । तेन सापराधमिवात्मानं शङ्के ।

There is yet another reason.

Reason : My Lord, what is that reason?

King : This woman of bad character thought thus : "My youth is gone and I am old. This ancient Man by nature is not attracted by pleasures. Therefore, I shall place His son (*Mind*) in His place of Supreme Lordship". Then Mind being very close to Him following the mother's wish created the towns of nine gates (bodies) as if he has attained His (*father's*) form. (*Thus*) Though he is one he divides himself into many and enters them (*bodies*). Then he attributes his actions to Him as (*the reflections of colour etc. are attributed*) to a crystal. (28).

Reason : (*Thoughtfully*) My Lord, the son also has become like his mother.

King : Then He was embraced by His grandson Egoism, the son of Mind. This wise Lord, experiencing the imaginations of the Mind, thus :

"I am born, this is my father, mother, body, wife, family, sons, friends, enemies, wealth, strength, knowledge and relations", sees various dreams having forgotten His own nature after falling into the sleep of ignorance. (29).

Reason : My Lord how can Awakening be born in the Supreme Lord from whom the awakening is driven away by long sleep?

King : (*Hangs down his head in shame*).

Reason : Why are you keeping silence bending down your head in great shame without replying to me?

King : Beloved, mostly women are jealous at heart. Therefore I consider myself guilty.

मतिः : अज्जउत्त, अण्णा ता इत्थियाओ जाओ सरसप्पउत्तस्स वा धम्मात्थवावारप्पत्थिअस्स भत्तुणो हिअअत्थिदं विहणन्दि ।

[आर्यपुत्र, आन्यास्ताः स्त्रियो याः सरसप्रवृत्तस्य वा धर्मार्थव्यापारप्रस्थितस्य वा भर्तुर्हृदयस्थितं विघटयन्ति ।]

राजा : प्रिये,

मानिन्याश्चिरविप्रयोगजनितासूयाकुलाया भवे-
च्छान्त्यादेरनुकूलनादुपनिषद्देव्या मया संगमः ।
तूष्णीं चेद्विषयानपास्य भवती तिष्ठेन्मुहूर्तं ततो
जाग्रत्स्वप्नसुषुप्तिधामविरहात्प्राप्तः प्रबोधोदयः ॥३०॥

मतिः : अज्जउत्त, जदि एवं कुलप्पहुणो दिढगंथिणिबद्धस्स वि बन्धमोक्खो भोदि तदो ताए णिच्चानुबन्धो जेव्व अज्जउत्तो भोदु त्ति सुट्ठु मे पिअं ।

[आर्यपुत्र, यद्येवं कुलप्रभोर्दृढग्रन्थिनिबद्धस्यापि बन्धमोक्षो भवति तदा तया नित्यानुबन्ध एवार्यपुत्रो भवत्विति सुष्ठु मे प्रियम् ।]

राजा : प्रिये, यद्येवं प्रसन्नासि सिद्धास्तर्ह्यस्माकं मनोरथाः ।
तथा हि—

बद्ध्वैको बहुधा विभज्य जगतामादिः प्रभुः शाश्वतः
क्षिप्त्वा यैः पुरुषैः पुरेषु परमो मृत्योः पदं प्रापितः ।
तेषां ब्रह्मभिदां विधाय विधिवत्प्राणान्तिकं विद्यया
प्रायश्चित्तमिदं मया पुनरसौ ब्रह्मैकतां नीयते ॥३१॥

तद्भवतु । प्रस्तुतविधानाय शमादीन्योजयामः ।

(इति निष्क्रान्तौ मतिविवेकौ ।)

इति श्रीकृष्णमिश्रयतिविरचिते प्रबोधचन्द्रोदये प्रथमोऽङ्कः ॥१॥

Reason : My Lord, those women are different who shatter the wishes of their husbands who do things out of love or who start doing things for the sake of righteousness.

King : Beloved,

The Goddess Sacred Lore who is jealous and offended with me due to long separation will be united with me through the help of Peace etc. Thus if you keep quiet for some time giving up all the sense objects then from the separation of the states of waking, dreaming and sleep, Awakening will be born. (30).

Reason : If the Lord of the family who is strongly bound can be freed from his bondage, let my Lord be always united with her (*Sacred Lore*). This surely is welcome to me.

King : Beloved, If you are thus happy, my wishes are fulfilled.

For

The one Supreme Eternal Lord who is the source of the worlds was divided into many and thrown into the cities (*bodies*) by men. I shall with the help of Knowledge bring about the end of those who divide Brahman through proper means and shall again establish his identity with Brahman. This shall be the atonement of my sins. (31).

Let it be so. Let us collect Tranquillity and others for the execution of our plan.

(*Exeunt—Reason and Discrimination*)

Thus ends the first Act of Prabodhacandrodaya composed by Sri Kṛṣṇa Miṣra.

द्वितीयोऽङ्कः ।

(ततः प्रविशति दम्भः ।)

दम्भः : आदिष्टोऽस्मि महाराजमहामोहेन । यथा--वत्स दम्भ, प्रतिज्ञातं सामात्येन विवेकेन प्रबोधोदयाय । प्रेषिताश्च तेषु तेषु तीर्थेषु शमदमादयः । स चायमस्माकमुपस्थितः कुलक्षयो भवद्भिरवहितैः प्रतिकर्तव्यः । तत्र पृथिव्यां परमं मुक्तिक्षेत्रं वाराणसीनाम नगरी । तद्भवांस्तत्र गत्वा चतुर्णामप्याश्रमाणां निःश्रेयसविघ्नार्थं प्रयततामिति । तदिदानीं वशीकृतभूयिष्ठा मया वाराणसी । संपादितश्च स्वामिनो यथानिर्दिष्ट आदेशः । तथा हि मदधिष्ठितैरिदानीम्--

वेश्यावेश्मसु सीधुगन्धिललनावक्त्रासवामोदितै-
नीत्वा निर्भरमन्मथोत्सवरसैरुन्निद्रचन्द्राः क्षपाः ।
सर्वज्ञा इति दीक्षिता इति चिरात्प्राप्ताग्निहोत्रा इति
ब्रह्मज्ञा इति तापसा इति दिवा धूर्तैर्जगद्वञ्च्यते ॥१॥

(विलोक्य ।) कोऽप्ययं पान्थो भागीरथीमुत्तीर्य सांप्रतमित एवाभिवर्तते । तथा च यथैषः--

ज्वलन्निवाभिमानेन ग्रसन्निव जगत्त्रयीम् ।
भर्त्सयन्निव वाग्जालैः प्रज्ञयोपहसन्निव ॥२॥

तथा तर्कयामि नूनमयं दक्षिणराढाप्रदेशादागतो भविष्यति । तदेतस्यार्यस्याहंकारस्य वृत्तान्तमनुस्मरिष्यामि । (इति परिक्रामति ।)

(ततः प्रविशत्यहंकारो यथानिर्दिष्टः ।)

अहंकारः : अहो, मूर्खबहुलं जगत् । तथाहि--

Act II

(*Enter Deceit*)

Deceit : The great King Delusion has commanded me thus "Son Deceit, Discrimination together with his ministers has promised the birth of Spiritual Awakening. Tranquillity, Self-restraint etc. and others are sent to various holy places. The destruction of our family is at hand. It must be prevented by you carefully. The city named Vārāṇasī is the best place in the world to attain liberation. Go there and try to obstruct the path of the liberation of all the four castes." Now Vārāṇasī is very much under my control. I have also executed the commands of my master. For, the people who are under my control—

Spend the moonlit nights in the house of courtesans and rejoice with intoxication the mouths of women which smell of liquor and delight in the sexual pleasures and in the day times pose that they know everything, as performers of sacrifice, as those who perform Agnihotra Sacrifice for a long time, as knowers of Brahman, as austere people. The world is deceived by these swindlers. (1).

(*Looking*) Who is this traveller that having crossed the Bhāgīrathī river is now coming towards this side. He looks as if he is burning with pride, as if he will devour the three worlds, as if he scoffs at people with his speech and as if he is laughing at people with his learning. (2).

I conjecture, he must be certainly coming from the southern country. I am reminded of the respectable Egoism. (*He takes a turn*).

(*Then enters Egoism as described*)

Egoism : Ah ! the world is filled with fools. For

नैवाश्रावि गुरोर्मतं न विदितं कौमारिलं दर्शनं
तत्त्वज्ञानमहो न शारिकगिरां वाचस्पतेः का कथा।
सूक्तं नापि महोदधेरधिगतं माहाव्रती नेक्षिता
सूक्ष्मा वस्तुविचारणा नृपशुभिः स्वस्थैः कथं स्थीयते ॥३॥

(विलोक्य।) एते तावदर्थावधारणविधुराः स्वाध्यायाध्ययनमात्रनिरता वेदविप्लावका एव। (पुनरन्यतो गत्वा।) एते च भिक्षामात्रगृहीतयतिव्रता मुण्डितमुण्डाः पण्डितंमन्या वेदान्तशास्त्रं व्याकुलयन्ति। (विहस्य।)

प्रत्यक्षादिप्रमासिद्धविरुद्धार्थावबोधिनः।
वेदान्ता यदि शास्त्राणि बौद्धैः किमपराध्यते ॥४॥

तदेतद्वाङ्मात्रश्रवणमपि गुरुतरदुरितोदयाय। (पुनरन्यतो गत्वा।) एते च शैवपाशुपतादयो दुरभ्यस्ताक्षपादमताः पशवः पाषण्डाः। अमीषां संभाषणादपि नरा नरकं यान्ति। तदेते दर्शनपथाद्दूरतः परिहरणीयाः।

(पुनरन्यतो गत्वा।) एते च—

गङ्गातीरतरङ्गशीतलशिलाविन्यस्तभास्वद्बृसी-
संविष्टाः कुशमुष्टिमण्डितमहादण्डाः करण्डोज्ज्वलाः।
पर्यायग्रथिताक्षसूत्रवलयप्रत्येकबीजग्रह-
व्यग्राग्राङ्गुलयो हरन्ति धनिनां वित्तान्यहो दाम्भिकाः ॥५॥

They have not heard of the views of Guru (*Prabhākara*) and have not known Kumārila' sphilo sophy. They do not have the correct knowledge of the text Śārika and what to speak of Vācaspati. They have not understood the sayings of Mahodadhi and have not looked into the work of Mahāvrata. Then how do these lazy minded people examine the truth which is very subtle ? (3). (*Looking*).

These are people who engage themselves only in learning the Vedic Texts without understanding the meaning and thus confuse the meaning of the Vedas. (*Looking at another side*) These are those who have accepted the life of holy persons just to be able to get alms, who with shaven heads consider themselves to be scholars and do harm to the science of Vedānta philosophy. (*laughing*)

If the Vedānta texts which teach things (*contradictory to the experience gained by perception etc.*) are sciences what error have the Buddhists committed. (4).

Therefore even hearing their words is for great harm. (*Going to the other side*) Here are the animal-natured heretics, Śaivas and Pāśupatas who have studied with great pain the views of Akṣapāda. Even by conversation with them people go to hell. They should be avoided even from a distance from coming into one's line of vision.

(*Again going to another side*) And these—
Seated on the shining (*Kuśa*) seats placed on the rocks that are cool on account of the waves on the shore of Gaṅgā, holding in their hands Kuśa grass and a big stick prominent with the Kamaṇḍalu, their finger tips engaged in fingering one by one of the beads of the rosary while repeating (*God's name*), these deceitful persons take away the wealth of the rich. (5).

(पुनरन्यतो गत्वा ।) एते त्रिदण्डव्यपदेशजीविनो द्वैताद्वैत-मार्गपरिभ्रष्टा एव । (अन्यतो गत्वा विलोक्य) अये, कस्यैतद्-द्वारोपान्तनिखातातिप्रांशुवंशकाण्डताण्डवितधौतसितसूक्ष्माम्बरस-हस्रमितस्ततो विन्यस्तकृष्णाजिनदृषदुपलसमिच्चषालोलूखल-मुसलमनवरतहुताज्यगन्धिधूमश्यामलितगगनमण्डलममरसरितो नातिदूरे विभात्याश्रममण्डलम् । नूनमिदं कस्यापि गृहमेधिनो गृहं भविष्यति । भवतु । युक्तमस्माकमतिपवित्रमेतद्द्वित्रिदिवस-निवासस्थानम् । (प्रवेशं नाटयति) । (विलोक्य च) अये,

मृद्बिन्दुलाञ्छितललाटभुजोदरोरः-
कण्ठोष्ठपृष्ठचुबुकोरुकपोलजानुः ।
चूडाग्रकर्णकटिपाणिविराजमान-
दर्भाङ्कुरः स्फुरति मूर्त इवैष दम्भः ॥६॥

भवतूपसर्पाम्येनम् (उपसृत्य) कल्याणं भवतु भवताम् ।

(दम्भो हुंकारेण निवारयति ।)

(ततः प्रविशति बटुः)

बटुः : (ससंभ्रमम् ।) ब्रह्मन्, दूरत एव स्थीयताम् । यतः पादौ प्रक्षाल्य एतदाश्रमपदं प्रवेष्टव्यम् ।

अहंकारः : (सक्रोधम् ।) आः पाप, तुरुष्कदेशं प्राप्ताः स्मः, यत्र श्रोत्रिया-नतिथीनासनपाद्यादिभिरपि गृहिणो नोपतिष्ठन्ति ।

दम्भः : (हस्तसंज्ञया समाश्वासयति ।)

(*Again going to another side*). These who support themselves by taking the guise of Tridaṇḍis are neither the followers of Dvaita nor Advaita. (*Looking at another direction*). Well, whose is this hermitage, not very far from the divine river (*Gaṅgā*) where thousands of fine washed white clothes swing on the high bamboo poles fixed very near the door and where, there on the ground are kept the black deer-skin, dṛṣad-upala,[1] samidh[2], caṣāla[3], ulūkhala[4] and musala[5] (*all accessories of Yoga*), and the sky is darkened by smoke fragrant with the oblations offered continually. Certainly this must be the house of a householder. Well, this is a holy place where we can stay for two or three days.

(*Acting as if entering and looking*), *Ah*!

This one with his forehead, arms, belly and chest, necks, lips, chins, thighs, temples and knees, marked with mud and with sprouts of darbha grass on his head, ears, waist and hand, appears to be Deceit personified. (6).

Well, I shall go near him. (*Going near*) Let there be happiness for you. (*Deceit wards him off with the sound 'hum'*)

(*The student enters*)

Student : (*Hurriedly*). Brahmin, stay at a distance. For you have to enter this hermitage only after washing your feet.

Egoism : (*Angrily*) Oh! sinner, we have come to the land of Turuṣkas (*Turkey perhaps*) where the house-holders do not receive the venerable guests even with offering them a seat and water to wash their feet.

Deceit : (*Pacifies him with the gesture of hand*)

---

1. a flat stone for grinding condiments.
2. sacrificial sticks for the sacred fire.
3. a wooden ring on the top of sacrificial Post.
4. a wooden mortar.
5. a pestle.

बटुः : एवमाराध्यपादा आज्ञापयन्ति दूरदेशादागतस्यार्यस्य कुलशीलादिकं न सम्यगस्माकं विदितम् ।

अहंकारः : आः कथमस्माकमपि कुलशीलादिकमिदानीं परीक्षितव्यम् ? श्रूयताम्—

गौडं राष्ट्रमनुत्तमं निरुपमा तत्रापि राढापुरी
भूरिश्रेष्ठकनाम धाम परमं तत्रोत्तमो नः पिता ।
तत्पुत्राश्च महाकुला न विदिताः कस्यात्र तेषामपि
प्रज्ञाशीलविवेकधैर्यविनयाचारैरहं चोत्तमः ॥ ७ ॥

(दम्भो बटुं पश्यति)

बटुः : (ताम्रघटीं गृहीत्वा ।) भगवन्, पादशौचं विधीयताम् ।

अहंकारः : (स्वगतम् ।) भवतु । कोऽत्र विरोधः ? एवं क्रियते । (तथा कृत्वोपसर्पति ।)

दम्भः : (दन्तान्संपीड्य बटुं पश्यति ।)

बटुः : दूरे तावत्स्थीयताम् । वाताहताः प्रस्वेदकणिकाः प्रसरन्ति ।

अहंकारः : अहो, अपूर्वमिदं ब्राह्मण्यम् ।

बटुः : ब्रह्मन्, एवमेतत् । तथाहि—

अस्पृष्टचरणा ह्यस्य चूडामणिमरीचिभिः ।
नीराजयन्ति भूपालाः पादपीठान्तभूतलम् ॥ ८ ॥

अहंकारः : (स्वगतम्) अये, दम्भग्राह्योऽयं देशः । (प्रकाशम्) भवतु । अस्मिन्नासने उपविशामि । (तथा कर्तुमिच्छति ।)

बटुः : मैवम् नाराध्यपादानामन्यैरासनमाक्रम्यते ।

अहंकारः : आः पाप, अस्माभिरपि दक्षिणराढाप्रदेशप्रसिद्धविशुद्धिभिर्नाक्रमणीयमिदमासनम् । शृणु रे मूर्ख,

नास्माकं जननी तथोज्ज्वलकुला सच्छ्रोत्रियाणां पुन-
र्व्यूढा काचन कन्यका खलु मया तेनास्मि ताताधिकः ।
अस्मच्छालकभागिनेयदुहिता मिथ्याभिशप्ता यत-
स्तत्संपर्कवशान्मया स्वगृहिणी प्रेयस्यपि प्रोज्झिता ॥९॥

Student : The Revered one says that we do not know for certain about you, your family and character, Revered sir, who have come from a far off country.

Egoism : What, even our family, character etc. have to be examined now? Listen.

Gauḍa is an unequalled country, there is a city called Rāḍhāpurī. There is a celebrated house called Bhūriśreṣṭhaka and our father is the worthiest there. Who has not heard of his noble sons? Among whom I am the best in intelligence, character, power of discrimination, courage, modesty and in performance of duties. (7).

(*Deceit looks at the student*)

Student : (*Taking the small copper pot*). Sir, please wash your feet.

Egoism : (*To himself*). Let it be, what objection is there? I shall do so. (*Goes near after doing so*).

Deceit : (*Bites his lip and looks at the student*)

Student : Stay farther off. Particles of your perspiration blown by the wind spread everywhere.

Egoism : Ah! this is a new kind of Brahminism.

Student : Brahmin, it is so. For

The kings of the earth even without touching his feet, radiate the space in front of his feet with the rays of the jewels on their head. (8).

Egoism : (*To himself*). Oh! this is a land overcome by deceit. (*Aloud*) Let it be, I shall sit on this seat. (*attempts to do so*).

Student : Don't do so. None else occupies the seat of the Revered one.

Egoism : Oh! sinner, this seat should not be occupied even by us whose purity is well known in the Southern Rāḍhā land. Hear you fool.

"My mother did not belong to a noble family but I married a girl from a respectable family. In this respect I am superior to my father. The daughter of the nephew of my brother-in-law was falsely accused but on account of her relation to this person, I left my wife though beloved to me." (9).

दम्भः : ब्रह्मन्, यद्यप्येवं तथाप्यस्माकमविदितवृत्तान्तो भवान् । तथाहि--

सदनमुपगतोऽहं पूर्वमम्भोजयोनेः
सपदि मुनिभिरुच्चैरासनेषूज्झितेषु ।
सशपथमनुनीय ब्रह्मणा गोमयाम्भः-
परिमृजितनिजोरावाशु संवेशितोऽस्मि ॥१०॥

अहंकारः : (स्वगतम्) अहो, दाम्भिकस्य ब्राह्मणस्यात्युक्तिः । (विचिन्त्य) अथवा दम्भोऽयम् । भवत्वेवं तावत् । (प्रकाशम्) आः किमेवं गर्वायसे ? (सक्रोधम्)

अरे क इव वासवः कथय कोऽत्र पद्मोद्भवो
वद प्रभवभूमयो जगति का मुनीनामपि ।
अवेहि तपसो बलं मम पुरन्दराणां शतं
शतं च परमेष्ठिनां पततु वा मुनीनां शतम् ॥ ११ ॥

दम्भः : (विलोक्य । सानन्दम् ।) अये, आर्यः पितामहोऽस्माकमहंकारः । आर्य, दम्भो लोभात्मजोऽहं भो अभिवादये ।

अहंकारः : वत्स, आयुष्मान्भव । बालः खल्वसि मया द्वापरान्ते दृष्टः । संप्रति चिरकालविप्रकर्षाद्वार्धक्यग्रस्ततया च न सम्यक्प्रत्यभिजानामि । अपि त्वत्कुमारस्यानृतस्य कुशलम् ?

दम्भः : अथ किम् । सोऽप्यत्रैव महामोहस्याज्ञया वर्तते । नहि तेन विना मुहूर्तमप्यहं प्रभवामि ।

अहंकारः : अथ तव मातापितरौ तृष्णालोभावपि कुशलौ ? ।

दम्भः : तावपि राज्ञो महामोहस्याज्ञयाऽत्रैव वर्तेते । तयोर्विना क्षणमपि न तिष्ठामि । आर्यमिश्रैः पुनः केन प्रयोजनेनात्र प्रसादः कृतः ।

अहंकारः : वत्स, मया महामोहस्य विवेकसकाशादत्याहितं श्रुतम् । तेन तद्वृत्तान्तं प्रत्येतुमागतोऽस्मि ।

Deceit : Brahmin even if it is so, you do not know about us. For—

Once I went to the abode of the Lotus-born (*Brahmā*), all of a sudden all the sages rose up from their seats. I was respectfully entreated by Brahmā and he immediately placed me on his thighs purified with cowdung water. (10).

Egoism : (*To himself*) What an exaggerated statement of a deceitful Brāhmaṇa ! (*Thinking*) Perhaps it is Deceit himself. Let it be so (*Aloud*). Why should you be so proud ? (*Angrily*).

Oh! who is Indra, pray who is the Lotus-born, which are the sources of the sages in the world, know that by the strength of my penance, let hundred Indras, hundred Brahmās and hundred sages fall. (11).

Deceit : (*Looking at him with delight*) Well, this is my revered grand-father Egoism. Revered one, I am Deceit the son of Greed, saluting you.

Egoism : My child, may you have long life. I saw you as a child at the end of Dvāparayuga. Now I do not recognise you properly because of long separation and old age. Is your son Falsehood well ?

Deceit : Of course. He is also here by the command of the great Moha. I cannot live without him even for a moment.

Egoism : And are your mother and father, Desire and Greed, well?

Deceit : They are also here by the command of the Grand Delusion. I cannot remain a moment without them. To what cause do we owe this favour of the Revered one (*towards us*).

Egoism : My child, I heard that Reason has done great harm to the great Delusion. I have come to ascertain the news.

दम्भः : स्वागतमेवार्यस्य । यतो महाराजस्यापीन्द्रलोकादत्रागमनं श्रूयते । अस्ति च किंवदन्ती यद्देवेन वाराणसी राजधानी वस्तुं निरूपितेति ।

अहंकारः : पुनः किं वाराणस्यां सर्वात्मना मोहस्यावस्थानकारणमिति ?

दम्भः : आर्य, ननु विवेकोपरोध एव। तथाहि--

विद्याप्रबोधोदयजन्मभूमिर्वाराणसी ब्रह्मपुरी निरत्यया ।
असौ कुलोच्छेदविधिं चिकीर्षुर्निर्वस्तुमत्रेच्छति नित्यमेवम् ॥१२॥

अहंकारः--(सभयम्) यद्यप्येवमशक्यप्रतीकार एवायमर्थः। यतः--

परममविदुषां पदं नराणां पुरविजयी करुणाविधेयचेताः ।
कथयति भगवानिहान्तकाले भवभयकातरतारकं प्रबोधम् ॥१३॥

दम्भः : सत्यमेतत्तथापि नैतत्कामक्रोधाभिभूतानां संभाव्यते । तथा ह्युदाहरन्ति तैर्थिकाः—

'यस्य हस्तौ च पादौ च मनश्चैव सुसंयतम् ।
विद्या तपश्च तीर्थं च स तीर्थफलमश्नुते ॥१४॥' इति ।

(नेपथ्ये) भो भोः पौराः, एष खलु संप्राप्तो देवो महामोहः । तेन,

निष्यन्दैश्चन्दनानां स्फटिकमणिशिलावेदिकाः संस्क्रियन्तां
मुच्यन्तां यन्त्रमार्गाः प्रचरतु परितो वारिधारा गृहेषु ।
उच्छ्रीयन्तां समन्तात्स्फुरदुरुमणयः श्रेणयस्तोरणानां
धूयन्तां सौधमूर्धस्वमरपतिधनुर्धामचित्राः पताकाः ॥१५॥

दम्भः : आर्य, प्रत्यासन्नोऽयं महाराजः । तत्प्रत्युद्गमनेन संभाव्यतामार्येण ।

Deceit : Welcome, Revered one. It is reported that the king is coming here from Indraloka. There is a rumour that he has decided to make Vārāṇasī his capital.

Egoism : And what is the cause of Delusion's whole-hearted stay in Vārāṇasī?

Deceit : Revered one, it is to obstruct Reason. For—

The safe (*indestructible*) city of Brahmā, Vārāṇasī is the birth place of knowledge and spiritual awakening. He (*Reason*) who desires to destroy our family wishes to stay here permanently. (12).

Egoism : (*Fearfully*) If it is so, it is impossible to fight against this purpose. For, here the conqueror of Tripura (*Lord Śiva*) full of compassion in his heart reveals to the ignorant people, who do not know the supreme Truth, in their last days the Spiritual awakening which helps them to cross the fear of mundane existence. (13).

Deceit : It is true but this is not possible for those who are overcome by Concupiscence and Anger. The holy people say thus.

He whose hands, legs, mind, knowledge, austerity and organ of generation are rightly employed, attains the fruit of (*this*) place of pilgrimage. (14).

(*Behind the curtain*). Hear you citizens ! the king Grand Delusion has arrived here.

Let the courtyards made of crystals and gems be sprinkled with sandal paste, let the fountain be open, let the streams of water spread to the houses around, let rows of festoons shining with big gems be hung high, and on the top of the mansions let many hued variegated flags resembling the bow of Indra fly.

Deceit : Revered one. The king has come. Let respect be given by your advancing to meet him.

अहंकारः : एवं भवतु । (निष्क्रान्तौ ।)

(प्रवेशकः ।)

(ततः प्रविशति महामोहो विभवतश्च परिवारः ।)

महामोहः : (विहस्य) अहो, निरङ्कुशा जडधियः ।

आत्मास्ति देहव्यतिरिक्तमूर्तिर्भोक्ता स लोकान्तरितः फलानाम् ।
आशेयमाकाशतरोः प्रसूनात्प्राथीयसः स्वादुफलप्रसूतौ ॥१६॥

इदं च स्वकल्पनाविनिर्मितपदार्थावष्टम्भेन जगदेवं दुर्विदग्धैर्वञ्च्यते । तथाहि—

यन्नास्त्येव तदस्ति वस्त्विति मृषा जल्पद्भिरेवास्तिकैर्-
वाचालैर्बहुभिस्तु सत्यवचसो निन्द्याः कृता नास्तिकाः ।
हंहो पश्यत तत्त्वतो यदि पुनश्छिन्नादितो वर्ष्मणां
दृष्टः किं परिणामरूपितचितेर्जीवः पृथक्कैरपि ॥१७॥

अपि च न केवलं जगदात्मैव तावदमीभिर्वञ्च्यते ।

तथाहि—

तुल्यत्वे वपुषां मुखाद्यवयवैर्वर्णक्रमः कीदृशो
योषेयं वसु चापरस्य तदमुं भेदं न विद्मो वयम्
हिंसायामथवा यथेष्टगमने स्त्रीणां परस्वग्रहे
कार्याकार्यविचारणा हि यदमी निष्पौरुषाः कुर्वते ॥१८॥

Egoism : Be it so (*They go out*).

(*Praveśaka*)

(*Then enters Grand Delusion pompously with his attendants*)

Gr. Delu. : (*Smiling*). The fools are without any check on them.

"(*The view*) that there is a soul separate from the body, which on reaching the other world enjoys rewards, is (*like*) the hope to get tasty fruits from the big flower of a tree in the sky." (16).

This world is deceived by the ignorant who accept the existence of what is the mere creation of their own imagination. For—

Them any talkative believers (*āstikas*) who jabber in vain that a thing which does not exist, exists, condemn the truth-speaking non-believers (*nāstikas*). Oh, consider from the point of reality. When the body is destroyed, has any one seen a soul separate from it which acquired consciousness as a result of transformation (*due to certain combination*). (17).

They deceive not only the world but also themselves. For—

If the bodies are alike in their different parts, the mouth, etc., how can there be a hierarchy of castes? We do not accept any difference between a woman and wealth belonging (to us or) to somebody else. Only those who are devoid of manliness consider whether an act should be done or not, whether it entails harm, whether to approach women at one's pleasure and seize the wealth of others. (18).

(विचिन्त्य, सश्लाघम् ।) सर्वथा लोकायतमेव शास्त्रं यत्र प्रत्यक्षमेव प्रमाणं पृथिव्यप्तेजोवायवस्तत्त्वानि, अर्थकामौ पुरुषार्थौ भूतान्येव चेतयन्ते । नास्ति परलोकः । मृत्युरेवापवर्गः । तदेतदस्मदभिप्रायानुबन्धिना वाचस्पतिना प्रणीय चार्वाकाय समर्पितम् । तेन च शिष्योपशिष्यद्वारेणास्मिल्लोके बहुलीकृतं तन्त्रम् ।

(ततः प्रविशति चार्वाकः शिष्यश्च ।)

चार्वाकः : वत्स, जानासि दण्डनीतिरेव विद्या । अत्रैव वार्तान्तर्भवति । धूर्तप्रलापस्त्रयी । स्वर्गोत्पादकत्वेन विशेषाभावात् ।

पश्य--

स्वर्गः कर्तृक्रियाद्रव्यविनाशे यदि यज्वनाम् ।
ततो दावाग्निदग्धानां फलं स्याद्भूरि भूरुहाम् ॥१९॥

अपि च ।

निहतस्य पशोर्यज्ञे स्वर्गप्राप्तिर्यदीष्यते ।
स्वपिता यजमानेन किं नु कस्मान्न हन्यते ॥२०॥

अपि च ।

मृतानामपि जन्तूनां श्राद्धं चेत्तृप्तिकारणम् ।
निर्वाणस्य प्रदीपस्य स्नेहः संवर्धयेच्छिखाम् ॥२१॥

शिष्यः : आचालिअ, जई एसो जेव्व पलमत्थो पुलिसस्स जं खज्जए पिज्जए ता किंति एदेहिं तित्थेहिं संसालसुहं पलिहलिअ आप्पा घोलघोलतलेहिं पलाअ-सांतवन-सट्ठका आप्पासनप्पहुदिहं दुखेहिं कुवो खविज्जदि ?

[आचार्य, यद्येष एव परमार्थः पुरुषस्य यत्खाद्यते पीयते तर्हि किमित्येतैस्तीर्थैः संसारसौख्यं परिहृत्यात्मा घोरघोरतरैः पराक-सान्तपन-षष्ठकालमाशन-प्रभृतिभिर्दुःखैः कस्मात्क्षिप्यते ?]

(*After thinking, proudly*). By all means materialism alone is the science, in whose view, the only means of knowledge is perception. The elements are earth, water, fire, and air. Wealth and pleasure are the sole aims of man. The elements move through original impulse. There is no other world. Emancipation is death. This science was composed by Vācaspati who followed our view and has given it to the Materialist. This science is popularised in the world by him through his disciples and their disciples.

(*Then enter the Materialist and his disciples*)

Material. : My child, know that knowledge consists only of statecraft. The science of Agriculture and trade is included in this. The three Vedas are incoherent talk of cheats. There is no difference just because they postulate heaven.

See—

If sacrifices obtain (*for one*) heaven by the destruction of the sacrificial matter through the action of the officiating priest, the trees burnt by the forest fire will bear ample fruit ? (19).

Moreover—

If it is assumed that an animal slain (*in sacrifices*) goes to heaven, why does not the sacrificer immolate his own father ? (20).

And—

If Śrāddha (*offering of rice balls to a dead person*) produces gratification to beings who are dead, then oil may rear the flame of an extinguished light. (21).

Disciple : Venerable teacher, if the sole aim of man is to eat and drink then why do these ascetics renounce the worldly pleasures and afflict themselves with severe tortures caused by parāka (*a sacrificial sword*) sāntapana (*a kind of rigid penance*) and taking food once in three days (*as an expiatory act*) ?

चार्वाकः : धूर्तप्रणीतागमप्रतारितानामाशामोदकैरियं तृप्तिर्मूर्खाणाम् ।
पश्य पश्य—

क्वालिङ्गनं भुजनिपीडितबाहुमूलं
भुग्नोन्नतस्तनमनोहरमायताक्ष्याः ।
भिक्षोपवासनियमार्कमरीचिदाहै-
र्देहोपशोषणविधिः कुधियां क्व चैषः ॥२२॥

शिष्यः : आचालिअ, एवं खु तित्थिआ आलवन्ति जं दुःखमिस्सिदं संसालसुहं पलिहलणीअं त्ति ।

[आचार्य, एवं खलु तीर्थिका आलपन्ति यद्दुःखमिश्रितं संसारसुखं परिहरणीयमिति] ।

चार्वाकः : (विहस्य ।) आः, दुर्बुद्धिविलसितमिदं नरपशूनाम् ।

त्याज्यं सुखं विषयसंगमजन्म पुंसां
दुःखोपसृष्टमिति मूर्खविचारणैषा ।
व्रीहीञ्जिहासति सितोत्तमतण्डुलाढ्या-
न्को नाम भोस्तुषकणोपहितान्हितार्थी ॥२३॥

महामोहः : अये, चिरेण खलु प्रमाणवन्ति वचनानि कर्णसुखमुपजनयन्ति ।
(विलोक्य, सानन्दम्) हन्त, प्रियसुहृन्मे चार्वाकः ।

चार्वाकः : (विलोक्य ।) एष महाराजो महामोहः । (उपसृत्य ।) जयतु जयतु महाराजः । एष चार्वाकः प्रणमति ।

महामोहः : चार्वाक, स्वागतं ते । इहोपविश्यताम् ।

चार्वाकः : (उपविश्य ।) एष कलेः साष्टाङ्गः प्रणामः ।

महामोहः : अये कले, भद्रमव्याहतम् ।

चार्वाकः : देवप्रसादात्सर्वत्र भद्रम् । निर्वर्तितकृत्यशेषश्च देवपादमूलं द्रष्टुमिति । यतः—

आज्ञामवाप्य महतीं द्विषतां निपाता-
न्निर्वर्त्य तां सपदि लब्धसुखप्रसादः ।
उच्चैःप्रमोदमनुमोदितदर्शनः सन्
धन्यो नमस्यति पदाम्बुरुहं प्रभूणाम् ॥२४॥

Material. : These fools who are deceived by the Vedas composed by cheats are contented with the sweetmeats of hopes. See,

Where is the embrace of the long-eyed ones, the embrace pressing the shoulders with one's arms and which is pleasing because of the prominent breasts compressed and where is begging, fasting, penance, exposure to the burning heat of the sun which emaciate the body of these fools. (22).

Disciple : Revered sir, these ascetics say that worldly pleasure is to be given up because it is mingled with miseries.

Material. : (*Laughing*) This is the expression of foolishness of these human animals.

It is the reasoning of fools that the pleasure which arises in men from contact with sensible objects is to be relinquished as they are accompanied by pain. What man seeking his true interest would fling away the berries of paddy, rich with finest white grains, because they are covered with husks and dust. (23).

Gr. Delu.: Well, It is after a long time, my ears are gratified by words which are authoritative (*Looking with joy*) Oh! it is my dear friend Materialist.

Material.: (*Looking*) This is king Delusion. (*going near*). May the king be victorious ! I, Materialist salute you.

Gr. Delu. : Welcome Materialist, be seated here.

Material.: (*sits*) Kali prostrates before you.

Gr. Delu. : Ah! Kali, unimpaired blessings be upon you!

Material.: By your grace all is good. He has accomplished everything (*ordered by you*) and wishes to (worship at) your feet. For—

After receiving the great command (*from you*) and having accomplished it by destroying the enemies he is now happy and delighted and with his great joy in countenance feels blessed and prostrates himself at the lotus feet of the Lord. (24).

महामोहः : अथ तस्मिन्कलौ कियत्संवृत्तम् ।

चार्वाकः : देव,

व्यतीतवेदार्थपथः प्रथीयसीं यथेष्टचेष्टां गमितो महाजनः ।
तदत्र हेतुर्न कलिर्न चाप्यहं प्रभोः प्रभावो हि तनोति पौरुषम् ॥२५॥

तत्रोत्तराः पथिकाः पाश्चात्यादच त्रयीमेव त्याजिताः। शमदमादीनां कैव कथा? अन्यत्रापि प्रायशो जीविकामात्रफलैव त्रयी । यथाहाचार्यः ।

अग्निहोत्रं त्रयो वेदास्त्रिदण्डं भस्मगुण्ठनम् ।
प्रज्ञापौरुषहीनानां जीविकेति बृहस्पतिः ॥२६॥

तेन कुरुक्षेत्रादिषु तावद्देवेन स्वप्नेऽपि विद्याप्रबोधोदयो नाशङ्कनीयः ।

महामोहः : साधु संपादितम् । महत्खलु तत्तीर्थं व्यर्थीकृतम् ।

चार्वाकः : देव, अन्यच्च विज्ञाप्यमस्ति ।

महामोहः : किं तत् ?

चार्वाकः : अस्ति विष्णुभक्तिर्नाम महाप्रभावा योगिनी । सा तु कलिना यद्यपि विरलप्रचारा कृता तथापि तदनुगृहीतान्वयमालोकयितुमपि न प्रभवामः । तदत्र देवेनावधातव्यमिति ।

महामोहः : (सभयमात्मगतम् ।) आः, प्रसिद्धमहाप्रभावा सा योगिनी स्वभावाद्विद्वेषिणी चास्माकं दुरुच्छेद्या सा । भवतु । (स्वगतम् ।) कार्यमत्याहितं भविष्यति । (प्रकाशम् ।) तत्र भद्र, अलमनया शङ्कया । कामक्रोधादिषु कुत्रेयमुदेष्यति ।

चार्वाकः : तथापि लघीयस्यपि रिपौ नानवहितेन जिगीषुणा भवितव्यम् ।

Gr. Delu. : And what has that Kali achieved?

Material.: Lord, he caused the virtuous forsake the path shown by the Vedas and act according to their own wish. It is the glory of my Lord neither mine nor Kali's for this achievement. (25).

The people of the north and west have forsaken the three Vedas, what to speak of tranquillity and self-restraint. In other places too the three Vedas are there just as a means of livelihood. The Ācārya (*Bṛhaspati*) has said:

"The oblations in the fire, the three Vedas, the carrying of three sticks tied together, and smearing oneself with ashes are the means of livelihood of those who are devoid of intelligence and manliness. (26).

There in Kurukṣetra and other places my Lord need not fear the birth of Knowledge or Spiritual Awakening even in a dream".

Gr. Delu. : Well done. That great holy place is rendered useless.

Material.: My Lord. There is something more to be reported.

Gr. Delu. : What is it ?

Material.: There is a Yogini of great power called Devotion to Viṣṇu. Though her popularity is lessened by Kali, we cannot even look at those who are blessed by her. Therefore, my Lord, you have to be on your guard against her.

Gr. Delu. : (*In fear to himself*). Oh! it is difficult to destroy her whose great power is well known and who is my natural enemy. Well. (*to himself*). Sometimes drastic action has to be taken. (*Loudly*) Then my dear, do not have any doubts. Where can she appear when Concupiscence and Anger are her enemies?

Material.: Even then one who desires victory should not remain unguarded even where the enemy is weak.

यतः—

विपाकदारुणो राज्ञां रिपुरल्पोऽप्यरुंतुदः ।
उद्वेजयति सूक्ष्मोऽपि चरणं कण्टकाङ्कुरः ॥२७॥

महामोहः : (नेपथ्याभिमुखमवलोक्य) कः कोऽत्र भोः ?

(प्रविश्य दौवारिकः ।)

दौवारिकः : जयतु जयतु । आज्ञापयतु देवः ।

महामोहः : भो असत्सङ्ग, आदिश्यन्तां कामक्रोधलोभमदमात्सर्यादयो यथा योगिनां विष्णुभक्तिर्भवद्भिरेवावहितैर्विहन्तव्येति ।

दौवारिकः : यदाज्ञापयति देवः ।

(इति निष्क्रान्तः ।)

(ततः प्रविशति पत्रहस्तः पुरुषः ।)

पुरुषः : हग्गे उक्कलदेशादो आगदोम्हि । अत्थि तत्थ साअलतीलसण्णिवेसे पुलिसोत्तमसग्गिदं देवदाअदणम् । तस्सि मदमाणेहिं भट्टकेहिं महालाअसआसं पेसिदोम्हि । (विलोक्य) एसा वालाणसी । एदं लाअउलम् । जाव प्पविसामि । (प्रविश्य) एसो भट्टको चव्वाकेण सद्धं किंवि मन्तअन्तो चिट्ठदि । ता उवसप्पामि णम् । (उपसृत्य) जेदु जेदु भट्टको । एदं पत्तं जाव णिलुप्पिअमाणं पेक्खदु भट्टको । (इति पत्रमर्पयति ।)

[अहमुत्कलदेशादागतोऽस्मि । अस्ति तत्र सागरतीरसंनिवेशे पुरुषोत्तमशब्दितं देवतायतनम् । तस्मिन्मदमानाभ्यां भट्टारकाभ्यां महाराजसकाशं प्रेषितोऽस्मि । एषा वाराणसी । इदं राजकुलम् । यावत्प्रविशामि । एष भट्टारकश्चार्वाकेण सार्धं किमपि मन्त्रयंस्तिष्ठति । तदुपसर्पाम्येनम् । जयतु जयतु भट्टारकः । इदं पत्रं तावन्निरूप्यमाणं प्रेक्षतु भट्टारकः] ।

महामोहः : (पत्रं गृहीत्वा) कुतो भवान् ?

पुरुषः : हग्गे पुलिसोत्तमादो आगदोम्हि ।

[अहं पुरुषोत्तमादागतोऽस्मि ।]

महामोहः : (स्वगतम्) कार्यमत्याहितं भविष्यति । (प्रकाशम्) चार्वाक, गच्छ । कर्तव्येष्ववहितेन भवता भवितव्यम् ।

चार्वाकः : यदाज्ञापयति देवः ।

(इति निष्क्रान्तः ।)

For--

Even a weak enemy may prove to be a fierce one in the end and inflict a mortal wound like a small thorn that afflicts the foot. (27).

Gr. Delu. : (*Looking behind the curtain*) Who is there ?

(*Enter the gatekeeper*)

Gatekeep : Victory to my Lord. Let my Lord command.

Gr. Delu. : Oh! 'Companion of the wicked', Go and direct Concupiscence, Anger, Greed, Arrogance, Spite and others that they should be on guard and kill the Yogini—Devotion to Viṣṇu.

Gatekeep: As your Lord commands.

(*Exit*)

(*A man enters with a letter*)

Man : I come from Utkala. There near the ocean there is a temple of God called Puruṣottama. I have been sent to the king by my masters, Arrogance, Deceit and Conceit. (*Looking*) This is Vārāṇasī. This is the place of the king. I shall enter (*Entering*). Here the master is talking something with the Materialist. I shall go near him (*Going near*) Victory to my Lord. Look at this letter which needs attention.

(*Gives the letter*)

Gr. Delu. : (*Taking the letter*) Where do you come from ?

Man : I have come from Puruṣottama.

Gr. Delu. : (*To himself*) Must be something very serious. (*Aloud*) Materialist go. Be alert while doing whatever is required.

Material.: As you command.

(*Exit*)

महामोहः : (पत्रं वाचयति ।)

'स्वस्ति श्रीवाराणस्यां महाराजाधिराजपरमेश्वरमहामोहपादान्पुरुषोत्तमायतनान् मदमानौ साष्टाङ्गपातं प्रणम्य विज्ञापयतः । यथा भद्रमव्याहृतम् । अन्यच्च देवी शान्तिर्मात्रा श्रद्धया सह विवेकस्य दौत्यमापन्ना विवेकसंगमाय देवीमुपनिषदमहर्निशं प्रबोधयति । अपि च कामसहचरोऽपि धर्मो वैराग्यादिभिरुपजप्त इव लक्ष्यते । यतः कामाद्विभिद्य कुतश्चिन्निगूढः प्रचरति । तदेतज्ज्ञात्वा तत्र देवः प्रमाणमिति ।

महामोहः : (सक्रोधम्) आः किमेवमतिमुग्धौ शान्तेरपि बिभ्यतः । कामादिषु प्रतिपक्षेषु कुतोऽस्याः संभवः । तथाहि—

धाता विश्वविसृष्टिमात्रनिरतो देवोऽपि गौरीभुजा-
श्लेषानन्दविघूर्णमाननयनो दक्षाध्वरध्वंसनः ।
दैत्यारिः कमलाकपोलमकरीलेखाङ्कितोरःस्थलः
शेतेऽब्धावितरेषु जन्तुषु पुनः का नाम शान्तेः कथा ॥२८॥

(पुरुषं प्रति वदति ।)

जाल्म, गच्छ । कामं सत्वरमुपेत्यादेशमस्माकं प्रतिपादय । तथा दुराशयो धर्म इत्यस्माभिरवगतम् । तदस्मिन्मुहूर्तमपि न विश्वसितव्यम् । दृढं बध्वा धारयितव्य इति ।

पुरुषः : जं देवो आणवेदि ।

[यद्देव आज्ञापयति] ।

(इति निष्क्रान्तः ।)

महामोहः : (स्वगतं विचिन्त्य) शान्तेः कोऽभ्युपायः । अथवा अलमुपायान्तरेण । क्रोधलोभावेव तावदत्र पर्याप्तौ । (प्रकाशम्) कः कोऽत्र भोः ?

(प्रविश्य दौवारिकः ।)

दौवारिकः : आज्ञापयतु देवः ।

Gr. Delu. : (*Reads the letter*).

Arrogance and Deceit from Puruṣottama beg to inform after prostrations, to the Great King Delusion, the king of kings residing in Vārāṇasī. "Goddess Peace with her mother Faith has entered into the service of Reason and persuades day and night Sacred Lore to be united with Reason. And Righteousness, the friend of Concupiscence seems to be influenced by Dispassionateness. He separating himself from Concupiscence roams about somewhere hidden. My Lord, who knows this, is now the authority."

Gr. Delu. : (*Angrily*) Ah! these two fools are afraid of even Peace. How is this possible when Concupiscence etc. are to oppose her? For, Brahmā engaged only in the creation of the world; the God (*Śiva*) the destroyer of the sacrifice of Dakṣa has eyes rolling out of joy born of the embrace of Gaurī's arms; the enemy of Demons (*Viṣṇu*) whose breast is marked with the decoration on the cheek of Kamalā (*Lakṣmī*) sleeps in the ocean. What to speak of Peace to be obtained by the other (*ordinary*) beings. (28).

(*Replies to the man*)

You wretch, go as fast as you can and deliver this message. We have come to know that Righteousness is meanminded Therefore he should not be trusted by us for a moment even. He should be bound fast.

Man : As you command sir. (*Leaves*)

Gr. Delu. : (*To himself after thinking*) What device is there against Peace? Or, rather, there is no need of any other device. Anger and Greed are strong enough (*to destroy Peace*). (*Aloud*) Who is there?

(*The Gatekeeper entering*)

Gatekeep : My Lord, command me.

महामोहः : तावदाहूयतां क्रोधो लोभश्च ।

पुरुषः : जं आणवेदि देवो ।

[यदाज्ञापयति देवः ।]

(इति निष्क्रान्तः ।)

(ततः प्रविशति क्रोधो लोभश्च ।)

क्रोधः : श्रुतं मया यथा शान्तिश्रद्धाविष्णुभक्तयो महाराजेन प्रतिपक्षमाचरन्तीति । अहो, मयि जीवति कथमासामात्मनि निरपेक्षितं चेष्टितम् । तथाहि—

अन्धीकरोमि भवनं बधिरीकरोमि
धीरं सचेतनमचेतनतां नयामि ।
कृत्यं न पश्यति न येन हितं शृणोति
धीमानधीतमपि न प्रतिसंदधाति ।।२९।।

लोभः : अये, मदुपगृहीता मनोरथसरित्परम्परामेव तावन्न तरिष्यन्ति किं पुनः शान्त्यादींश्चिन्तयिष्यन्ति । पश्य पश्य सखे—

सन्त्येते मम दन्तिनो मदजलप्रम्लानगण्डस्थला
वातव्यायतपातिनश्च तुरगा भूयोऽपि लप्स्येऽपरान् ।
एतल्लब्धमिदं लभे पुनरिदं लब्धाधिकं ध्यायतां
चिन्ताजर्जरचेतसां बत नृणां का नाम शान्तेः कथा ।।३०।।

क्रोधः : सखे, विदितस्त्वया मत्प्रभावः ।

त्वाष्ट्रं वृत्रमघातयत्सुरपतिश्चन्द्रार्धचूडोऽच्छिन-
द्देवो ब्रह्मशिरो वसिष्ठतनयानाघातयत्कौशिकः ।

अपि च

विद्यावन्त्यपि कीर्तिमन्त्यपि सदाचारावदातान्यपि
प्रोच्चैःपौरुषभूषणान्यपि कुलान्युद्धर्तुं मीशः क्षणात् ।।३१।।

लोभः : तृष्णे, इतस्तावत् ।

(प्रविश्य तृष्णा ।)

तृष्णा : किं आणवेदि अज्जउत्तो ।

[किमाज्ञापयत्यार्यपुत्रः ।]

लोभः : प्रिये, श्रूयताम्—

Delusion : Call Anger and Greed.

Man : As you command sir. (*Exit*)

(*Then enter Anger and Greed*)

Anger : I have heard that Peace, Faith and Devotion to Viṣṇu are hostile to the king. Ah ! How is it possible that they act in disregard of themselves while we are living. For—

I will make the world blind and deaf and steadily convert the animate into inanimate. So that they do not pay regard to their duties, do not listen to good advice, and the wise will not remember what he has learnt. (29).

Greed : Those who are caught by me do not cross the successive rivers of desire. Then how will they think of Peace, etc. See my friend.

"These are my elephants whose temples are washed with ichor, and these horses are swifter than the wind" "I shall get some thing more", "this has been acquired", "I shall get this", thus these men who are thinking of something more than they have already got, whose minds are shattered because of worries, how can they have peace ? (30).

Anger : My dear friend, you know my greatness.

The Lord of gods (*Indra*) killed Vṛtra the son of Tvaṣṭṛ. The half-moon-crested (*Śiva*) cut the head of Brahmā and Kauśika (*Viśvāmitra*) killed the sons of Vasiṣṭha. Moreover—

I am capable of uprooting families possessing knowledge, fame, pure by their actions and clothed in great might. (31).

Greed : Desire come here.

(*Desire enters*)

Desire : What does my Lord command ?

Greed : My beloved, listen.

क्षेत्रग्रामवनाद्रिपत्तनपुरद्वीपक्षमामण्डल-
प्रत्याशायतसूत्रबद्धमनसां लब्धाधिकं ध्यायताम् ।
तृष्णे देवि यदि प्रसीदसि तनोष्यङ्गानि तुङ्गानि चे-
त्तद्गोः प्राणभृतां कुतः शमकथा ब्रह्माण्डलक्षैरपि ॥३२॥

तृष्णा : अज्जउत्त, सअं जेव्व दाव अहं एदस्सिं अत्थे णिच्चं अहिजुत्ता। संपदं अज्जउत्तस्स अण्णाए बह्मण्डकोटिओवि ण मे उदरं पूरइस्संदि ।

[आर्यपुत्र, स्वयमेव तावदहमस्मिन्नर्थे नित्यमभियुक्ता । सांप्रतमार्यपुत्रस्याज्ञया ब्रह्माण्डकोट्योऽपि न मे उदरं पूरयिष्यन्ति ।]

क्रोधः : हिंसे, इत आगम्यताम् ।

(प्रविश्य हिंसा ।)

हिंसा : एसम्हि । आणवेदु अज्जउत्तो ।

[एषास्मि । आज्ञापयत्वार्यपुत्रः ।]

क्रोधः : प्रिये, तावत्त्वया सह धर्मचारिण्या मातृपितृवधोऽपि ममेषत्कर एव । तथाहि--

केयं माता पिशाची क इव हि जनको भ्रातरः केऽत्र कीटा
वध्योऽयं बन्धुवर्गः कुटिलविटसुहृच्चेष्टिता ज्ञातयोऽमी ।

(हस्तौ निष्पीड्य ।)

आगर्भं यावदेषां कुलमिदमखिलं नैव निःशेषयामि
स्फूर्जन्तः क्रोधवह्नेर्न दधति विरतिं तावदङ्गे स्फुलिङ्गाः ॥३३॥

(विलोक्य) एष स्वामी । तदुपसर्पामः । (सर्वे उपसृत्य) जयतु जयतु देवः ।

महामोहः : श्रद्धायास्तनया शान्तिरस्मद्द्वेषिणी । सा भवद्भिरवहितैर्निग्राह्येति ।

सर्वे : यदादिशति देवः ।

(इति निष्क्रान्ताः ।)

Oh ! Goddess Desire if you are pleased and if you can nourish the bodies of those whose minds are bound by the long cord of hopes, to attain fields, villages, forest, cities, town, islands and the earth itself, and who are always eager to acquire more, then where is the question of Tranquillity for the living beings even after acquiring lakhs of worlds. (32).

Desire : My Lord, On my own I am always engaged in this object. Now by your command crores of worlds will not fill my belly.

Anger : Injury, please come here.

(*Injury having entered*)

Injury : Here I am. Command my Lord.

Anger : My beloved, when you are there as my wife, even the murder of father and mother is but a small matter for me. For—

who is this demoness my mother, who is my father, who are my worm-like brothers? Relations are fit to be slain, and also the people of the family who are influenced by their wicked and dandy type friends. (*Clenching his hands*). The gleaming sparks of the fire of anger will not subside in my body until I have massacred the entire family of these people, even to the child in the womb. (33).

(*Looking*) Here is our Lord. Let us go near him. (*All going near*). Victory to my Lord.

Delusion : Peace the daughter of Faith is our enemy. She is to be killed by you with great care.

All : As you order. (Exit.)

महामोहः : श्रद्धायास्तनया इत्युपक्षेपेणोपायान्तरमपि हृदयमारूढम् । तथाहि । शान्तेर्माता श्रद्धा । सा च परतन्त्रा । तत्केनाप्युपायेनोपनिषत्सकाशात्तावच्छ्रद्धापकर्षणं कर्तव्यम् । ततो मातृवियोगदुःखादतिमृदुलतया शान्तिरुपरता भविष्यति । श्रद्धां व्याक्रष्टुं मिथ्यादृष्टिरेव विलासिनी परं प्रगल्भेति तदस्मिन्विषये सैव नियुज्यताम् । (पार्श्वतो विलोक्य) विभ्रमावति, सत्वरमाहूयतां मिथ्यादृष्टिर्विलासिनी ।

विभ्रमावती : जं देवो आणवेदि ।

[यद्देव आज्ञापयति ।]

(निष्क्रम्य मिथ्यादृष्ट्या सह प्रविशति ।)

मिथ्यादृष्टिः : सहि, चिरविट्ठस्स महाराअस्स कहं मुहं पेक्खिस्स । णं खु मं महाराओ उवालहिस्सदि ।

[सखि, चिरदृष्टस्य महाराजस्य कथं मुखं प्रेक्षिष्ये । न खलु मा महाराज उपालम्भिष्यते ।]

विभ्रमावती : सहि, तुअ मुहदंसणेण अप्पाणं जेव्व महाराओ ण वेदस्सदि । कुदो उवालहिस्सदि ?

[सखि, त्वन्मुखदर्शनेनात्मानमेव महाराजो न वेत्स्यति । कुत उपालम्भिष्यते ?]

मिथ्यादृष्टिः : सहि, किं मं अलीअसोहग्गां संभाविअ विलम्बेसि ।

[सखि, किं मामलीकसौभाग्यां संभाव्य विडम्बयसि ।]

विभ्रमावती : सहि, संपदं जेव्व पेक्खिस्से अलिअत्तणं सोहग्गस्स । अण्णच्च णिद्दाघुम्माउले प्पिअसहीए लोअणे पेक्खेमि । ता किं खु प्पिअसहीए लोअणस्स विणिद्ददाए कालणम् ?

[सखि, सांप्रतमेव प्रेक्षिष्येऽलीकत्वं सौभाग्यस्य । अन्यच्च निद्राघूर्णाकुले प्रियसख्या लोचने पश्यामि । तर्हि किं खलु प्रियसख्या लोचनस्य विनिद्रतायाः कारणम् ?]

मिथ्यादृष्टिः : सहि, एकवल्लहावि जा इत्थिआ भवई ता एवि णिद्दा दुल्लहा । किं उण अम्हाणं सअललोअवल्लहाणम् ।

[सखि, एकवल्लभापि या स्त्री भवति तस्या अपि निद्रा दुर्लभा । किं पुनरस्माकं सकललोकवल्लभानाम् ।]

Delusion : The mention of the daughter of Faith brings another means to my mind. That is—Mother of Peace is Faith. She is dependent on others. Therefore we must somehow remove Faith from the Sacred Lore. Then Peace being tender (hearted) will die due to the pangs of separation from her mother. To catch Faith wanton Heresy is really capable. So let her be employed in this job. (*Looking to one side*) Error, call the wanton Heresy immediately.

Error : As your Lord commands.

(*Goes out and enters with Heresy*)

Heresy : Friend, how shall I look at the face of the king who has not been seen by me for a long time. Will the king not abuse me ?

Error : Friend, seeing your face, the king will not recognize himself. How will he abuse you ?

Heresy : Friend ! why do you mock (at me) by falsely fancying me to be fortunate.

Error : Friend, I shall presently see how false your good fortune is. Moreover I see the eyes of my dear friend drowsy. What then is the cause for the sleeplessness of my friend's eye ?

Heresy : Friend, a woman who is the beloved of one man does not get enough sleep, what to say of us who are the beloved of the whole world.

वभ्रमावती : के के उण प्पिअसहीए वल्लहा ?

[के के पुनः प्रियसख्या वल्लभाः ?] ।

मिथ्यादृष्टिः सहि, पढमं महाराओ, अदो उवरि कामो, क्कोहो, लोहो, अहंकालो त्ति । अधवा अलं विसेसेण । एत्थ कुले जो जादो बालो ट्ठविरो जुवाणोवि हिअअणिहिदए मए विणा रद्दिदि-अहाइं ण अहिरमई ।

[सखि प्रथमं महाराजः, अत उपरि कामः, क्रोधः, लोभः, अहंकारश्च। अथवालं विशेषेण । अस्मिन्कुले यो जातो बालः स्थविरो युवापि हृदयनिहितया मया विना रात्रिदिवमान्नाभिरमते ।]

विभ्रमावती : णं एत्थ कामस्स रदी, क्कोहस्स हिंसा, लोहस्स तिण्हा परमप्पिआ सुणीअदि । तासं कधं पिअदमाणं निच्चं रमन्दी इस्सं ण संजाणेसि ।

[नन्वत्र कामस्य रतिः, क्रोधस्य हिंसा, लोभस्य तृष्णा, प्रियतमेति श्रूयते । तासां कथं प्रियतमान्नित्यं रमयन्तीर्ष्यां न संजनयसि ।]

मिथ्यादृष्टिः : सहि, इस्सेत्ति कहं भणीअदि ? ता अवि मए विणा मुहुत्तंवि ण तुस्संति ।

[सखि, ईर्ष्येति कथं भण्यते ? ता अपि मया विना मुहूर्तमपि न तुष्यन्ति ।]

विभ्रमावती : सहि, अदो जेव्व भणामि तुहसरिसी सुहआ इत्थिआ पुहिवीए णत्थि । जाए सोअग्गमहद्धिविहुरिअहिअआ सावतिओ प्पसाअं पडिच्छन्ति । सहि, अण्णच्च भणामि । एवं णिद्दाउलण-अणविसंठुलक्खलन्तचलणनेउलझंकालमहलाए गदीए महाराअं संभावयंदी संकिदहिअअं करिस्सदि पिअसहीति तक्केमि ।

[सखि, अत एव भणामि त्वत्सदृशी सुभगास्यां पृथिव्यां नास्ति । यस्याः सौभाग्यमाहात्म्यविधुरितहृदयाः सपत्न्यः प्रसादं प्रतीच्छन्ति । सखि, अन्यद्भणामि । एवं निद्राकुलनयनविसंस्थुलस्खलच्चरणनूपुरझङ्कारमुखरया गत्या महाराजं संभावयन्ती शङ्कितहृदयं करिष्यति प्रियसखीति तर्कयामि ।]

मिथ्यादृष्टिः : किं एत्थ संकिदव्वं । णं अम्हाणं महाराअणिउत्ताणं जेव्व एसो अविणओ । अविअ सहि, दंसणमत्तप्पसण्णाणं पुरिसाणं पुरो कीरिसं भअम् ?

[किमत्र शङ्कितव्यम् । नचास्माकं महाराजनियुक्तानामेवैषोऽविनयः । अपिच सखि, दर्शनमात्रप्रसन्नानां पुरुषाणां पुरतः कीदृशं भयम् ?]

Error : Who are the husbands of my dear friend ?

Heresy : Friend, first of all the king, then Concupiscence, Anger, Greed and Egoism. Or let me not go into the details. Whoever is born in this family, boy, old or youth does not enjoy day and night without me who reside in their heart.

Error : But I hear that Peace is the beloved of Concupiscence, Injury of Anger and Desire of Greed. How is that you do not create jealousy in them while enjoying (with their husbands) every day ?

Heresy : Why do you talk about jealousy ? They also do not rejoice for a moment without me.

Error : Friend, that is why I say that there is no one as fortunate as you are in this world. Even the co-wives whose hearts are devoid of the good fortune you have, want to please you. Friend, let me tell you something else. I am afraid my dear friend that your approaching the king with your gait, with the jingling sound of your ornaments on the legs caused by your faulty steps due to the drowsiness in your eyes, will create doubt in the king's mind.

Heresy : What is there to doubt ? Is it not that our immodesty is due to the king's own orders ? Moreover friend, what fear is there in front of those people who are pleased at the mere sight (of me).

महामोहः : (विलोक्य ।) अये, संप्राप्तेव प्रिया मिथ्यादृष्टिः । या एषा—

श्रोणीभारभरालसा दरगलन्माल्योपवृत्तिच्छला-
ल्लीलोत्क्षिप्तभुजोपदर्शितकुचोन्मीलन्नखाङ्कावलिः ।
नीलेन्दीवरदामदीर्घतरया दृष्ट्या धयन्ती मनो
दोषान्दोलनलोलकङ्कणरणत्कारोत्तरं सर्पति ॥३४॥

विभ्रमावती : एसो महाराओ । उवसप्पदु पिअसही ।

[एष महाराजः । उपसर्पतु प्रियसखी ।]

मिथ्यादृष्टिः : (उपसृत्य ।) जअदु जअदु महाराओ ।

[जयतु जयतु महाराजः ।]

महामोहः : प्रिये,

दलितकुचनखाङ्कमङ्कपालीं रचय ममाङ्कमुपेत्य पीवरोरु ।
अनुहर हरिणाक्षि शंकराङ्कस्थितहिमशैलसुताविलासलक्ष्मीम् ॥३५॥

(मिथ्यादृष्टिः सस्मितं तथा करोति ।)

महामोहः : (आलिङ्गनसुखमभिनीय ।) अहो, प्रियायाः परिष्वङ्गात्परावृत्तं नवयौवनम् । तथाहि—

यः प्रागासीदभिनववयोविभ्रमावाप्तजन्मा
चित्तोन्माथी विविधविषयोपप्लवानन्दसान्द्रः ।
वृत्तोरन्तस्तिरयति तवाश्लेषजन्मा स कोऽपि
प्रौढः प्रेमा नव इव पुनर्मान्मथो मे विकारः ॥३६॥

मिथ्यादृष्टिः : महाराअ, अहंवि संपदं नवजोवणा संवुत्ता । ण खु भावाणुबन्धो प्पेमा कालेणावि विघडिअदि । आणवेदु महाराओ किंणिमित्तं भट्टिणा सुमरिदम्हि ।

[महाराज अहमपि सांप्रतं नवयौवना संवृत्ता । न खलु भावानुबन्धः प्रेमा कालेनापि विघटते । आज्ञापयतु महाराजः किंनिमित्त भट्टारकेण स्मृतास्मि ।]

महामोहः : प्रिये,

स्मर्यते सा हि वामोरु या भवेद्धृदयाद्बहिः ।
मच्चित्तभित्तौ भवती शालभञ्जीव राजते ॥३७॥

Delusion : (*Looking*) Here is my beloved Heresy. She comes beautifully with the bracelets making a tinkling sound when she moves her arms (while walking), fatigued by the weight of her hips, exhibiting the rows of nail-marks on her breasts when she raises her arms sportfully on the pretext of keeping in place the garland which has slightly slipped (from its place) and attracting the mind with her glances from eyes as long as a garland of blue lotuses. (34).

Error : Here is the king. Let my dear friend go near him.

Heresy : (*Going near*) Hail to the king.

Delusion : Beloved, you with big thighs sit down on my knee and exhibiting the nail marks on your breasts embrace me. Oh ! dear-eyed one, imitate the beauty of the sport of (Pārvatī) the daughter of Himālya seated on the lap of Śaṅkara. (35).

(*Heresy does so with a smile*)

Delusion : (*Experiencing the pleasure of embrace*) youth has come back to me by the embrace of (my) beloved. For—

A strong and new emotion of love born out of your embrace disturbs my (mental) state, arouses emotions which in olden days used to arise from the flurry of the mind, which agitated the mind (emotion) which is full of happiness gained from various objects of pleasure. (36).

Heresy : King, I too have become young now. Time cannot break off the love caused by (similar) disposition of mind. Command Great King, why have I been remembered by (my) Lord ?

Delusion : Dear,

Oh ! the beautiful-thighed one, only the one who is outside the mind be remembered. (But) you shine as the (painted) doll in the wall of my mind.

मिथ्यादृष्टिः : महाप्पसादो ।

[महान्प्रसादः ।]

महामोहः : यथैव प्रकाशितैरङ्गैः सर्वत्र विचरसि तथैव प्रवर्तितव्यम् । अन्यच्च दास्याः पुत्री श्रद्धा विवेकेन सहोपनिषदं संयोजयितुं कुट्टिनीभावं प्रतिपन्ना । अतः—

प्रतिकूलामकुलजां पापां पापानुवर्तिनीम् ।
केशेष्वाकृष्य तां रण्डां पाषण्डेषु निवेशय ॥३८॥

मिथ्यादृष्टिः : एद्दहमेत्तके विसए अलं भट्टिणो अहिणिवेसेण । वअणमत्तकेण जेव्व भट्टिणो दासी सद्धा सव्वं अण्णां करिस्सदि । सा खु मए मित्था धम्मो, मित्था मोक्खो, मित्था वेअमग्गो, मित्था सुहविग्घअराइं, सात्थपलविदाइं, मित्था सग्गफलं ति भणिअन्ती वेअमग्गं जेव्व पलिहलिस्सदि, किं उण उवणिसहम् । अविअ । विसआणन्दविमुक्के मोक्खे दोसाणं दंसअन्तीए उवणिसदोवि विरत्ता कलिस्सदि अचिलं मए सद्धा ।

[एतावन्मात्रेऽपि विषये अलं भर्तुरभिनिवेशेन । वचनमात्रेणैव भर्तुर्दासी श्रद्धा सर्वामाज्ञां करिष्यति । सा खलु मया मिथ्या धर्मो, मिथ्या मोक्षो, मिथ्या वेदमार्गो, मिथ्या सुखविघ्नकराणि शास्त्रप्रलपितानि, मिथ्या स्वर्गफलमिति भण्यमाना वेदमार्गमेव परिहरिष्यति, किं पुनरुपनिषदम् । अपिच । विषयानन्द-विमुक्ते मोक्षे दोषान्दर्शयन्त्योपनिषदाऽपि विरक्ता करिष्यतेऽचिरं मया श्रद्धा] ।

महाराजः : यद्येवं सुष्ठु मे प्रियं सम्पादितं प्रियया । (पुनरालिङ्गय चुम्बति ।)

मिथ्यादृष्टिः : भट्टिणोप्पआसे एव्वं प्पउत्तेण लज्जेमि ।

[भट्टारकस्य प्रकाशे एवं प्रवृत्तेन लज्जामि] ।

महामोहः : तद्भवतु । स्वागारमेव प्रविशामः ।

(इति निष्क्रान्ताः सर्वे ।)

इति श्रीकृष्णमिश्रविरचिते प्रबोधचन्द्रोदयनाम्नि नाटके द्वितीयोऽङ्कः ॥२॥

Heresy : Great is the favour (shown by you). Even then, command my Lord.

Delusion : You should act in such a way that you roam about everywhere with your limbs displayed. And also, Faith, the daughter of a slave acts as a 'go between' in bringing together Discrimination and Sacred Lore.

Therefore,

catch by the hair that whore who is opposed to me, who is not born in a good family and who follows sinners. (38).

Heresy : If this is all that my Lord wants, enough of anxiety. My Lord's slave, Faith will obey all your orders by the mere saying of them. She will give up the even path of Vedas, when I tell her that Righteousness is false, Liberation is false, the path of Vedas is false, false are the sayings of Śāstras which are obstacles in the path of happiness, and false is the fruit in heaven. What to say of (giving up) Sacred Lore ? Moreover, I shall very soon separate Faith from the Sacred Lore, pointing out to her the weak points in Liberation where there is no enjoyment of pleasure.

King : If so, definitely my beloved has done me a favour. (*Again embraces her and kisses her*).

Heresy : When my Lord behaves so in public I feel shy.
Delusion : Let it be. Let us enter our abode.

(*Exeunt Omnes.*)

तृतीयोऽङ्कः ।

(ततः प्रविशति शान्तिः करुणा च ।)

शान्तिः : (सास्रम् ।) मातः मातः, क्वासि । देहि मे प्रियदर्शनम् । ततः—

मुक्तातङ्ककुरङ्गकाननभुवः शैलाः स्खलद्वारयः
पुण्यान्यायतनानि संततपोनिष्ठाश्च वैखानसाः ।
यस्याः प्रीतिरमीषु सात्रभवती चण्डालवेश्मोदरं
प्राप्ता गौः कपिलेव जीवति कथं पाषण्डहस्तं गता ॥१॥

अथवालं जीवितसंभावनया । यतः—

मामनालोक्य न स्नाति न भुङ्क्ते न पिबत्यपः ।
न मया रहिता श्रद्धा मुहूर्तमपि जीवति ॥२॥

तद्विना श्रद्धया मुहूर्तमपि शान्तेर्जीवितं विडम्बनमेव । तत्सखि करुणे, मदर्थं चितामारचय । यावदचिरमेव हुताशनप्रवेशेन तस्याः सहचरी भवामि ।

करुणा : (सास्रम् ।) सहि एव्वं विसमज्जलणज्झालाउलकादुःसहाइं अक्खराइं जप्पन्ती सव्वधा विलुत्तजीविदं मं करेसि । ता प्पसीददु मुहुत्तं जीविदं धारेदु पिअसही । जाव इदो तदो पुण्णेसु अस्समेसु मुणिअणसमाउलेसु भाईरहीतीरेसु णिउणं णिरुवेम्हि कआवि महामोहभीदिआ कहमवि पच्छण्णा णिवसदि ।

[सखि, एवं विषमज्वलनज्वालोल्कादुःसहान्यक्षराणि जल्पन्ती सर्वथा विलुप्तजीवितां मां करोषि । तस्मात्प्रसीदतु मुहूर्तं जीवितं धारयतु प्रियसखी । यावदितस्ततः पुण्येष्वाश्रमेषु मुनिजनसमाकुलेषु भागीरथीतीरेषु निपुणं निरूपयामि कदाचिन्महामोहभीत्या कथमपि प्रच्छन्ना निवसति ।]

शान्तिः : सखि, किमन्विष्यते । अन्वेषितैव—

नीवाराङ्कितसैकतानि सरितां कूलानि वैखानसै-
राक्रान्तानि समिच्चषालचमसव्याप्ता गृहा यज्वनाम् ।
प्रत्येकं च निरूपिताः प्रतिपदं चत्वार एवाश्रमाः
श्रद्धायाः क्वचिदप्यहो खलु मया वार्तापि नाकर्णिता ॥३॥

Act III

(*Enter Peace and Pity*)

Peace : (*With tears*) Mother, mother, where are you ? Give me your beloved view. Then.

Her Ladyship whose delight was in forests where deer were free from fear, in mountains where waters used to flow, in holy places and in ascetics always engaged in austerities, how does she (now) like a brown cow entering the house of a butcher, having been delivered into the hands of a Nihilist, survive? (1).

Or there is no use of hoping that she will be alive.

Faith does not bathe, eat or drink water without seeing me. Without me she does not even survive for a moment. (2).

Therefore without faith, the life of Peace for a moment is a ridicule. Therefore Friend Pity, make the fire ready for me, so that without any delay I shall accompany her by entering the fire.

Pity : (*with tears*) Friend, you are taking away my life completely by uttering such unbearable words which are like the flames of a fierce fire. Therefore, be pleased and keep yourself alive for a moment. In the meantime I shall cleverly investigate whether out of fear from Delusion, she somehow is hiding in sacred hermitages that are here and there, or on the banks of Bhāgīrathī crowded with sages.

Peace : Friend, what do you search for ? She has been already sought for. I have looked for her everywhere, on the banks of rivers inhabited by the ascetics, where the sands are sprinkled with grains. I have searched every house of the sacrificers where the sacrificial fuel, the wooden ring on the top of the sacrificial post and sacrificial utensils are kept and also among the four classes of men, but nowhere have I even heard of Faith. (3).

करुणा : सहि, एव्वं भणामि : जइ सा जेव्व सत्तई सद्धा तदो ताए ण एरिसीं दुग्गदिं संभावेमि । ण खु तारिसीओ पुण्णमयी सदीओ एतारिसीं असंभावणिज्जं विपत्तिं अणुहवन्दि ।

[सखि, एवं भणामि : यदि सैव सात्त्विकी श्रद्धा तदा तस्या नेदृशीं दुर्गतिं संभावयामि । न खलु तादृश्यः पुण्यमय्यः सत्य एनादृशीमसंभावनीयां विपत्तिमनुभवन्ति ।]

शान्तिः : सखि, किंनु प्रतिकूले विधातरि न संभाव्यते ? तथाहि—

श्रीदेवी जनकात्मजा दशमुखस्यासीद्गृहे रक्षसो
नीता चैव रसातलं भगवती देवत्रयी दानवैः ।
गन्धर्वस्य मदालसां च तनयां पातालकेतुश्छलाद्-
दैत्येन्द्रोऽपजहार हन्त विषमा वामा विधेर्वृत्तयः ॥४॥

एवं विधिविलसितमेतदिति संप्रधार्यम् । तद्भवतु । पाखण्डालयेष्वेव तावदनुसरावः ।

करुणा : सहि, एव भोदु । (इति परिक्रामतः ।)

[सखि, एवं भवतु ।]

(अग्रतो विलोक्य ।)

करुणा : (सत्रासम् ।) सहि, रक्खसो रक्खसो ।

[सखि, राक्षसो राक्षसः ।]

शान्तिः : कोऽसौ राक्षसः ?

करुणा : सहि, पेक्ख पेक्ख । जो एसो गलन्तमलपिच्छिलबीहत्सदुप्पेक्खदेहच्छवी उल्लुंचिअचिउरनुक्कवसणदुद्दंसणो सिहिसिहण्डपिच्छिआहत्थो इदो जेव्व अहिवट्टदि ।

[सखि, पश्य पश्य । य एष गलन्मलपिच्छिलबीभत्सदुःप्रेक्ष्यदेहच्छविः उल्लुञ्चितचिकुरमुक्तवसनदुर्दर्शनः शिखिशिखण्डपिच्छिकाहस्त इत एवाभिवर्तते ।]

शान्तिः : सखि, नायं राक्षसः । निर्वीर्यः खल्वयम् ।

करुणा : ता को एसो भविस्सदि ?

[तर्हि क एष भविष्यति ?]

Pity : Friend, I say this. If she is the same Faith of the nature of purity I cannot even imagine such a plight for her. Ladies like her cannot undergo a tragic calamity like this.

Peace : Friend, when fate is adverse what is not possible ?

For,

The daughter of Janaka (Sītā), the goddess of prosperity, lived in the house of the ten-headed Rākṣasa (*Rāvaṇa*). The Goddess Trayī (three Vedas) was taken to hell by the demons. Madālasā, the daughter of a Gandharva, was taken away by a stratagem by Pātālaketu, the lord of the demons. Alas ! the workings of Fate are difficult and perverse. (4).

Let it be so. Let us go to the abodes of Nihilists considering that all this is the play of Fate.

Pity : Friend, be it so. (*They both walk*)

(*Looking ahead*)

Pity : (*Fearfully*) Friend, a demon ! a demon !

Peace : Who is this demon ?

Pity : Friend, see ! see ! His body slimy due to the trickling dirt and therefore disgustful to look at, and with the hair of his head plucked out and (wearing) no clothes, he looks ugly. He is coming this side with a peacock feather in his hands.

Peace : Friend, this is not a demon. He is someone without manliness.

Pity : Then, who can he be ?

शान्तिः : सखि, पिशाच इति शङ्के ।

करुणा : सहि, पप्फुरन्तमहामऊहमालोब्भासिअभुअणन्तरे जलदि प्पचण्डमात्तण्डमण्डले कहं पिसाआणं अवआसो ?

[सखि, प्रस्फुरन्महामयूखमालोद्भासितभुवनान्तरे ज्वलति प्रचण्डमार्तण्डमण्डले कथं पिशाचानामवकाशः ?]

शान्तिः : तर्हि अनन्तरमेव नरकविवरादुत्तीर्णः कोऽपि नारकी भविष्यति । (विलोक्य विचिन्त्य च) आः, ज्ञातम् । महामोहप्रवर्तितोऽयं दिगम्बरसिद्धान्तः । तत्सर्वथा दूरे परिहरणीयमस्य दर्शनम् । (इति पराङ्मुखीभवति ।)

करुणा : सहि, मुहुत्तकं चिट्ठ । जाव एत्थ सद्धां अण्णेसामि ।

[सखि, मुहूर्तकं तिष्ठ । यावदत्र श्रद्धामन्वेषयामि ।]

(उभे तथा स्थिते ।)

(ततः प्रविशति यथानिर्दिष्टो दिगम्बरसिद्धान्तः ।)

दिगम्बरः : ॐ णमो अलिहन्ताणम् । णवदुवालग्घलमज्झे अप्पा दीवेव्व जलदि । एसो जिणवलभासिदो पलमत्थो जं मोक्ससुखदो (इति परिक्रामति) । (आकाशे) अलेले सावका, सुणुद्धं—

[ॐनमोऽर्हद्भ्यः । नवद्वारपुरीमध्ये आत्मा दीप इव ज्वलति । एष जिनवरभाषितः परमार्थोऽयं मोक्षसुखदः । अरेरे श्रावकाः, शृणुध्वम्—]

मलमअपुग्गलपिण्डे सअलजलेहिं वि केलिसी सुद्धी ।
अप्पा विमलसहाओ लिसिपलिचलणेहिं जाणव्वो ॥५॥

किं भणत्थ-केलिसं लिसिपरिचलणं ति । ता सुणुध—

दूले चलणपणामो, किदसक्कालं च भोअणं मिट्ठम् ।
इस्सामलं ण कज्जं, लिसिणं दालाणं लमन्ताणम् ॥६॥

[मलमयपुद्गलपिण्डे सकलजलैरपि कीदृशी शुद्धिः ।
आत्मा विमलस्वभावः ऋषिपरिचरणैर्ज्ञातव्यः ॥

किं भणथ-कीदृशमृषिपरिचरणमिति । तच्छृणुध्वम् ।

दूरे चरणप्रणामः कृतसत्कारं च भोजनं मिष्टम् ।
ईर्ष्यामलं न कार्यं ऋषीणां दारान्रममाणानाम् ॥

(नेपथ्याभिमुखमवलोक्य) सद्धे, इदो दाव । (उभे सभयमालोकयतः ।)

श्रद्धे इतस्तावत् ।]

Peace : Friend, I presume that he may be an evil spirit.

Pity : Friend, where is the possibility of evil spirits when the bright Sun is shining and is illumining the world with the chain of his luminous rays ?

Peace : Then he must be some one who has recently come up from the pit of the hell. (*Looking at him and thinking*). Ah ! I know. He is a Digambara (Jain) sent by the Grand Delusion. By all means the sight of him should be avoided from a distance. (*Thus turns away*).

Pity : Friend, wait for a moment. I shall look for faith here.

(*Both wait*)

(*Then enters the Jaina as described*)

Jaina : Prostrations to Arhata. The self shines like a lamp in the middle of the town of nine gates (the body). This is the truth uttered by the great Jina. This is the giver of happiness in the form of liberation. (*Walks*) (*In the air*). Listen, Oh Disciples !

With all the waters how can the lump of impure matter (body) be purified ? The self which is of pure nature is to be known through the service of sages. (5).

What do you say—What kind of service of the sages ? Listen.

From a distance one should prostrate oneself at their feet and should welcome them and give them sweet food. One should not pollute with jealousy the sages when they enjoy the wives. (6).

(*Looking towards the back curtain*) Faith, come over here. (*Both look with fear*)

(ततः प्रविशति तदनुरूपवेषा श्रद्धा ।)

श्रद्धा : किं आणवेदि लाउलम् ।

[किमाज्ञापयति राजकुलम् ।]

दि० : सावकाणां कुलं मुहुत्तमेकं वि मा पलिहलिस्सदि भवदी ।

[श्रावकाणां कुटुम्बं मुहूर्तमात्रमपि मा परिहरिष्यति भवती ।]

श्रद्धा : जं आणवेदि लाउलम् ।

[यदाज्ञापयति राजकुलम् ।]

(इति निष्क्रान्ता।)

करुणा : समस्ससदु पिअसही । णं खु णाममेत्तकेण पियसहीए भेदव्वं । जदो सुदं मए हिंसासआसादो जं अत्थि पासण्डाणं वि तमसः सुदा सद्धेति । तेण एसा तामसी सद्धा भविस्सदि ।

[समाश्वसितु प्रियसखी । न खलु नाममात्रेण प्रियसख्या भेतव्यम् । यतः श्रुतं मया हिंसासकाशाद्यदस्ति पाषण्डानामपि तमसः सुता श्रद्धेति । तेनैषा तामसी श्रद्धा भविष्यति ।]

शान्तिः : (समाश्वस्य) सखि, एवमेवैतत् । तथाहि—

दुराचारा सदाचारां दुर्दर्शा प्रियदर्शनाम् ।
अम्बामनुसरत्येषा दुराशा न कथंचन ॥७॥

तद्भवतु तावत् । सौगतालयेष्वप्यसावन्विष्यताम् ।

(शान्तिकरुणे परिक्रामतः)

(ततः प्रविशति भिक्षुरूपः पुस्तकहस्तो बुद्धागमः ।)

भिक्षुः : (विचिन्त्य) भो भो उपासकाः

सर्वे क्षणक्षयिण एव निरात्मकाश्च
यत्रार्पिता बहिरिव प्रतिभान्ति भावाः ।
सैवाधुना विगलिताखिलवासनत्वा-
द्धीसन्ततिः स्फुरति निर्विषयोपरागा ॥८॥

(परिक्रम्य पुनः सश्लाघम् ।) अहो, साधुरयं सौगतधर्मो यत्र सौख्यं मोक्षश्च ।

(*Then enter Faith in a befitting dress*)

Faith : What is the command of the one belonging to the family of (our) king ?

Jaina : You should not leave the family of disciples even for a moment.

Faith : As the Royal self commands. (*Exit*)

Pity : Be comforted my dear friend. You should not fear by merely hearing the name of my friend (Faith). For, I have heard from Injury that the Nihilists too have a Faith who is the daughter of the quality, Darkness. Therefore this must be the Faith belonging to Darkness.

Peace : (*Comforting herself*) Friend, it is so. For,

This one with wicked thoughts and bad behaviour and ugly looks can in no way imitate (my) mother who is of good behaviour and of pleasant looks. (7).

Be it so. Let us look for her in the abodes of Buddhists.

(*Peace and Pity walk forward*)

(*Enters Buddhist mendicant with a book in his hand*)

Buddhist : (*Thinking over*) Oh ye worshippers !

All elements of existence are momentary and devoid of self. They appear as if they were outside (had objective existence, but are only) super-imposed on the flux of consciousness, which shines without any object-tinge, when all the 'perfumes' (vāsanās) are dropped. (8).

(*Walking around and continuing proudly*) How good is the religion of the Buddha where there is (Sensual) enjoyment as well as liberation.

तथाहि—

आवासो लयनं मनोहरमभिप्रायानुरूपा वणिङ्-
नार्यो वाञ्छितकालमिष्टमशनं शय्या मृदुप्रस्तराः ।
श्रद्धापूर्वमुपासिता युवतिभिः क्लृप्ताङ्गदानोत्सव-
क्रीडानन्दभरैर्व्रजन्ति विलसज्ज्योत्स्नोज्ज्वला रात्रयः ॥६॥

करुणा सहि, को एसो तरुणतालतलुप्पलम्बो लम्बन्तकसाअपिसङ्ग-चिउरो मुण्डिदसचूडमुण्डपिण्डो इदो जेव्व आअच्छदि ?

[सखि, क एष तरुणतालतरुप्रलम्बो लम्बमानकषायपिशङ्गचिकुरो मुण्डित-सचूडमुण्डपिण्ड इत एवागच्छति ?]

शान्तिः : सखि, बुद्धागम एषः ।

भिक्षुः : (आकाशे) भो भो उपासकाः भिक्षवश्च, श्रूयतां भगवतः सुगतस्य वाक्यामृतम् । (पुस्तकं वाचयति) पश्याम्यहं दिव्येन चक्षुषा लोकानां सुगतिं दुर्गतिं च । क्षणिकाः सर्वे संस्काराः । नास्त्यात्मा स्थायी । तस्माद्भिक्षुषु दारानाक्रमत्सु नेर्षितव्यम् । चित्तमलं हि तद्यदीर्ष्यानाम । (नेपथ्याभिमुखमवलोक्य ।) श्रद्धे, इतस्तावत् ।

(प्रविश्य श्रद्धा ।)

श्रद्धा : आणवेदु लाउलम् ।

[आज्ञापयतु राजकुलम् ।]

भिक्षुः : उपासकान्भिक्षूंश्च चिरमालिङ्ग्य स्थीयताम् ।

श्रद्धा : जं आणवेदि लाउलम् । (इति निष्क्रान्ता ।)

[यदाज्ञापयति राजकुलम् ।]

शान्तिः : सखि, इयमपि तामसी श्रद्धा ।

करुणाः : एवं णेदम् ।

[एवमेतत् ।]

क्षपणकः : (भिक्षुमालोक्योच्चैःशब्दम् ।) अलेले भिक्खुअ, इदो दाव । किंपि पुच्छिस्सम् ।

[अरेरे भिक्षुक, इतस्तावत् । किमपि पृच्छामि]

भिक्षुः : (सक्रोधम् ।) आः पाप पिशाचाकृते, किमेवं प्रलपसि ?

For—

(Living in) beautiful houses, (possessing) prostitutes who are to their liking, (having) food of their taste at any time they desire, (sleeping on) soft beds, they who meditate with faith (on Buddha) spend the nights bright with moon light, with happiness derived from sporting with young women offering their bodies. (9).

Pity : Friend, who is this one as tall as a young palm tree, with long fragrant tawny hair, his head shaven in the centre, coming this side.

Peace : This is a Buddhist.

Mendicant : (*In the air*) Oh ! worshippers and mendicants, listen to Lord Sugata's sayings of nectar. (*Reads from the book*) "I see with a divine eye how people rise and fall (in transmigration). All conformations are momentary. There is no lasting self. Therefore when mendicants take (your) wives you should not feel jealous. Jealousy is only an impurity of the mind. (*Looking towards the back curtain*) Faith, please come over here.

(*Entering*)

Faith : May your Royal self command.

Mendicant : You should remain always embracing the worshippers and mendicants.

Faith : As the Royal self commands.

(*Exit*)

Peace : Friend, this is also Faith belonging to Darkness.

Pity : It is so.

Jaina : (*Looking at the Buddhist, loudly*) Oh Mendicant, come this side. I shall ask you something.

Mendicant : (*Angrily*) Oh sinner, you who look like an evil spirit, what do you prattle ?

क्षपणक: : अले, मुञ्च कोहम् । साच्छगदं पुच्छामि ।
[अरे, मुञ्च क्रोधम् । शास्त्रगतं पृच्छामि ।]

भिक्षु: : अरे क्षपणक, शास्त्रकथामपि वेत्सि । भवतु । प्रतीक्षामस्तावत् (उपसृत्य) किं पृच्छसि ?

क्षपणक: : भण दाव क्खणविणासिणा तुए कस्स किदे एदं व्वदं धाली-अदि ?
[भण तावत्क्षणविनाशिना त्वया कस्य कृते इदं व्रतं धार्यते ?]

भिक्षु: : अरे श्रूयताम् । अस्मत्संततिपतित: कश्चिद्विज्ञानलक्षण: समुच्छिन्नवासनो मोक्ष्यते ।

क्षपणक: : अले मुलुक्ख, कस्सिवि मण्णन्तले कोवि मुक्को भविस्सदि । तदो दे संपदं णट्ठस्स कीरिसं उवआलं कलिस्सदि ? अण्णं च पुच्छामि । केण दे ईरिसो धम्मो उवदिट्ठो ?

[अरे मूर्ख, कस्मिन्नपि मन्वन्तरे कोऽपि मुक्तो भविष्यति । ततस्ते सांप्रतं नष्टस्य कीदृशमुपकारं करिष्यति ? अन्यच्च पृच्छामि । केन ते ईदृशो धर्म उपदिष्ट: ?]

भिक्षु: : नूनं सर्वज्ञेन भगवता बुद्धेनोक्तोऽयमेव धर्म: ।

क्षपणक: : अले, सव्वण्णो बुद्धोत्थि त्ति कधं तुए णादम् ?
[अरे, सर्वज्ञो बुद्ध इति कथं त्वया ज्ञातम् ?]

भिक्षु: : ननु रे यदागमैरेव प्रसिद्धो बुद्ध: सर्वज्ञ इति ।

क्षपणक: : अले उज्झिअबुद्धअ, जयि तस्स भासिदेण सव्वण्णत्तं पडिवज्जेसि ता अहं वि सव्वं जाणामि । तुमंपि पिदुपिदामहेहिं सद्धं सत्तपुलिसं अम्हाणं दासो त्ति ।

[अरे उज्झितबुद्धक, यदि तस्य भाषितेन सर्वज्ञत्वं प्रतिपन्नोऽसि तदहमपि सर्वं जानामि । त्वमपि पितृपितामहै: सह सप्तपुरुषमस्माकं दास इति ।]

भिक्षु: : (सक्रोधम्) आ: पाप, पिशाच मलपङ्कधर, कस्तवाहं दास: ?

Jaina : Do not be angry. I shall ask you something dealing with the scriptures.

Mendicant: Oh Jaina, do you know anything of scriptures? Well, let us see. (*Going near*) What is your question?

Jaina : Please, say, for whose sake do you, who perish in a moment, keep this observance?

Mendicant: Oh! listen, Somebody characterised by pure consciousness who has fallen into the flux of (Consciousness which is) my person, will attain liberation, when he is freed from all Vāsanās.

Jaina : Oh fool! at some period somebody will be liberated. Then how does it benefit you who are lost now? I shall ask another question. Who advised you this kind of philosophy?

Mendicant: Certainly this philosophy is given by the all-knowing Lord Buddha himself.

Jaina : How do you know that Buddha is all knowing?

Mendicant: It is well known through his teaching that Buddha is all-knowing.

Jaina : You who are devoid of intelligence, if you think he is all-knowing from his own sayings, then I also (say that I) know everything. You with your father and forefathers are my slaves for seven generations.

Mendicant: (*Angrily*) Oh sinner! evil spirit, dirty one, who am I to be your slave?

क्षपणकः : अले विहालदासीभुअङ्ग दुट्ठपलिव्वज्जिअ, दिट्ठंदो एसो मए दंसिदो । ता पिअं दे विस्सद्धं भणामि । बुद्धाणुसासणं पलिहलिअ अलिहन्ताणुसासणं जेव्व अनुसालिअ दिअवलमदं जेव्व धालेदु भवम् ।

[अरे विहारदासीभुजङ्ग दुष्टपरिव्राजक, दृष्टान्त एष मया दर्शितः । तत् प्रियं ते विस्रब्धं भणामि । बुद्धानुशासनं परिहृत्यार्हतानुशासनमेवानुसृत्य दिगम्बरमतमेव धारयतु भवान् ।]

भिक्षुः : आः पाप, स्वयं नष्टः परानपि नाशयितुमिच्छसि ।

स्वाराज्यं प्राज्यमुत्सृज्य लोके निन्द्यामनिन्दितः ।
अभिवाञ्छति को नाम भवानिव पिशाचताम् ॥१०॥

अपिच, आर्हतमपि धर्मवेदनं कः श्रद्दधाति ?

क्षपणकः : गहणक्खत्तचालचन्दसूल्लोपलाअलुप्पलाहपलमत्थाण्णाणसंधाणदंसणेण णिलुविदं सव्वणंतणं भअवदो अलिहन्तस्स ।

[ग्रहनक्षत्रचारचन्द्रसूर्योपरागलुप्तलाभपरमार्थज्ञानसंधानदर्शनेन निरूपितं सर्वज्ञत्वं भगवतोऽर्हतः ।]

भिक्षुः : अरे, अनादिप्रवृत्तज्योतिर्वातीन्द्रियज्ञानेन प्रतारितेन भगवतेदमतिकष्टं व्रतमाश्रितम् । तथाहि—

ज्ञातुं वपुःपरिमितः क्षमते त्रिलोकीं
जीवः कथं कथय संगतिमन्तरेण ।
शक्नोति कुम्भनिहितः सुशिखोऽपि दीपो
भावान्प्रकाशयितुमप्युदरे गृहस्य ॥११॥

तस्माल्लोकद्वयविरुद्धादार्हतमताद्वरं सुगतमतमेव साक्षात्सुखावहमतिरमणीयं पश्यामः ।

शान्तिः : सखि, अन्यतो गच्छावः ।

करुणा : एवं भोदु । (इति परिक्रामतः ।)

[एवं भवतु ।]

शान्तिः : (पुरो विलोक्य) एष पुरस्तात्सोमसिद्धान्तः । भवतु । अत्रापि तावदनुसरावः ।

(ततः प्रविशति कापालिकरूपधारी सोमसिद्धान्तः ।)

सोमसिद्धान्तः : (परिक्रम्य) ।

Jaina : You paramour of prostitutes, wicked recluse, I gave only an example. I shall say something favourable to you in confidence. Give up Buddha's doctrine and accept the doctrine of Arhata and embrace Jainism.

Mendicant: Oh sinner, having lost yourself you want to destroy others too.

In this world which respectable person will give up his great freedom and will desire to be come an evil spirit like you. (10).

Moreover, who has faith in the teachings of the philosophy of Arhata ?

Jaina : Lord Arhata's all knowingness is established by seeing his correct knowledge of the course of the planets, stars and the eclipse of the Moon and Sun, and also how to get back what is lost.

Mendicant: You who have been cheated by the super sensuous knowledge of astrology which existed from time immemorial have accepted this difficult observance. For,

Tell me how the soul, limited by the body, without association with anything else can know the three worlds. Can a lamp having bright flame, but placed in a jar. illuminate the things inside a house. ? (11).

Therefore, we see that the doctrine of Buddha which is attractive and which gives direct happiness is better than the doctrine of Arhata which contradicts both the worlds.

Peace : Let us go somewhere else.

Pity : Let it be so. (*They Walk forward*).

Peace : (*Looking in front*) Here in front (of us) is the follower of Somasiddhānta. Well, let us go there also.

(*Enter Somasiddhānta wearing the dress of a Kāpālika*).

Kāpālika: (*Walking around*)

नरास्थिमालाकृतचारुभूषणः
श्मशानवासी नृकपालभोजनः ।
पश्यामि योगाञ्जनशुद्धचक्षुषा
जगन्मिथो भिन्नमभिन्नमीश्वरात् ॥१२॥

क्षपणकः : को एसो कावालिअव्वदं पुलिसो धालेदि ? ता णं वि पुच्छिस्सम् । (उपसृत्य) अलेले कावालिअ, णलात्थिमुण्डमालाधारिअ, कीलिसो तुम्ह धम्मो, कीलिसो तुम्ह मोक्खो ?

[क एष कापालिकं व्रतं पुरुषो धारयति ? तदेनमपि पृच्छामि । अरेरे कापालिक, नरास्थिमण्डमालाधारक, कीदृशस्तव धर्मः कीदृशस्तव मोक्षः ?]

कापालिकः : अरे क्षपणक, धर्मं तावदस्माकमवधारय ।

मस्तिष्कान्त्रवसाभिपूरितमहामांसाहुतीर्जुह्वतां
वह्नौ ब्रह्मकपालकल्पितसुरापानेन नः पारणा ।
सद्यःकृत्तकठोरकण्ठविगलत्कीलालधारोज्ज्वलै-
रर्च्यो नः पुरुषोपहारबलिभिर्देवो महाभैरवः ॥१३॥

भिक्षुः : (कर्णौ पिधाय) बुद्ध बुद्ध, अहो दारुणा धर्मचर्या !

क्षपणकः : अलिहन्त अलिहन्त, अहो घोलपावकालिणा केणावि विप्पलद्धो वलाओ ।

[अर्हन् अर्हन्, अहो घोरपापकारिणा केनापि विप्रलब्धो वराक. ।]

कापालिकः : (सक्रोधम्) आः पाप पाखण्डापसद, मुण्डितमुण्ड, चूडालकेश, केशलुञ्चक, अरे, विप्रलम्भकः किल चतुर्दशभुवनोत्पत्तिस्थिति-प्रलयप्रवर्तको वेदान्तप्रसिद्धसिद्धान्तविभवो भगवान्भवानीपतिः ? दर्शयामस्तर्हि धर्मस्यास्य महिमानम् ।

हरिहरसुरज्येष्ठश्रेष्ठान्सुरानहमाहरे
वियति वहतां नक्षत्राणां रुणध्मि गतीरपि ।
सनगनगरीमम्भः पूर्णां विधाय महीमिमां
कलय सकलं भूयस्तोयं क्षणेन पिबामि तत् ॥१४॥

I, who am adorned with a garland of human bones, who live in the cremation ground and who eat out of a human skull, with an eye purified by the ointment of Yoga, see the world having differences within itself but being non-different from God. (12).

Jaina : Who is this man observing the Kāpālika way of life ? I shall ask him also. Oh Kāpālika, wearing the garland of human bones and skulls! what kind of religion is yours and what is the nature of your liberation ?

Kāpālika: Oh Jaina monk, you better know our religion. We who offer oblations into the fire in the form of human flesh, steeped, brains, entrails and marrow break our fast with alcohol kept in the skull of a Brāhmaṇa. God Mahābhairava has to be worshipped with human offerings, lustrous with streams of blood flowing from the stiff threat which is freshly cut. (13).

Mendicant; (*Shutting his ears*) Buddha, Buddha. How fierce is this observance of religion.

Jaina : Arhat, Arhat, this poor man is deceived by someone who does frightful sin.

Kāpālika: (*Angrily*) Oh sinner, the lowest of Nihilists, the shaven and the unshaven one, the one with a lock hair on the head, the plucker of hair, (you say) that Lord Bhavānīpati (Śiva) whose greatness is the doctrine established in the Vedānta, who is the creator, sustainer and destroyer of the fourteen worlds, is a deceiver ? We shall show you the greatness of this religion.

I can bring here Hari and Hara (Viṣṇu and Śiva) who are the senior and superior gods (and also) the (other) gods. I can obstruct the course of the stars moving in the sky. I can flood with water this earth with its mountains and towns; and think of this, (I can) drink all that water again in a moment. (14).

क्षपणकः : अले कावालिअ, अदो जेव्व भणामि केणावि इन्दजालिणा माआं दंसीअ विप्पलद्धोऽसि त्ति ।

[अरे कापालिक, अत एव भणामि केनापीन्द्रजालिना मायां दर्शयित्वा विप्रलब्धोऽसीति ।]

कापालिकः : आः पाप, पुनरपि परमेश्वरमैन्द्रजालिकमित्याक्षिपसि । तन्न मर्षणीयमस्य दौरात्म्यम् । (खड्गमाकृष्य) तदलमस्य ।

एतत्करालकरवालनिकृत्तकण्ठ-
नालोच्चलद्बहुलफेनिलबुद्बुदौघैः ।
सार्धं डमड्डमरुडांकृतिहूतभूत-
वर्गेण भर्गगृहिणीं रुधिरैर्धिनोमि ।।१५।।

(इति खड्गमुद्यच्छति ।)

क्षपणकः : (सभयम्) महाभाअ, अहिंसापलमो धम्मो त्थि । (भिक्षोरङ्कं प्रविशति)

[महाभाग, अहिंसा परमो धर्मोऽस्ति ।]

भिक्षुः : (कापालिकं वारयन्) भो भो महाभाग, कौतुकप्रयुक्तवाक्कलहेनायुक्तमेतस्मिंस्तपस्विनि प्रहर्तुम् ।

कापालिकः : (खड्गं प्रतिसंहरति ।)

क्षपणकः : (समाश्वस्य ।) महाभाओ जदि संहलिदघोललोसावेसो संवुत्तो तदो अहं किंवि पुच्छिदुमिच्छेमि ।

[महाभागो यदि संहृतघोररोषावेगः संवृत्तस्ततोऽहं किमपि प्रष्टुमिच्छामि ।]

कापालिकः : पृच्छ ।

क्षपणकः : सुदो तुम्हाणं पलमो धम्मो । अध केलिसो सोक्खमोक्खो ?

[श्रुतो युष्माकं परमो धर्मः । अथ कीदृशः सौख्यमोक्षः ?]

कापालिकः : शृणु--

दृष्टं क्वापि सुखं विना न विषयैरानन्दबोधोज्झिता
जीवस्य स्थितिरेव मुक्तिरुपलावस्था कथं प्रार्थ्यते ।
पार्वत्याः प्रतिरूपया दयितया सानन्दमालिङ्गितो
मुक्तः क्रीडति चन्द्रचूडवपुरित्यूचे मृडानीपतिः ।।१६।।

Jaina : Oh Kāpālika! that is why I say that some magician has deceived you by showing his magic.

Kāpālika : Oh Sinner! again you are insulting the supreme lord by calling him a magician. His wickedness is unpardonable. (*Taking out his sword*). Enough of this. I shall please the wife of Bharga (Śiva) with the blood springing out in thick foamy streams of bubbles from the threat which is cut with this frightful sword, along with the hosts of ghosts called by the booming sound of the Ḍamaru. (15). (*Raises his sword*).

Jaina : (*Fearfully*) Good sir, non-injury is the highest virtue.

Mendicant: (*Keeping off Kāpālika*) Oh good sir ! it is not proper to strike this poor man who out of curiosity started a quarrel of words.

Kāpālika: (*Withdraws the sword*)

Jaina : (*Cheering up*) Oh great sir! if your violent anger is subsided I shall ask you a question.

Kāpālika: Ask.

Jaina : I have heard about your excellent religion. But what is the nature of happiness and liberation (according to you) ?

Kāpālika: Listen.

Nowhere is happiness seen without objects of pleasure. If liberation is a stage of the self without the experience of pleasure, how can a state equal to that of a stone be desired? Mṛḍānīpati (Śiva) has said that the liberated one having a body (equal to that of Śiva whose body is decorated) with the crest-ornament of the moon, enjoys the pleasant embrace of his beloved who is an image of Pārvatī. (16),

भिक्षुः : महाभाग, अश्रद्धेयमेतदवीतरागस्य मुक्तिरिति ।

क्षपणकः : अले कावालिअ, जइ ण कुप्पसि तवो भणामि । सलीली सलागी मुक्केति विलुद्धम् ।

[अरे कापालिक, यदि न कुप्यसि तर्हि भणामि । शरीरी सरागी मुक्त इति विरुद्धम् ।]

कापालिकः : (स्वगतम्) अये अश्रद्धाक्षिप्तमनयोरन्तःकरणम् । भवत्वेवं तावत् । (प्रकाशम्) श्रद्धे, इतस्तावत् ।

(ततः प्रविशति कापालिनीरूपधारिणी श्रद्धा ।)

करुणा : सहि, पेक्ख पेक्ख रजसस्सुदा सद्धा । एसा—

विप्पट्टणीलुप्पललोललोअणा
नरत्थिमालाकिदचालुभूसणा ।
णिअम्बपीणत्थणभालमन्थला
विहादि पुण्णेन्दुमुही विलासिणी ॥१७॥

[सखि, पश्य पश्य रजसः सुता श्रद्धा । या एषा—
विस्पष्टनीलोत्पललोललोचना
नरास्थिमालाकृतचारुभूषणा ।
नितम्बपीनस्तनभारमन्थरा
विभाति पूर्णेन्दुमुखी विलासिनी ॥१७॥

श्रद्धा : (परिक्रम्य) एसम्हि । आणवेदु सामी ।

[एषास्मि । आज्ञापयतु स्वामी ।]

कापालिकः : प्रिये, एनं दुरभिमानिनं भिक्षुं तावद्गृहाण । (श्रद्धा भिक्षुमालिङ्गति ।)

भिक्षुः : (सानन्दं परिष्वज्य रोमाञ्चमभिनीय जनान्तिकम्) अहो, सुखस्पर्शा कापालिनी ! तथाहि—

रण्डाः पीनपयोधराः कति मया चण्डानुरागाद्भुज-
द्वन्द्वापीडनपीवरस्तनभरैर्नो गाढमालिङ्गिताः ।
बुद्धेभ्यः शतशः शपे यदि पुनः कुत्रापि कापालिनी-
पीनोत्तुङ्गकुचावगूहनभवः प्राप्तः प्रमोदोदयः ॥१८॥

Mendicant: Good Sir, it is unbelievable that one who has not subdued his passion can attain liberation.

Jaina : Oh Kāpālika ! if you do not get angry I shall speak. It is contradictory that a corporeal being who has not subdued his passion be liberated.

Kāpālika: (*Aside*) The mind of these people are polluted by having no faith. Let it be so. (*Aloud*) Faith, please come over here.

(*Enter Faith dressed up as Kāpālin*).

Pity : Friend, See this is Faith, the daughter of Passion.

This coquettish woman appears with her sleepy eyes tremulous like the blue lotus, beautifully adorned with the garland of human bones, bent with the weight of her buttock and large breasts, her face resembling the full moon. (17).

Faith : (*Walking forward*) Here I am, command me.

Kāpālika : My dear, catch hold of this vain mendicant.

(*Faith embraces the Mendicant*)

Mendicant: (*Embracing her with pleasure and showing horripilation, Aside*) Oh! how delightful is the touch of this Kāpālinī ! For—

How often have I ardently embraced widows with swelling breasts, pressing their big breasts with my arms with great passion ! but by the Buddhas I swear a hundred times that nowhere have I attained such pleasure as derived from the embrace of big swelling bosom of this Kāpālinī. (18).

अहो पुण्यं कापालिकचरितमहो श्लाघ्यः सोमसिद्धान्तः। आश्चर्योऽयं धर्मः। भो महाभाग, सर्वथा बुद्धानुशासनमस्माभिरुत्सृष्टम्। प्रविष्टाः स्मः पारमेश्वरं सिद्धान्तम्। तदाचार्यस्त्वं शिष्योऽहम्। प्रवेशय मां पारमेश्वरीं दीक्षाम्।

क्षपणकः : अले भिक्खुअ, कावालिणीपलसदूसिदं तुमम्। ता दूलं अपसल।

[अरे भिक्षो, कापालिनीस्पर्शदूषितस्त्वम्। तद्दूरमपसर।

भिक्षुः : आः पाप, वञ्चितोऽसि रे कापालिन्या परिरम्भमहोत्सवेन।

कापालिकः : प्रिये, क्षपणकं गृहाण। (कापालिनी क्षपणकमालिङ्गति।)

क्षपणकः : (सरोमाञ्चम्।) अहो अरिहन्त, अहो अरिहन्त, कापालिनीए पलसस्हं। सुन्दलि, देहि देहि पुणोवि अङ्कपालिम्। (स्वगतम्) अरे, महन्तो क्खु इन्दिअविआलो उपत्थिदो। ता अत्थि कोवि उवाओ? किं एत्थ जुत्तम्? भोदु। पिच्छिआए ढंकिस्सम्।

[अहो अर्हन्! अहो अर्हन्! कापालिन्याः स्पर्शसुखम्। सुन्दरि, देहि देहि पुनरप्यङ्कपालीम्। अरे, महान्खल्विन्द्रियविकार उपस्थितः। तदस्ति कोऽप्युपायः किमत्र युक्तम्? भवतु पिच्छिकया छादयिष्यामि।

अयि पीणघणत्थणसोहणि पलितत्थकुलङ्गविलोअणि।
जइ लमसि कावालिणीभावेंहि सावका किं कलिस्संदि॥१९॥

अहो कावालिअदंसणं जेव्व इक्कं सौक्खमोक्खसाहणम्। भो कावालिअ, हग्गे तुह्के सम्पदं दासो संवुत्तो। मंपि महाभैरवानुशासणे दिक्खय।

अयि पीनघनस्तनशोभने परित्रस्तकुरङ्गविलोचने।
यदि रमसे कापालिनीभावैः श्रावका किं करिष्यन्तीति॥

अहो कापालिकदर्शनमेवैकं सौख्यमोक्षसाधनम्। भो कापालिक, अहं तव सांप्रतं दासः संवृत्तः। मामपि महाभैरवानुशासने दीक्षय।

कापालिकः : उपविश्यताम्।

(उभौ तथा कुरुतः।)

(कापालिको भाजनं समादाय ध्यानं नाटयति।)

श्रद्धा : भअवं, सुलाए पूलितं भाअणम्।

[भगवन्, सुरया पूरितं भाजनम्।]

Excellent is the practice of the Kāpālika. Praiseworthy is the Soma Siddhānta. Wonderful is this religion. Oh good sir, we have forsaken the doctrine of Buddha completely. We have accepted the doctrine of Parameśvara. Therefore, you are my teacher and I am your disciple. Initiate me into the teachings of Parameśvara.

Jaina : Oh mendicant ! you are polluted by the touch of the Kāpālīn; Go far away.

Mendicant: Fool, you have missed the great experience of the embrace of the Kāpālinī.

Kāpālika: My dear, catch hold of the Jaina. (Kāpālinī embraces the Jaina)

Jaina : (*With horripilation*) Oh Arhat! the pleasure of the touch of the Kāpālinī ! Oh beautiful one! embrace me again (to himself). My emotions are greatly excited. Is there any remedy for it ? What shall I do ? I shall hide it with this bunch of peacock feathers.

Oh you who are beautiful with big and fully developed breasts, with eyes like the timid deer, if you enjoy with me with the Kāpālinī ways of making love, what can the Digambaras do? (19).

Certainly the Kāpālika's philosophy is the only means to give happiness and liberation. Oh Kāpālika! I have become your slave now. Initiate me into the teachings of Mahābhairava.

Kāpālika: Be seated.

(*Both do so*)

(*Kāpālika taking up a vessel meditates*)

Faith : Lord, the vessel is filled with alcohol.

कापालिकः : (पीत्वा शेषं भिक्षुक्षपणकयोरर्पयति ।)

इदं पवित्रममृतं पीयतां भवभेषजम् ।
पशुपाशसमुच्छेदकारणं भैरवोदितम् ॥२०॥

(उभौ विमृशतः ।)

क्षपणकः : **अम्हाणं अलिहन्ताणुमासणे सूलापाणं णत्थि ।**

[अस्माकमार्हतानुशासने सुरापानं नास्ति ।]

भिक्षुः : कथं कापालिकोच्छिष्टां सुरां पास्यामि ।

कापालिकः : (विमृश्य जनान्तिकम् ।) **किं विमृशसि श्रद्धे, पशुत्वमनयोर्नाद्याप्यपनीयते । तेनास्मद्वदनसंसर्गदोषादपवित्रां सुरामेतौ मन्येते । तद्भवती स्ववक्त्रासवपूतां कृत्वाऽनयोरुपनयतु । यतस्तैर्थिका अपि वदन्ति 'स्त्रीमुखं तु सदा शुचि' इति ।**

श्रद्धा : **जं भअवं आणवेदि ।** (पानपात्रं गृहीत्वा पीतशेषमुपनयति)

[यद्भगवानाज्ञापयति ।]

भिक्षुः : **महाप्रसादः** (इति चषकं गृहीत्वा पिबति ।) **अहो सुरायाः सौन्दर्यम् ।**

निपीता वेश्याभिः सह न कतिवारान्सुवदना-
मुखोच्छिष्टास्माभिर्विकचबकुलामोदमधुरा ।
कपालिन्या वक्त्रासवसुरभिमेतां तु मदिरा-
मलब्धां जानीमः स्पृहयति सुधायै सुरगणः ॥२१॥

क्षपणकः : **अले भिक्खुअ, मा सव्वं पिब । कावालिणीवअणोच्छिट्टं मइलं मदत्थंवि धालेसु ।**

[अरे भिक्षो, मा सर्वं पिब । कापालिनीवदनोच्छिष्टां मदिरां मदर्थमपि धारय ।]

(भिक्षुः क्षपणकाय चषकमुपनयति ।)

Kāpālika: (*Drinks and then offers the remaining to the Mendicant and Jaina*)

Drink this pure nectar which is the medicine for worldly existence; Bhairava has said that this is the instruement to remove the bondage of the soul. (20).

(*Both consult each other*)

Jaina : In our ordinance of the Arhata drinking alcohol is not permitted.

Mendicant: How shall I drink the alcohol left over by the Kāpālika.

Kāpālika: (*Thinking over and Aside*) Faith, what are you thinking. The beastly nature of these people is not yet removed. Therefore they think that this alcohol which has come in contact with my mouth is impure. Therefore you purify it with the liquor of your mouth and then take it to them; for, even the holy people say that "the mouth of a woman is always pure".

Faith : As my lord commands. (*Taking the vessel and after drinking from it to the mendicant*).

Mendicant: Great is the favour (*takes the vessel and drinks from it*) Ah the beauty of the alcohol !

How many times have we drunk alcohol with prostitutes, the alcohol which is made sweet with the fragrance of the fully opened bakula blossoms and which is left over after coming in contact with the mouth of beautiful faced women. We think that the gods crave for nectar (only) because they do not get the alcohol which is made fragrant with the nectar of the mouth of the Kāpālinī. (21).

Jaina : Oh mendicant ! do not drink the whole thing. Keep some alcohol which is left over from the mouth of the Kāpālinī.

(*The mendicant takes the vessel to the Jaina*)

क्षपणकः : (पीत्वा) अहो, सुराए महुलत्तणम्, अहो सादो अहो गन्धो, अहो सुलहित्तणम् । चिलं खु अलिहन्ताणुसासणे णिवडिदे पडिवञ्चिदोम्हि ईदिसेण सुलालसेण । अले भिक्खुअ, घोलन्ति मं अङ्गाइं । ता सुविस्सम् ।

[अहो सुराया मधुरत्वम्, अहो स्वादः, अहो गन्धः, अहो सुरभित्वम् । चिरं खलु अर्हदनुशासने निपतितः प्रतिवञ्चितोऽस्मीदृशेन सुरारसेन । अरे भिक्षो, घूर्णन्ति ममाङ्गानि तर्हि स्वप्स्यामि ।]

भिक्षुः : एवं कुर्वः । (तथा कुरुतः ।)

कापालिकः : प्रिये, अमूल्यक्रीतं दासद्वयं लब्धम् । तन्नृत्यावस्तावत् ।

(उभौ नृत्यतः ।)

क्षपणकः : अले भिक्खुअ, एसो कावालिओ अहवा आचालिओ कावालिनीए सद्धं सोहणं णच्चेदि । ता एदाए सद्धं अम्हेवि णच्चावः ।

[अरे भिक्षुक, एष कापालिकोऽथवाचार्यः कापालिन्या सार्धं शोभनं नृत्यति । तस्मादेताभ्यां सार्धमावामपि नृत्यावः ।]

भिक्षुः : आचार्य, महाश्चर्यमेतद्दर्शनम् । यत्राक्लेशमभिमतार्थसिद्धयः संपद्यन्ते ।

(मदस्खलितं नृत्यतः ।)

क्षपणकः : (अयि 'पीणत्थणि' इत्यादि पूर्वमेवोक्त्वा ।)

कापालिकः : कियदेतदाश्चर्यं पश्यसि ?

अत्रानुज्झितचक्षुरादिविषयासङ्गेऽपि सिध्यन्त्यमू-
रत्यासन्नमहोदयाः प्रणयिनाप्यष्टौ महासिद्धयः ।
वश्याकर्षविमोहनप्रशमनप्रक्षोभणोच्चाटन-
प्रायाः प्राकृतसिद्धयस्तु विदुषां योगान्तरायाः परम् ॥२२॥

क्षपणकः : अले कापालिअ, (विमृश्य) अहवा आचालिअ, आचालिअलाअ, कुलाचालिअ ।

[अरे कापालिक, अथवा आचार्य, आचार्यराज, कुलाचार्य ।]

भिक्षुः : (विहस्य) अयमनभ्यासातिशयपीतया मदिरया दूरमुन्मनीकृतस्तपस्वी । तत्क्रियतामस्य मदापनयनम् ।

कापालिकः : एवं भवतु । (इति स्वमुखोच्छिष्टं ताम्बूलं क्षपणकाय ददाति ।)

Jaina : (*After drinking*) Ah ! the sweetness of the alcohol; what taste, what smell, what fragrance ! By falling into the teachings of Arhata, I have been deceived for a long time from drinking this kind of alcohol. Oh mendicant ! my limbs stagger. So let me sleep.

Mendi. : Let us do so (*they do so*).

Kāpālika : My dear, we have obtained two slaves without any payment. So let us dance (*Both dance*).

Jaina : Oh mendicant ! this Kāpālika, rather Master, dances beautifully with the Kāpālinī. So let us also dance with them.

Mendi. : Master, this is a wonderful philosophy where without any difficulty one's wishes are fulfilled. (They both dance staggeringly due to intoxication).

Jaina : (*Repeats verse* 19).

Kāpā. : What do you see wonderful in this ?

Here (in our philosophy) even without giving up attachment towards the objects of the (senses) eyes etc., the eight great Siddhis are attained by the desirous and their excellent results are near at hand. The primitive Siddhis, however, like subjection, attraction, causing bewilderment, subduing, exciting, and causing to quit, are obstacles of Yoga for the wise. (22).

Jaina : Oh Kāpālika ! or Master ! or king of Masters!

Mendi. : (*Laughing*) This poor man is very much out of his senses, through the liquor which he is not used to drink. Therefore, let his drunkenness be removed.

Kāpā. : Let it be so. (*He gives the chewed betel etc. from his mouth to the Jaina*).

क्षपणकः : (स्वस्थीभूय) आचालिअ, एव्वं पुच्छिस्सम्। जादिसी तुम्हाणं सुलाए आहलणसिद्धी किं तादिसी सिद्धी इत्थिआसु पुलिसेसु अवि अत्थि ?

[आचार्य, इदं पृच्छामि। यादृशी युष्माकं सुराया आहरणसिद्धिः किं तादृशी सिद्धिः स्त्रीषु पुरुषेष्वप्यस्ति ?]

कापालिकः : किं विशेषेण पृच्छ्यते। पश्य—

विद्याधरीं वाथ सुराङ्गनां वा
नागाङ्गनां वाप्यथ यक्षकन्याम्।
यद्यन्ममेष्टं भुवनत्रयेऽपि
विद्याबलात्तत्तदुपाहरामि ॥२३॥

क्षपणकः : भो, एदं मए गणिदेण ण्णादं। जं सव्वेवि अम्हे महामोहस्स किंकले त्ति।

[भो, इदं मया गणितेन ज्ञातम्। यत्सर्वेऽपि वयं महामोहस्य किङ्करा इति।]

उभौ : यथाज्ञातमायुष्मता। एवमेतत्।

क्षपणकः : ता लाअकज्जं किंवि मन्तिदव्वम्।

[तर्हि राजकार्यं किमपि मन्त्रितव्यम्।]

कापालिकः : किं तत् ?

क्षपणकः : सत्तस्स सुदा सद्धा महालाअस्स अण्णाए आहलिअदु त्ति।

[सत्त्वस्य सुता श्रद्धा महाराजस्याज्ञयाह्रियतामिति।]

कापालिकः : कथय क्वासौ दास्याः पुत्री ? एष तामचिरमेव विद्याबलादुपाहरामि।

(क्षपणकः खटिकामादाय गणयति।)

शान्तिः : सखि, अम्बागतमिव हताशानामालापं शृणोमि तदवधानेन तावदाकर्णयावः।

करुणा : सहि एव्वं करेम्ह। (उभे तथा कुरुतः।)

[सखि, एवं कुर्मः।]

क्षपणकः : (गाथां गणयित्वा।)

णत्थि जले णत्थि थले णत्थि गिलिगव्हलेसु णत्थि पाआले।
सा विण्णुभत्तिसहिदा वसदि हिअए महम्माणम् ॥ २४ ॥

[नास्ति जले नास्ति स्थले नास्ति गिरिगह्वरेषु नास्ति पाताले।
सा विष्णुभक्ति सहिता वसति हृदये महात्मनाम् ॥]

Jaina : (*Becoming normal*) Master, let me ask you this. Do women and men possess the power of attracting as much as this liquor of yours?

Kāpā. : Why do you ask this question specially ? See.

Whatever I desire in these three worlds, be it a Vidyādhara woman or the wife of a god or of a Nāga or a Yakṣa girl, I shall bring her here through the power of my knowledge. (23).

Jaina : Well, I have known through the calculation (of the stars) that we are all servants of Grand Delusion.

Both : You have correctly understood. It is so.

Jaina : Let us think of some service to the king.

Kāpā. : What is that?

Jaina : By the command of the king, Faith, the daughter of purity, should be brought.

Kāpā. : Say, who is this daughter of a slave? I shall bring her here immediately through the power of my knowledge.

(*Jaina takes a chalk and calculates.*)

Peace : Friend, it seems that these hopeless people are talking about my mother. So let us listen to it carefully.

Pity : Friend, let us do so. (*Both do so*)

Jaina : (*Concluding after calculating a religious verse*).

Not in water, not in land, not in the caves of mountain and not in hell, she along with devotion to Viṣṇu lives in the heart of great souls. (24).

करुणा : (सानन्दम्) सहि, दिट्ठिआ वड्ढसि विण्णुभत्तिए देवीए पास्सवत्तिणी सद्धेत्ति ।

[सखि, दिष्ट्या वर्धसे विष्णुभक्त्या देव्याः पार्श्ववर्तिनी श्रद्धेति ।]

(शान्तिः हर्षं नाटयति ।)

भिक्षुः : अथ धर्मस्य कामादपक्रान्तस्य कुत्र प्रवृत्तिः ?

क्षपणकः : (पुनर्गणयित्वा ।)

णत्थि जले णत्थि वणे णत्थि गिलिगव्हलेसु णत्थि पाआले ।
विण्णुभत्तीए सहिदो वसदि हिअए महम्माणम् ।। २५ ।।

[नास्ति जले नास्ति वने नास्ति गिरिगह्वरेषु नास्ति पाताले ।
विष्णुभक्त्या सहितो वसति हृदये महात्मनाम् ।।]

कापालिकः : (सविषादम्) अहो महत्कष्टमापतितं महाराजस्य । तथाहि—

मूलं देवी सिद्धये विष्णुभक्ति-
स्तां च श्रद्धानुव्रता सत्त्वकन्या ।
कामान्मुक्तस्तत्र धर्मोऽप्यभूच्चे-
त्सिद्धं मन्ये तद्विवेकस्य कृत्यम् ।।२६।।

तथापि तावदसुव्ययेनापि स्वामिनः प्रयोजनमनुष्ठेयम् । तन्महाभैरवीं विद्यां धर्मश्रद्धयोराहरणाय प्रस्थापयामः (इति निष्क्रान्ताः सर्वे ।)

शान्तिः : आवामप्येवं हताशानां व्यवसायं देव्यै विष्णुभक्त्यै निवेदयावः ।

(इति निष्क्रान्ते ।)

इति श्रीकृष्णमिश्रविरचिते प्रबोधचन्द्रोदयनाम्नि नाटके तृतीयोऽङ्कः ।। ३ ।।

Pity : (*Happily*) Friend, you are fortunate. Faith is living with devotion to Viṣṇu.

Peace : (*Acts as if she is happy.*)

Mendi. : Then where is Righteousness operating when he is taken away from Concupiscence.

Jaina : (*Calculating again*)

Not in water, not in the forest, not in the caves of mountains, and not in hell. He remains in the heart of great souls along with Devotion to Viṣṇu. (25).

Kāpā. : (*Sorrowfully*) What great danger has fallen on King Delusion. For—

Devotion to Viṣṇu (herself) is enough cause for the achievement of the fruit. Faith, the daughter of purity, is with her. If Righteouness separated from Concupiscence is also there, then definitely I consider that Discrimination has achieved his end. (26).

Even then, we have to fulfil our lord's purpose even at the loss of our lives. Therefore let us send Mahābhairavī-knowledge to bring Righteousness and Faith. (*Exeunt omnes.*)

Peace : Let us also inform of the attempt of these hopeless people to goddess Devotion to Viṣṇu.

(*Exeunt both*)

चतुर्थोऽङ्कः ।

(ततः प्रविशति मैत्री ।)

मैत्री : सुदं मए मुदिताए सआसादो जधा महाभैरवीसङ्गसणसम्भमादो भअवदीए विण्णुभत्तीए परित्तादा प्पिअसही सद्धेति । ता उक्कण्ठिदेण हिअएण पिअसहीं सद्धां कदा पेक्खिस्सम् । (परिक्रामति ।)

[श्रुतं मया मुदितायाः सकाशाद्यथा महाभैरवीसङ्ग्रसनसंभ्रमाद्भगवत्या विष्णुभक्त्या परित्राता प्रियसखी श्रद्धेति तदुत्कण्ठितेन हृदयेन प्रियसखीं श्रद्धां कदा प्रेक्षिष्ये ।

(ततः प्रविशति श्रद्धा ।)

श्रद्धा : (सभयोत्कम्पम् ।)

घोरां नारकपालकुण्डलवतीं विद्युच्छटां दृष्टिभि-
र्मुञ्चन्तीं विकरालमूर्तिमनलज्वालापिशङ्गैः कचैः ।
दंष्ट्राचन्द्रकलाङ्कुरान्तरलसज्जिह्वां महाभैरवीं
पश्यन्त्या इव मे मनः कदलिकेवाद्याप्यहो वेपते ॥१॥

मैत्री : (स्वगतम्) अए, एसा मे पिअसही सद्धा भअसमुब्भान्तहिअआकलिदकम्पतरलेहिं अङ्गेहिं किंवि मन्तअन्ती संमुहागदंवि मं ण लक्खेदि । ता आलविस्सं दाव । (प्रकाशम्) पिअसहि सद्धे, किंति तुमं उक्कलिदहिअआ मंवि ण विलोएदि ।

[अये, एषा मे प्रियसखी श्रद्धा भयसमुद्भ्रान्तहृदयाकलितकम्पतरलैरङ्गैः किमपि मन्त्रयन्ती संमुखागतामपि मां न लक्षयति। तस्मादालपिष्यामि तावत् । प्रियसखि श्रद्धे, किमिति त्वमुत्कलितहृदया मामपि न विलोकयसि ।

श्रद्धा : (विलोक्य सोच्छ्वासम्) अये मे प्रियसखी मैत्री !

कालरात्रिकरालास्यदन्तान्तर्गतया मया ।
दृष्टासि सखि सैव त्वं पुनरत्रैव जन्मनि ॥२॥

तदेहि गाढं परिष्वजस्व माम् ।

ACT IV

Enter Friendship

Friend. : I have heard from Joy, that my dear friend Faith is saved by the goddess, Devotion to Viṣṇu, from the fear of being devoured by Mahābhairavī. When shall I, whose heart is worried, see my beloved friend ? (*Walks on*).

Enter Faith.

Faith : (*Trembling with fear*). Alas, my mind trembles even now like a flag as if I am seeing the frightful Mahābhairavī, with ear rings of human skulls, ejecting lightning from her eyes, dreadful, with her hair which is tawny in colour like the flame of fire, and with her tongue tolling in between her tusks shining like the digit of the moon. (1).

Friend. : (*Aside*). Ah! this is my friend Faith, with her limbs trembling because her heart is filled with fear; she is muttering something to herself and she does not notice me though I am in front of her. Therefore let me talk to her. My dear friend Faith, why is that you with your heart perturbed do not even see me?

Faith : (*Looks on and with a deep sigh*). Ah! my dear friend Friendship! Friend, Am I who have been held in between the teeth in the mouth of Mahābhairavī which is as frightful as the night of destruction, beholding you again in this very birth. (2).

So, come, embrace me tightly.

मैत्री : (तथा कृत्वा) सहि तधा विण्णुभत्तिणिब्भत्थिदप्पभावाए महाभैरवीए कहं दे अज्जवि वेवन्दि अङ्गाइं ?

[सखि, तदा विष्णुभक्तिनिर्भर्त्सितप्रभावाया महाभैरव्याः कस्मात्तेऽद्यापि वेपन्तेऽङ्गानि ?

(श्रद्धा घोरामित्यादि पठति ।)

मैत्री : (सत्रापत्) अहो, हदासा घोलदंसणा। अध ताए आगदाए किं किदम् ।

[अहो हताशा घोरदर्शना । अथ तयागतया किं कृतम् ?]

श्रद्धा :

श्येनावपातमवपत्य पदद्वये मा-
मादाय धर्ममपरेण करेण घोरा ।
वेगेन सा गगनमुत्पतिता नखाग्र-
कोटिस्फुरत्पिशितपिण्डयुतेव गृध्री ॥ ३ ॥

मैत्री : हद्धी हद्धी। (इति मूर्च्छति।)

[हा धिक् हा धिक् ।]

श्रद्धा : सखि, समाश्वसिहि समाश्वसिहि ।

मैत्री : (आश्वस्य) तदो तदो ।

[ततस्ततः ।]

श्रद्धा : ततः परमस्मदीयार्तनादोपजातदयार्द्रचित्तया देव्या—

भ्रूभङ्गभीमपरिपाटलदृष्टिपात-
मुद्गाढकोपकुटिलं च तथा व्यलोकि ।
सा वज्रपातहतशैलशिलेव भूमौ
व्याभुग्नजर्जरशिरोस्थि यथा पपात ॥ ४ ॥

मैत्री : दिट्ठिआ मए दिट्ठा कुद्धसादूलमुहादो विब्भट्टा मिईव क्खेमेण संजीविदा पिअसही ।

[दिष्ट्या मया दृष्टा क्रुद्धशार्दूलमुखाद्विभ्रष्टा मृगीव क्षेमेण संजीविता प्रियसखी ।

Friend. : (*Doing so*) Friend, why are your limbs trembling even now out of fear from that Mahābhairavī whose power is weakened by devotion to Viṣṇu ?

Faith. : (*Repeats the verse "My mind trembles etc"*)

Friend. : (*Fearfully*) Alas! the cruel, fearful one. Then when she came what did she do ?

Faith : She, the fearful one fell upon me like a hawk, caught hold of my legs and catching hold of Righteousness with the other hand suddenly jumped up into the sky like a female vulture carrying a piece of flesh glittering at the tip of her nails. (3).

Friend. : Woe me, Woe me (*Faints*).

Faith : Friend, be comforted, be comforted.

Friend. : (*Recovering*) And then!

Faith : Then the goddess (Devotion to Viṣṇu) whose heart being moved by compassion by (hearing) our helpless cry, looked (at them) thus with great anger, with her eyes red, frightful and the eyebrows curved. Then she (Mahābhairavī) fell down on the earth with her skull broken and shattered like a mountain rock (rent) by the stroke of a thunder-bolt. (4).

Friend. : Fortunately I have seen my friend, safely rescued like a she deer slipped down from the mouth of an angry tiger.

श्रद्धा : ततो देव्या समुपजाताभिनिवेशभुक्तमेवमस्य दुरात्मनो महामोहहतकस्य मामप्यवज्ञाय प्रवर्तमानस्य समूलमुन्मूलनं करिष्यामीति। आदिष्टा चाहं देव्या। यथा गच्छ श्रद्धे, ब्रूहि विवेकम्। कामक्रोधादीनां निर्जयायोद्योगः क्रियताम्। ततो वैराग्यं प्रादुर्भविष्यति। अहं च यथासमयं प्राणायामाद्यनुप्राणनेन युष्मत्सैन्यमनुग्रहीष्यामि। ऋतंभरावयश्च देव्यः शान्त्यादिकौशलेनोपनिषद्देव्या संगतस्य भगवतः प्रबोधोदयमनुविधास्यन्तीति। तदहमिदानीं विवेकसंनिधिं प्रस्थिता। त्वं पुनः किमाचरन्ती दिवसानतिवाहयसि?

मैत्री : अम्हेवि विण्णुभत्तीए अण्णाए चतस्सो बहिणीओ विवेअसिद्धिकालणेण महाप्पणं हिअए अहिवट्टम्हो। (संस्कृतमाश्रित्य) तथाहि—

[वयमपि विष्णुभक्तेराज्ञया चतस्रो भगिन्यो विवेकसिद्धिकारणेन महात्मनां हृदयेऽभिवर्तामहे।]

ध्यायन्निमां सुखिनि दुःखिनि चानुकम्पां
पुण्यक्रियासु मुदितां कुमतावुपेक्षाम्।
एवं प्रसादमुपयाति हि रागलोभ-
द्वेषादिदोषकलुषोऽप्ययमन्तरात्मा ॥ ५ ॥

तदेवं चतस्रोऽपि भगिन्यो वयं तदभ्युदयकारणेनैव वासरान्नयामः। कुत्रेदानीं प्रियसखी महाराजमालोकयति?

श्रद्धा : देव्या एतदेवमुक्तम्। अस्ति राढाभिधानो जनपदः। तत्र भागीरथीपरिसरालंकारभूते चक्रतीर्थे मीमांसानुगतया मत्या कथंचिद्धार्यमाणप्राणो व्याकुलेनान्तरात्मना विवेक उपनिषद्देव्याः संगमार्थं तपस्तपस्यतीति।

मैत्री : ता गच्छदु पिअसही। अहंवि स्सकं णिओअं अणुचिट्ठामि।

[तद्गच्छतु प्रियसखी। अहमपि स्वकं नियोगमनुतिष्ठामि।]

श्रद्धा : एवं भवतु।

(इति निष्क्रान्ते।)

(विष्कम्भकः।)

Faith : Then, the goddess uttered thus with firm resolve: "I shall uproot this wicked and wretched Delusion who acts ignoring even me". The goddess has ordered me thus: "Faith, go and tell Discrimination, 'Make an effort to defeat Concupiscence and Anger. Then Dispassionateness will appear. I shall at the appropriate time bless your Army with the help of Control of Breath etc. The goddesses like Bearer of Truth etc. will bring about the Rise of Spiritual Awakening in the Lord who is united with goddess Sacred Lore through the skill of Peace etc.". Therefore, I am going to Discrimination now. With what activities do you spend your days?

Friend. : By the command of Devotion to Viṣṇu, we four sisters also reside in the hearts of great men for the success of Discrimination. (*Adapting Sanskrit*) For—

In dealing with a happy person, the innerself should feel me (Friendship); in associating with an unhappy one, (feel) compassion; to good actions it should respond with joy, and to bad thoughts with indifference. Thus the innerself, though still tainted by attachment, greed, spite etc., attains sedateness. (5).

Thus we four sisters spend the days for the sake of his success. Now where will my dear friend find the king?

Faith : The Goddess has said thus: "There is a place named Rāḍhā. There in Cakratīrtha adorned by the surroundings of river Bhāgīrathī, Discrimination with a perturbed mind, along with Reason who is accompanied by Mīmāṁsā, somehow manages to live and is doing penance for his union with goddess Sacred Lore".

Friend. : You go then my dear friend. I shall also perform my duty.

Faith : Be it so,

(*Both exit*)

(*Interlude*)

(ततः प्रविशति राजा प्रतीहारी च।)

राजा : आः पाप महामोहहतक, सर्वथा हतस्त्वयायं महाजनः। तथाहि—

शान्तेऽनन्तमहिम्नि निर्मलचिदानन्दे तरङ्गावली-
निर्मुक्तेऽमृतसागराम्भसि मनाङ्भग्नोऽपि नाचामति ।
निःसारे मृगतृष्णिकार्णवजले श्रान्तोऽपि मूढः पिब-
त्याचामत्यवगाहतेऽभिरमते मज्जत्यथोन्मज्जति ॥६॥

अथवा संसारचक्रवाहकस्य महामोहस्याबोधो मूलम्। तस्य च तत्त्वावबोधादेव निवृत्तिः। यतः—

अमुष्य संसारतरोरबोधमूलस्य नोन्मूलविनाशनाय ।
विश्वेश्वराराधनबीजजातात्तत्त्वावबोधादपरोऽभ्युपायः ॥७॥

'प्रायः सुकृतिनामर्थे देवा यान्ति सहायताम् ।
अपन्थानं तु गच्छन्तं सोदरोऽपि विमुञ्चति ॥'

इति तत्त्वविदो व्याहरन्ति। तथा तु देव्या विष्णुभक्त्या संदिष्टम् 'उद्योगः कामादिविजयविषये क्रियताम्' इति। अहमपि भवदर्थे गृहीतपक्षेति। तत्र कामस्तावत्प्रथमो वीरो वस्तुविचारेणैव जीयते। तद्भवतु। तमेव तावद्विजयार्थमादिशामि। वेदवति, आहूयतां वस्तुविचारः।

प्रतीहारी : जं देवो आणवेदि।

[यद्देव आज्ञापयति।]

(इति निष्क्रम्य वस्तुविचारेण सह प्रविशति।)

वस्तुविचारः : अहो निर्विचारसौन्दर्याभिमानवर्धिष्णुना कामहतकेन वञ्चितं जगत्। अथवा दुरात्मना महामोहेनैव।

(Then enter King and the Gate-Keeper)

King : Oh Sinner, Wretched Great Delusion! you have by all means killed this great man. For

Though immersed in the immortal ocean of pure intelligence and bliss, which is quiet, of endless greatness and free from rows of waves, Man does not take even a sip from it. Instead, he seeks refreshment by drinking the essenceless water of the sea of a mirage, bathes in it, enjoys it, and plunges into it again and again. (6).

Or rather, ignorance is the root of great delusion which is the bearer of the wheel of saṁsāra. That can be removed only through the knowledge of Truth. For—

To uproot the tree of saṁsāra grown from ignorance, there is no other means than realization of Truth, born of the seed of worship of the Lord of the Universe. (7).

"Usually, in regard to good people, gods are of help. But one who goes on the wrong path is abandoned even by his brother." Thus say the knowers of Truth. Goddess Devotion to Viṣṇu has sent this message. "Exert yourself to defeat Concupiscence etc. I am also on your side. There, the foremost warrior, Concupiscence will be defeated by Investigation into Truth." "Let it be so. I shall give orders to him to go and be victorious. Vedavatī, please call Investigation into Truth.

Door Keeper: As my Lord commands. (*Goes out and comes back with Investigation into Truth*).

Investi. : The univesrse is deceived by the wretched Concupiscence who increases thoughtless vanity caused by beauty. Or rather it is (deceived) by the wicked Grand Delușion.

तथाहि—

कान्तेत्युत्पललोचनेति विपुलश्रोणीभरेत्युन्नम-
त्पीनोत्तुङ्गपयोधरेति सुमुखाम्भोजेति सुभ्रूरिति ।
दृष्ट्वा माद्यति मोदतेऽभिरमते प्रस्तौति विद्वानपि
प्रत्यक्षाशुचिपुत्तिकां स्त्रियमहो मोहस्य दुश्चेष्टितम् ॥८॥

अपिच यथावस्तु विचारयताममन्दमतीनामपि पिशितपङ्कावनद्धास्थिपञ्जरमयी स्वभावदुर्गन्धिर्बीभत्सवेषा नारीति नास्ति विरतिः । तदत्र विस्पष्ट एवेतरगुणाध्यासः । तथाहि—

मुक्ताहारलता रणन्मणिमया हैमास्तुलाकोटयो
रागः कुङ्कुमसंभवः सुरभयः पौष्पा विचित्राः स्रजः ।
वासश्चित्रदुकूलमल्पमतिभिर्नार्यामहो कल्पितं
बाह्यान्तः परिपश्यतां तु निरयो नारीति नाम्ना कृतः ॥९॥

(आकाशे) आः पाप कामचण्डाल, किमनालम्बनमेवं भवता व्याकुलीक्रियते जनः । तथा ह्ययमेवाभिमन्यते—

बाला मामियमिच्छतीन्दुवदना सानन्दमुद्वीक्षते
नीलेन्दीवरलोचना पृथुकुचोत्पीडं परीरम्भते ।

अरे मूढ,

का त्वामिच्छति का च पश्यति पशो मांसास्थिभिर्निर्मिता
नारी वेद न किंचिदत्र स पुनः पश्यत्यमूर्तः पुमान् ॥१०॥

प्रतीहारी : इदो आगच्छेदु महाभाओ।

[इत आगच्छतु महाभागः ।]

(इत्युभौ परिक्रामतः ।)

प्रतीहारी : एसो महाराओ उवविट्ठो चिट्ठदि । ता उवसप्पदु भवम् ।

[एष महाराज उपविष्टस्तिष्ठति । तदुपसर्पतु भवान् ।

वस्तुविचारः : (उपसृत्य ।) जयतु जयतु देवः । एष वस्तुविचारः प्रणमति ।

For—

Even a wise man seeing a woman who is an idol of all visible impurities, as the beloved, lotus-eyed one, as one with heavy hips, as one with raised and heavy breasts, as one with beautiful face like a lotus, as one with beautiful eye-brows gets deluded, rejoices, enjoys and praises. Alas ! the wicked action of Delusion. (8).

Moreover, even those people who are not dull-witted and who investigate into truth do not refrain (from woman) thinking that woman is (only) a mass of flesh built up with bones and possessing by nature a stinking and disgusting garb. Therefore it is clear that there is a super-imposition of qualities belonging to something else. For—

Pearl necklaces jingling with precious stones, golden anklets, red colour due to the saffron (which they have applied), many-hued fragrant flower garlands, silken clothes of different types—all these are fancied on woman by fools but for those who examine both the exterior and interior (of things) hell is named as woman. (9).

(*Behind the scene*) Oh ! sinner Concupiscence—you of the low caste, why do you agitate people with out any reason. Thus he thinks: "This girl whose face is like the moon and whose eyes are like the blue lotus desires me, (thinking thus) he looks at her with pleasure and embraces her pressing her big breasts." Oh fool ! who desires you, who beholds you ! Oh ! you animal, woman is made of flesh and bones and she does not know anything here but he the formless man (the inner self) alone sees. (10).

Door K. : This way, Respected Sir.

(*Both walk on*)

Door K. : Here is the king sitting. Go near him, sir.

Investi : (*Approaching*). May the Lord be victorious! Investigation into Truth salutes you.

राजा : इहोपविश्यताम् ।

वस्तुविचारः : (उपविश्य ।) देव, एष ते किंकरः संप्राप्तः, आज्ञयानुगृह्यताम् ।

राजा : महामोहेन सहास्माकं संप्रवृत्तः सङ्ग्रामः । तदत्र कामस्तस्य प्रथमो वीरः । तस्य च प्रतिवीरतयास्माभिर्भवान्निरूपितः ।

वस्तुविचारः : धन्योऽस्मि । येन स्वामिनाहमेव संभावितः ।

राजा : अथ कया शस्त्रविद्यया भवान्कामं जेष्यति ?

वस्तुविचारः : आः पञ्चशरः कुसुमधन्वा कामो जेतव्य इत्यत्रापि शस्त्रग्रहणापेक्षा ? पश्य—

दृढतरमपिधाय द्वारमारात्कथंचि-
त्स्मरणमपरिवृत्तौ दर्शने योषितां च ।
परिणतिविरसत्वं देहबीभत्सतां वा
प्रतिमुहुरनुचिन्त्योन्मूलयिष्यामि कामम् ॥११॥

राजा : साधु साधु ।

वस्तुविचारः : अपिच—

विपुलपुलिनाः कल्लोलिन्यो नितान्तपतज्झरी-
मसृणितशिलाः शैलाः सान्द्रद्रुमा वनभूमयः ।
यदि शमगिरो वैयासिक्यो बुधैश्च समागमः
क्व पिशितवसामय्यो नार्यस्तथा क्व च मन्मथः ॥१२॥

नारीति नाम प्रधानमस्त्रं कामस्य । तेन तस्यां जितायां तत्सहायाः सर्व एव विफलारम्भा भङ्गमासादयिष्यन्ति । तथाहि—

चन्द्रश्चन्दनमिन्दुधामधवला रात्रिर्द्विरेफावली-
झङ्कारोन्मुखरा विलासविपिनोपान्ता वसन्तोदयः ।
मन्द्रध्वानघनोदयाश्च दिवसा मन्दाः कदम्बानिलाः
शृङ्गारप्रमुखाश्च कामसुहृदो नार्यां जितायां जिताः ॥१३॥

King : Be seated here.

Investi. : (*Sitting*) Lord, here your servant has arrived. Bless him by your command.

King : We have started a battle with Great Delusion. There Concupiscence is the chief fighter. We have appointed you as his opponent.

Investi. : I am blessed that I have been honoured by my Lord himself.

King : With what science of weapons will you defeat Concupiscence ?

Investi. : Ah ! Does one need any weapon to defeat Concupiscence, the five-arrowed and the flower-bowed one? See I shall uproot Concupiscence ?

At the sight of women if it (the mind) refuses to come back, (I shall) some-how immediately shut the door of memory and at every moment reminding the mind that in the end it (lust) leaves an insipid taste and the loathsomeness of the body, I shall uproot Concupiscence. (11).

King : Well, Well.

Investi. : Again, as long as these rivers with spacious banks, mountains whose rocks are smooth because of the constant flow of the streams (on them), the forest areas crowded with trees, the peace-giving words of Vyāsa and coming in contact with wise people—when these are there what place have women made of flesh and marrow and what place has Cupid ? (12)

Woman is the principal weapon of Cupid. Therefore, if she is won all the other auxiliary weapons are destroyed because their actions become fruitless. For—

Moon, sandal paste, the bright night with the moon's lustre, the pleasure gardens humming with the sound of the rows of bees, the days when clouds with roaring sound arise, the soft breeze from the Kādamba trees and the friends of Cupid, Sentiment of love and others, are all defeated when woman is defeated. (13).

तदलमतिविलम्बेन । आदिशतु स्वामी ।

सोऽहं प्रकीर्णैः परितो विचारैः
शरैरिवोन्मथ्य बलं परेषाम् ।
सैन्यं कुरूणामिव सिन्धुराजं
गाण्डीवधन्वेव निहन्मि कामम् ।।१४।।

राजा : (सप्रसादम् ।) तत्सज्जीभवतु भवाञ्शत्रुविजयाय ।

वस्तुविचारः : यदादिशति देवः ।

(इति प्रणम्य निष्क्रान्तः)

राजा : वेत्रवति, क्रोधस्य विजयाय क्षमैवाहूयताम् ।

प्रतीहारी : जं देवो आणवेदि ।

[यद्देव आज्ञापयति ।]

(इति निष्क्रम्य क्षमया सह प्रविशति ।)

क्षमा :

क्रोधान्धकारविकटभ्रुकुटीतरङ्ग-
भीमस्य सान्ध्यकिरणारुणरौद्रदृष्टेः ।
निष्कम्पनिर्मलगभीरपयोधिधीरा
धीराः परस्य परिवादगिरः सहन्ते ।।१५।।

(सश्लाघमात्मानं निर्वर्ण्य) अहो, अहम् ।

क्लमो न वाचां शिरसो न शूलं
न चित्ततापो न तनोर्विमर्दः ।
न चापि हिंसादिरनर्थयोगः
श्लाघ्या परं क्रोधजयेऽहमेका ।।१६।।

(इत्युभे परिक्रामतः ।)

प्रतीहारी : एसो देवो । ता उवसप्पतु पिअसही ।

[एष देवः । तदुपसर्पतु प्रियसखी ।]

क्षमा : (उपसृत्य ।) जयतु जयतु देवः । एषा देवस्य दासी क्षमा साष्टाङ्गं प्रणमति ।

राजा : क्षमे अत्रोपविश्यताम् ।

क्षमा : (उपविश्य ।) आज्ञापयतु देवः । किमर्थमाहूतो दासीजनः ।

राजा : अस्मिन्सङ्ग्रामे दुरात्मा क्रोधस्त्वया जेतव्यः ।

Therefore let us not delay much. Let my Lord command. I shall shatter the strength of the enemies by scattering the arrows of reason all over and then kill Concupiscence (Cupid) as Arjuna first destroyed the army of the Kurus and afterwards (killed) the king of Sindhus. (14).

King : (*With pleasure*) Then be you ready for the defeat of the enemy.

Investi : As my Lord commands.

(*Salutes him and goes out*)

King : Vetravati, call Patience to defeat Anger.

Door K. : As you command.

(*Goes out and returns with Patience*)

Patience : Brave men who are firm like the deep, clear, unruffled ocean bear the abusive words of another who looks dreadful with wavelike movements of his arched eyebrows due to blinding anger and whose wrathful eyes are red like the sun's rays in the twilight. (15).

(*Looking at herself with pride*) How wonderful am I !

There is neither fatigue due to talking nor head-ache, nor mental strain, nor jestling of the body nor anything to do with calamity caused by violence, I the praiseworthy one alone am capable of defeating Anger. (16).

(*Both walk forward*)

Door K. : Here is the Lord, go to him, my dear friend.

Patience : (*Going near*) Victory to you my Lord. Your servant Patience prostrates before you.

King : Patience, be seated here.

Patience : (*sitting*) Command my Lord ! What for is this servant called ?

King : In this battle the wicked Anger should be defeated by you.

क्षमा : देवस्याज्ञया महामोहमपि जेतुं पर्याप्तास्मि किं पुनः क्रोधं तनुचरमात्रम् । तदहमचिरादेव—

तं पापकारिणमकारणबाधितारं
स्वाध्यायदेवपितृयज्ञतपःक्रियाणाम् ।
क्रोधं स्फुलिङ्गमिव दृष्टिभिरुद्वमन्तं
कात्यायनीव महिषं विनिपातयामि ॥१७॥

राजा : क्षमे, शृणुमस्तावत्क्रोधविजयोपायम् ।

क्षमा : देव, विज्ञापयामि ।

क्रुद्धे स्मेरमुखावधीरणमथाविष्टे प्रसादक्रमो
व्याक्रोशे कुशलोक्तिरात्मदुरितोच्छेदोत्सवस्ताडने ।
धिग्जन्तोरजितात्मनोऽस्य महती दैवादुपेता विप-
द्दुर्वारेति दयारसार्द्रमनसः क्रोधस्य कुत्रोदयः ॥१८॥

राजा : साधु साधु ।

क्षमा : देव, क्रोधस्य विजयादेव हिंसापारुष्यमानमात्सर्यादयोऽपि विजिता एव भविष्यन्ति ।

राजा : तत्प्रतिष्ठतां भवती विजयाय ।

क्षमा : यदाज्ञापयति देवः ।

(इति निष्क्रान्ता ।)

राजा : (प्रतीहारीं प्रति) वेगवति, आहूयतां लोभस्य जेता संतोषः ।

प्रतीहारी : जं देवो आणवेदि ।

[यद्देव आज्ञापयति ।]

(इति निष्क्रम्य संतोषेण सह प्रविशति ।)

Patience : By your command I can even defeat Great Delusion. Let alone Anger who is a mere follower of his. I shall very soon—

As Kātyāyanī slew the (demon) Mahiṣa, I shall slay Anger of sinful actions, who obstructs, without any reason, study of one's own branch of the Vedas, rituals due to gods and manes and performing sacrifices and austerities, and who is as if he is emitting fire sparks through his eyes. (17).

King : Patience, let us hear the means by which you are going to defeat Anger.

Patience : My Lord, I shall let you know.

In dealing with an angry man, disregard him with a smiling, if he is possessed (with wrath) composure is the right course; if he abuses you, ask him about his health, if he beats you, it is a happy occasion for you to destroy your own evil actions. For him who thinks: 'Fie upon him who has no self-restraint, for it will be difficult for him to ward off great calamity caused by fate, and whose heart is soft with the milk of kindness, there is no rise of anger. (18).

King : Good, good.

Patience : My Lord, by the defeat of Anger itself, Violence, Harshness, Conceit, Spite and others are also as well defeated.

King : Then leave you for victory.

Patience : As my Lord commands.

(*Exit*)

King . (*To the door-keeper*) Vegavati, please call Contentment, the conqueror of Greed.

Door K. : As my Lord commands.

(*Exit and returns with Contentment*)

संतोषः : (विचिन्त्य सानुक्रोशम् ।)

फलं स्वेच्छालभ्यं प्रतिवनमखेदं क्षितिरुहां
पयः स्थाने स्थाने शिशिरमधुरं पुण्यसरिताम् ।
मृदुस्पर्शा शय्या सुललितलतापल्लवमयी
सहन्ते संतापं तदिह धनिनां द्वारि कृपणाः ॥१६॥

(आकाशे) अरे मूर्ख, लुब्ध, दुरुच्छेदः खल्वयं भवतो व्यामोहः ।

तथाहि—

समारम्भा भग्नाः कति कति न वारांस्तव पशो
पिपासोस्तुच्छेऽस्मिन्द्रविणमृगतृष्णार्णवजले ।
तथापि प्रत्याशा विरमति न ते मूढ शतधा
विदीर्णं यच्चेतो नियतमशनिग्रावघटितम् ॥२०॥

इदं च ते लोभान्धस्य चेष्टितं चेतसि चमत्कारमातनोति ।
यतः—

लभ्यं लब्धमिदं च लभ्यमधिकं तन्मूललभ्यं ततो
लब्धं चापरमित्यनारतमहो लब्धं धनं ध्यायसि ।
नैतद्वेत्सि पुनर्भवन्तमचिरादाशापिशाची बला-
त्सर्वग्रासमियं ग्रसिष्यति महालोभान्धकारावृतम् ॥२१॥

अपि च—

धनं तावल्लब्धं कथमपि तथाप्यस्य नियतो
व्ययो वा नाशो वा तव सति वियोगोऽस्त्युभयथा ।
अनुत्पादः श्रेयान्किमु कथय पथ्योऽथ विलयो
विनाशो लब्धस्य व्यथयतितरां न त्वनुदयः ॥२२॥

Content : (*Thinking compassionately*). Without any trouble, in every forest, fruit of trees is available according to one's own desire, cool and sweet water of holy rivers is available here and there, a bed soft to touch, made of tender leaves of graceful creepers (when these things are there) only people who are void of judgment suffer distress at the door of rich people. (19).

(*Behind the scenes*) Oh fool ! Greed, your delusion cannot be easily removed. For—

In this sea of mirage in the form of wealth you are desirous of drinking water ! Oh thoughtless one ! how many times have your attempts failed ! Even, then, oh fool, your desire does not stop. That your mind is not broken into hundred pieces, sure it is made of diamond. (20).

You who are blind due to avarice your action produces strange effect on the mind. For.

Money which is due has been obtained, more should be obtained, and from that I have obtained more money (in the form of interest) from the capital thus I have attained other money too, thus endlessly you are thinking of the wealth you have got. But you who are covered with the darkness of Great Greed do not know that you yourself will be completely devoured by this demoness Hope. (21).

Morcover—

Wealth has been obtained. Even then you are definitely going to spend or loose it, in both the cases, you will be separated from it. Which do you prefer ? Not having wealth or the loss of it ? Loss of what has been obtained is very painful but not as not having wealth is. (22).

किंच—

मृत्युर्नृत्यति मूर्ध्नि शश्वदुरगी घोरा जरारूपिणी
त्वामेषा ग्रसते परिग्रहमयैर्गृध्रैर्जगद्ग्रस्यते ।
धूत्वा बोधजलैरबोधबहुलं तल्लोभजन्यं रजः
संतोषामृतसागराम्भसि मनाङ्मग्नः सुखं जीवति ॥२३॥

प्रतीहारी : एसो सामी । ता उवसप्पतु महाभाओ ।
[एष स्वामी । तदुपसर्पतु महाभागः ।]

(तथा कृत्वा)

संतोषः : जयतु जयतु स्वामी । एष संतोषः प्रणमति ।

राजा : इहोपविश्यताम् ।

(इति स्वसंनिधावुपवेशयति ।)

संतोषः : (सविनयमुपविश्य) एष प्रेष्यजनः । आज्ञाप्यतां देवेन ।

राजा : विदितप्रभाव एव भवान् । तदलमत्र विलम्बेन । लोभं जेतुं वाराणसीं प्रतिष्ठीयताम् ।

संतोषः : यदाज्ञापयति देवः । सोऽहम्—

नानामुखं विजयिनं जगतां त्रयाणां
देवद्विजातिवधबन्धनलुब्धवृत्तिम् ।
रक्षोधिनाथमिव दाशरथिः प्रसह्य
निर्जित्य लोभमवशं तरसा पिनष्मि ॥२४॥

(इति निष्क्रान्तः ।)

(ततः प्रविशति विनीतवेषः पुरुषः ।)

पुरुषः : देव, संभृतानि विजयप्रयाणमङ्गलानि । प्रत्यासन्नश्च मौहूर्तिकावेदितः प्रस्थानसमयः ।

राजा : यद्येवं सेनाप्रस्थानायादिश्यन्तां सेनापतयः ।

पुरुषः : यदाज्ञापयति देवः ।

(इति निष्क्रान्तः ।)

(नेपथ्ये ।)

Moreover,

Death dances constantly over your head, old age like a frightful serpent swallows you, the world is swallowed by the vultures who are your family. Wash off with the water of knowledge that dust (Rajas) which is born of Greed and consists mainly of ignorance. He who is immersed (even) a little in the water of the nectar-ocean of Contentment, lives happily. (23).

D. Keeper: Here is my Master. Please go near him.

(*Doing so*)

Content. : Victory to my Lord. Contentment prostrates.

King : Please be seated here (*makes him sit near*).

Content. : (*Sitting down humbly*) Here I am whom you sent for. Let my Lord command.

King : Your greatness is known. Therefore, let us not delay. To defeat Greed, start for Vārāṇasī.

Content. : I shall speedily, using my strength, conquer and shatter the helpless Greed, like the son of Daśaratha (Rāma), shattering the King of the Rākṣasas (Rāvaṇa) who had many faces (like Greed who acts in many ways), who was the conqueror of the three worlds and whose job was the killing and the binding of the gods and the twice-born (Brāhmaṇas), like that of a hunter. (24).

(*Exit*)

(Then enters a man in simple dress).

Man : My Lord, all the auspicious rites necessary for a victorious journey have been performed. And also the time fixed by the astrologers for your departure has come.

King : Then let the generals be told to order the army to march.

Man : As the Lord commands.

(*Behind the scenes*)

भो भोः सैनिकाः,

सज्ज्यन्तां कुम्भभित्तिच्युतमदमदिरामत्तभृङ्गाः करीन्द्रा
युज्यन्तां स्यन्दनेषु प्रसभजितमरुच्चण्डवेगास्तुरङ्गाः ।
कुन्तैर्नीलोत्पलानां वनमिव ककुभामन्तराले सृजन्तः
पादाताः संचरन्तु प्रसभमसिलसत्पाणयोऽप्यश्ववाराः ॥२५॥

राजा : भवतु। कृतमङ्गलाः प्रतिष्ठामहे। (पारिपार्श्वकं प्रति) सारथिरादिश्यतां साङ्ग्रामिकं रथं सज्जीकृत्वानयेति ।

पारिपार्श्वकः : यदाज्ञापयति देवः । (इति निष्क्रान्तः ।)

(ततः प्रविशति यथोक्तं रथमादाय सारथिः ।)

सारथिः : जीव, सज्जीकृतोऽयं रथः । तदारोहत्वायुष्मान् ।

राजा : (कृतमङ्गलविधिरारोहणं नाटयति ।)

सारथिः : (रथवेगं निरूपयित्वा) आयुष्मन्, पश्य पश्य ।

उद्धूतपांसुपटलानुमितप्रबन्ध-
धावत्खुराग्रचयचुम्बितभूमिभागाः ।
निर्मथ्यमानजलधिध्वनिघोरहेष-
मेते रथं गगनसीम्नि वहन्ति वाहाः ॥२६॥

इयं च नातिदूरे दर्शनपथमवतीर्णा त्रिभुवनपावनी वाराणसी नाम नगरी ।

अमी धारायन्त्रस्खलितजलभङ्कारमुखरा
विभाव्यन्ते भूयः शशिकररुचः सौधशिखराः ।
विचित्रा यत्रोच्चैः शरदमलमेघान्तविलस-
त्तडिल्लेखालक्ष्मीं वितरति पताकावलिरियम् ॥२७॥

Soldiers!

Get the elephants ready, drinking whose ichor flowing from their wall-like temples the bees are intoxicated, harness to the chariots the swift horses who have defeated in speed even the wind, let the foot-soldiers piercing the space in the sky with their spears, as if creating a lake of blue lotuses there, move (forward) and also the cavalry with swords shining in their hands. (25).

King : Well. As the auspicious rites have been performed, I shall march. (*to his attendant*). Order the charioteer to get ready the war chariot and bring it.

Attend. : As the Lord commands. (*Exit*).

(*Then enters the charioteer bringing the chariot as already described*).

Char. : My Lord! The chariot is ready. Let the Lord with long life be pleased to enter.

King : (*Having done the auspicious rites acts ascending the chariot*).

Chariot. : (*Showing the speed of the chariot*) See, see! These horses are carrying the chariots—the terrific sound of which equals the sound of the ocean being churned, to the borders of the sky. The fact that while running with speed the host of hoofs of the horses slightly touch the surface of the ground can be inferred by the layers of dust raised (26).

Here at close sight is the holy city of Vārāṇasī, which purifies the three worlds.

The tops of its mansions are seen again resplendant as the rays of the moon, noisy with the sound of water flowing from the fountains where the rows of many coloured flags on high spread the beauty of lightning which appears at the edge of the pure clouds in autumn. (27).

एताश्च प्रतिमुकुलं लग्नमधुपावलीरणितमुखरा जृम्भभरविगलन्मकरन्दबिन्दुदुर्दिनाः कुसुमसुरभयो नातिदूरे श्यामायमानघनच्छदच्छायातरवो नगरपर्यन्तोद्यानभूमयः। यत्रैते मरुतोऽपि गृहीतयाशुपतव्रता धूलिमुद्धूलयन्तास्तापसा इव लक्ष्यन्ते।

तथाहि—

तोयार्द्राः सुरसरितः सिताः परागै-
रर्चन्तश्च्युतकुसुमैरिवेन्दुमौलिम्।
प्रोद्गीतां मधुपरुतैः स्तुतिं पठन्तो
नृत्यन्ति प्रचललताभुजैः समीराः ॥२८॥

राजा : (सानन्दमालोक्य।)

सैषान्तर्दधती तमोविघटनादानन्दमात्मप्रभं
चेतः कर्षति चन्द्रचूडवसतिर्विद्येव मुक्तेः पदम्।
भूमेः कण्ठविलम्बिनीव कुटिला मुक्तावलिर्जाह्नवी
यत्रैवं हसतीव फेनपटलैर्वक्रां कलामैन्दवीम् ॥२९॥

सूतः : (परिक्रम्य) आयुष्मन्, पश्य पश्य। तदिदं सुरसरित्परिसरालंकारभूतं भगवतः पावनमनादेरादिकेशवस्य विष्णोरायतनम्।

राजा : (सहर्षम्।) अरे,

एष देवः पुराविद्भिः क्षेत्रस्यात्मेति गीयते।
अत्र देहं समुत्सृज्य पुण्यभाजो विशन्ति यम् ॥३०॥

सूतः : आयुष्मन्, पश्य पश्य। एते तावत्कामक्रोधलोभादयोऽस्मद्दर्शनमात्रादितो देशाद्दूरमतिक्रामन्ति।

Not far off and surrounding the city are gardens, with trees with thick foliage, which darken the place and give shade, which are fragrant with flowers, and which hum with the sound of bees around each bud and which create the appearance of a rainy day through the dripping of honey from the blossoming flowers, where even the winds sprinkling dust appear as mendicants of the Pāśupata sect. For

The winds dance with their arms in the form of moving creepers, are wet by the water of Gaṅgā, strewn with white pollen dust, worship the moon-crested one (Śiva) with fallen flowers and sing his praise through the sound of bees. (28).

King : (*Looking with joy*)

This city which is the abode of him who wears the moon as his crest, which is the place for (attaining) salvation, attracts the mind like knowledge giving bliss with the light of (enlightening) the self through the destruction of darkness (ignorance); here (in this city) the Gaṅgā river taking a bend appears to be a pearl necklace clinging round the neck of earth, and she with layers of foam appears to be laughing at the curved moon's digit. (29).

Chariot. : (*Turning around*) King with long life! See, see this in the holy temple of Lord Viṣṇu, the beginningless Ādikeśava, which decorates the banks of the river of gods (Gaṅgā).

King : (*With joy*) Well,

This is the God who is praised by the ancient Knowers to be the Soul of this place (self within the body). Laying aside the body here the virtuous people enter Him (become one with him). (30).

Chariot. : Look! Look! these people, Concupiscence, Anger Greed and others at the mere sight of us are going far away from this place.

राजा : एवमेतत् । तद्भवतु । स्वाभीष्टसिद्धये भगवन्तं नमस्यामः । (रथादवतीर्य प्रविश्यावलोक्य च ।) जय जय भगवन्, अमरचयचक्रचूडामणिश्रेणिनीराजितोपान्तपादद्वयाम्भोज राजन्नखद्योतखद्योतकिर्मीरितस्वर्णपीठस्फुरद्द्वैतविभ्रान्तिसंतानसंतप्तवन्दारुसंसारनिद्रापहारैकदक्ष क्षमामण्डलोद्धारसंभारसंघट्टदंष्ट्राग्रकोटिस्फुरच्छैलचक्र क्रमाक्रान्तलोकत्रय प्रबलभुजबलोद्धृतगोवर्धनच्छत्रनिवारिताखण्डलोद्योजिताकाण्डचण्डाम्बुवाहातिवर्षत्रसद्गोकुलत्राणविस्मापिताशेषविश्व प्रभो विबुधरिपुवधूवर्गसीमन्तसिन्दूरसन्ध्यामयूखच्छटोन्मार्जनोद्दामधामाधिप त्रस्तदैत्येन्द्रवक्षस्तटीपाटनाकुण्टभास्वन्नखश्रेणिपाणिद्वयत्रस्तविसारिरक्तार्णवामग्नलोकत्रय त्रिभुवनरिपुकैटभोद्दण्डकण्ठास्थिकूटस्फुटोन्मार्जितोद्दामचक्रस्फुरज्ज्योतिरुल्लासितोद्दामदोर्दण्डखण्डेन्दुचूडा प्रियप्रौढदोर्दण्डविभ्रान्त मन्थाचलक्षुब्धदुग्धाम्बुधिप्रोत्थितश्रीभुजवल्लीसंश्लेषसंक्रान्तपीनस्तनाभोगपत्रावलीलाञ्छितोरःस्थल स्थूलमुक्ताफलोदारहारप्रभामण्डलस्फुरत्कुण्ठवैकुण्ठ भक्तस्य लोकस्य संसारमोहच्छिदं देहि बोधोदय देव तुभ्यं नमः ।

(निर्गमनं नाटयित्वा विलोक्य च) साधुरयमेवास्माकं निवासोचितो देशः । तदत्रैव स्कन्धावारं निवेशयामः ।

(इति निष्क्रान्तौ ।)

King : It is so. Well. Let us worship the Lord for the fulfilment of our desire. (*Descends from the chariot, enters and looks*). Victory Oh Lord! the edges of your lotus-like feet are illumined by the rows of crest jewels (from the prostrated heads) of the host of gods, your golden foot-rest is made to appear dotted by the glow-worm like bright nails (of your feet), you alone are an expert in removing the sleep of worldly existence of your devotees who are suffering from the chains of illusions caused by (the belief in) Dvaita, (the rows of mountains shone on the edge) when your tusks you raised the earth and the mountains knocked against each other; you with your (three) strides encompassed the three worlds, you made the whole world wonder by holding up the mountain Govardhana with your strong arms, and used it as an umbrella and stopped the deluge of rains coming from the thick clouds out of season sent by Indra, and saved the cowherds; Oh Lord! you the possessor of great valour are known to remove the Sindūra which shines like the rays of the Sun at the dusk, from the fore-heads of the wives of the enemies of gods; the three worlds were drowned in the ocean of blood flowing from both the hands that had rows of shining nails which were not made blunt when you broke open the breast of the frightened Daitya King (Hiraṇyakaśipu), your strong arms shine from the light coming out of your powerful Cakra (discus) which has broken the bones of the strong neck of Kaiṭabha, the enemy of the three worlds. You are the beloved of the one who wears the digit of the Moon on his head (Śiva). Your chest is marked by the designs drawn on the big breasts of Lakṣmī, which was transferred (to your chest) when she embraced with her arms, Lakṣmī who came up from the milky ocean which was churned with the help of churning mountain by your strong arms, Oh Vaikuṇṭha! your neck shines with the lustre coming from the necklace made of big pearls, I prostrate before you, give your devotee the knowledge which will dispel the ignorance of Saṁsāra.

(*Acts as if proceeding and looking around*) Well, this is the right place where we can stay. Therefore let us pitch the tent here itself. (*Exeunt*)

पञ्चमोऽङ्कः

(ततः प्रविशति श्रद्धा ।)

श्रद्धा : (विचिन्त्य) प्रसिद्धः खल्वयं पन्थाः । यतः—

निर्दहति कुलविशेषं ज्ञातीनां वैरसंभवः क्रोधः ।
वनमिव घनपवनाहततरुवरसंघट्टसंभवो दहनः ॥१॥

(सास्रम् ।) अहो दुर्वारो दारुणः सोदरव्यसनजन्मा शोकानलः, यो विवेकजलधरशतैरपि न मन्दीक्रियते ! तथाहि—

ध्रुवं ध्वंसो भावी जलनिधिमहीशैलसरिता-
मतो मृत्योः शीर्यत्तृणलघुषु का जन्तुषु कथा ।
तथाप्युच्चैर्बन्धुव्यसनजनितः कोऽपि विषमो
विवेकप्रोन्माथी दहति हृदयं शोकदहनः ॥२॥

येन तथा कुलप्रकृतिष्वपि भ्रातृषु कामक्रोधादिषु कथाशेषतां गतेषु ।

निकृन्ततीव मर्माणि देहं शोषयतीव मे ।
दहतीवान्तरात्मानं क्रूरः शोकाग्निरुत्थितः ॥३॥

(विचिन्त्य ।) आदिष्टास्मि देव्या विष्णुभक्त्या । वत्से श्रद्धे, अहमत्र हिंसाप्रायसमरदर्शनपराङ्मुखी । तेन वाराणसीमुत्सृज्य शालिग्रामाभिधाने भगवतः क्षेत्रे कंचित्कालमतिपालयामि । त्वं तु यथावृत्तमागत्य मे निवेदयिष्यसीति । तदहं देव्याः सकाशं गत्वा सर्वमेतत्समरवृत्तान्तमावेदयामि । (परिक्रम्यावलोक्य च ।) एतच्चक्रतीर्थम्, यत्रासौ संसारसागरोत्तारतरणिकर्णधारो भगवान्हरिः स्वयं प्रतिवसति । (प्रणम्य ।) इयं च महामुनिभिरुपास्यमाना भगवती विष्णुभक्तिः शान्त्या सह किमपि मन्त्रयते । यावदुपसर्पामि । (इति परिक्रामति ।)

ACT V

(*Enters Faith*)

Faith : (*Thinking*) This fact is well known that—

Anger born out of hatred amongst kinsmen destroys the entire family as fire caused by friction among big trees hit by a violent wind, burns up the forest. (1).

(*Weeping*) Alas ! it is impossible to ward off the fire of grief caused by the death of brothers. This (fire) cannot be quenched even with hundreds of (rain) clouds of reason. For—

Destruction is certain (even) of the ocean, earth, mountains and rivers. Then what to say of the death of beings as insignificant as grass. Even then a certain vehement or impassable fire of grief caused by the death of relatives suppressing the reason is burning my heart very much. (2).

Thus on the death of my relations—Concupiscence, Anger etc., who are by nature fierce, a fierce fire of grief is aroused which cuts asunder my vitals, dries up my body, as if it is burning my inner self. (3).

(*Musing*) Goddess Devotion to Viṣṇu has commanded me: "My child, Faith, I abhor the sight of battles full of violence (violent battles). Therefore I shall leave Vārāṇasī and shall spend sometime in a place called Śāligrāma the abode of God. You will come and inform me as and how things happen." Therefore I shall go to the goddess (Viṣṇu Bhakti) and give her the entire account of the battle. (*Turning round and looking*). This is Cakratīrtha, where Lord Hari, himself dwells, the pilot of the boat which helps to cross the ocean of Saṁsāra. (*Prostrating*). This is the goddess Devotion to Viṣṇu, reverenced by great sages, saying something to Peace I shall go near. (*Turns*).

(ततः प्रविशति विष्णुभक्तिः शान्तिश्च ।)

शान्तिः : देवि, प्रबलचिन्ताकुलहृदयामिव भवतीमालोकयामि ।

विष्णुभक्तिः : वत्से, एतस्मिन्वीरवरक्षये महति सांपराये जाते न जाने बलवता महामोहेनाभियुक्तस्य वत्सविवेकस्य कीदृशो वृत्तान्त इति दुःस्थितमिव मे हृदयम् ।

शान्तिः : किमत्र विचिन्त्यते । ननु भगवती चेत्कृतानुग्रहा तन्नियतमेव राज्ञो विवेकस्य विजय इति जानामि ।

विष्णुभक्तिः : वत्से,

यदप्यभ्युदयः प्रायः प्रमाणादवधार्यते ।
कामं तथापि सुहृदामनिष्टाशङ्कि मानसम् ॥४॥

विशेषतश्च श्रद्धायाश्चिरमनागमनं मनसि संदेहमारोपयति ।

श्रद्धा : (उपसृत्य ।) भगवति, प्रणमामि ।

वष्णुभक्ति : श्रद्धे स्वागतम् ।

श्रद्धा : देव्याः प्रसादेन ।

शान्तिः : अम्ब, प्रणमामि ।

श्रद्धा : पुत्रि, मां परिष्वजस्व ।

शान्तिः : (तथा करोति ।)

श्रद्धा : वत्से, देव्या विष्णुभक्तेः प्रसादान्मुनिजनचेतः पदं प्राप्नुहि ।

विष्णुभक्तिः : अथ तत्र किं वृत्तम् ?

श्रद्धा : यद्देव्याः प्रतिकूलमाचरतामुचितम् ।

विष्णुभक्तिः : तद्विस्तरेणावेदय ।

(*Then enter Devotion to Viṣṇu and Peace*)

Peace : Goddess, Some deep thought seems to trouble your heart.

D. Viṣṇu : Child, My mind is troubled.

In this great battle which destroys the best of warriors, I do not know what has happened to my child Discrimination who is opposed to that strong Great Delusion. (On this account) my heart is troubled.

Peace : What is there to think ? I know that when the goddess has blessed the King, Discrimination's victory is certain.

D. Viṣṇu : Child,

Even when usually one is certain of victory, one's mind is apprehensive of unfavourable things happening to friends. (4).

Especially since Śraddhā has not come, my mind has become doubt-ridden.

Faith : (*Going near*) goddess, I prostrate.

D. Viṣṇu : Faith, you are welcome.

Faith : By your grace.

Peace : Mother, I bow to you.

Faith : Daughter, embrace me.

Peace : (*Does so*)

Faith : Child, by the grace of Devotion to Viṣṇu, you shall occupy a place in the hearts of sages.

D. Viṣṇu : Now what is the news ?

Faith : Those who act against you were dealt with properly.

D. Viṣṇu : Tell me in detail.

श्रद्धा : आकर्णयतु भवती । देव्यामादिकेशवायतनादपक्रान्तायामेव किंचिदुत्सृष्टपाटलिम्नि भगवति भास्वति, विजयघोषणाहूयमानानेकवरवीरबहुलतरसिंहनादबधिरितदिगन्ते संततरथतुरङ्गखुरखण्डितक्ष्मामण्डलोच्छलद्विपुलरजःपटलान्तरितकिरणमालिनि प्रबलतरकर्णतालास्फालनोच्छलत्समदकरिकुम्भसिन्दूरसन्ध्यायमानदशदिशि प्रलयजलधरध्वानभीषणे तेषामस्माकं संनद्धे सैन्यसागरे महाराजमहामोहस्य महाराजेन नैयायिकदर्शनं दौत्येन प्रहितम् । गत्वा च तेनोक्तो महामोहः ।

विष्णोरायतनान्यपास्य सरितां कूलान्यरण्यस्थलीः
पुण्यः पुण्यकृतां मनांसि च भवान्म्लेच्छान्व्रजेत्सानुजः
नो चेत्सन्तु कृपाणदारितभवत्प्रत्यङ्गधाराक्षर-
द्रक्तस्फीतविदीर्णवक्त्रविसरत्फेङ्कारिणः फेरवाः ॥ ५ ॥

विष्णुभक्तिः : ततस्ततः ?

श्रद्धा : ततो देवि, विकटललाटतटताण्डवितभ्रुकुटिना क्रुद्धेन महामोहेनाभिहितम् । अनुभवत्वस्य दुर्नयपरिपाकस्य विवेकहतकः फलमित्यभिधाय स्वयं पाखण्डागमाः पाखण्डतर्कशास्त्रैः समं समराय प्रथमं समुद्योजिताः । अत्रान्तरेऽस्माकमपि सैन्यशिरसि—

वेदोपवेदाङ्गपुराणधर्मशास्त्रेतिहासादिभिरुच्छ्रितश्रीः ।
सरस्वती पद्मधरा शशाङ्कसंकाशकान्तिः सहसाविरासीत् ॥ ६ ॥

Faith : Listen goddess. When you came away from the abode of Ādikeśava, when Sun god shed his redness a little (was rising), when the extremes of the (four) quarters were deafened by the roaring noise, like that of the lions, of the many great warriors trumpeting victory, the Sun was obscured incessantly by huge layers of dust raised from the earth by the chariots and the hoofs of the horses, when the ten directions were made to look like dusk by the Sindūra on the temples of the wild elephants flying when they flapped their huge ears, there in the ocean of armies whose noise was fierce with its sound like that of clouds during the deluge, (when) their and our armies were ready King (Discrimination) sent the Naiyāyika as a messenger to King Delusion with the message :

"You with your brothers go away from the abode of Viṣṇu, from the banks of rivers, from the holy places in the forests, and from the minds of pious people and reside among the Mlecchas (barbarians). If you do not go, the howling jackals with their faces smeared by the blood flowing from your body cut by the sword, shall roam about." (5).

D. Viṣṇu : Well, then,

Faith : Then, Oh goddess! King Delusion whose eyebrows were dancing on his broad forehead, out of anger said: 'Let the wretched Discrimination experience the fruit of this bad conduct' and then he himself sent first to the battle the heretic scriptures along with heretic logic. In the meantime at the head of our army,

Suddenly appeared the lotus bearing Sarasvatī, whose lustre is equal to that of the moon, and whose beauty is increased by Vedas, Vedāṅgas, Purāṇas, Dharmaśāstras, Itihāsa and others. (6).

विष्णुभक्तिः : ततस्ततः ?

श्रद्धा : ततो देवि, वैष्णवशैवसौरादयो देव्याः सकाशमागताः ।

विष्णुभक्तिः : ततस्ततः ?

श्रद्धा : तदनन्तरं च—

साङ्ख्यन्यायकणादभाषितमहाभाष्यादिशास्त्रवृता
स्फूर्जन्न्यायसहस्रबाहुनिकरैरुद्द्योतयन्ती दिशः ।
मीमांसा समरोत्सुकाविरभवद्धर्मेन्दुकान्तानना
वाग्देव्याः पुरतस्त्रयी त्रिनयना कात्यायनीवापरा ।।७।।

शान्तिः : अये, कथं पुनः स्वभावप्रतिद्वन्द्विनामागमानां तर्काणां च समवायः संपन्नः ?

श्रद्धा : पुत्रि,

समानान्वयजातानां परस्परविरोधिनाम् ।
परैः प्रत्यभिभूतानां प्रसूते संगतिः श्रियम् ।।८।।

येन वेदप्रसूतानां तेषामवान्तरविरोधेऽपि वेदसंरक्षणाय नास्तिकपक्षप्रतिक्षेपणाय शास्त्राणां साहित्यमेव । आगमानां च तत्त्वं विचारयतामविरोध एव ।

तथाहि—

ज्योतिः शान्तमनन्तमद्वयमजं तत्तद्गुणोन्मीलना-
द्ब्रह्मेत्यच्युत इत्युमापतिरिति प्रस्तूयतेऽनेकधा ।
तैस्तैरेव सदागमैः श्रुतिमुखैर्नानापथप्रस्थितै-
र्गम्योऽसौ जगदीश्वरो जलनिधिर्वारां प्रवाहैरिव ।।९।।

D. Viṣṇu : Well, then ?

Faith : Then, Oh goddess! the Vaiṣṇavas, Śaivas and Sauras came near the goddess (Sarasvatī).

D. Viṣṇu : And then?

Faith : After that

There appeared in front of the goddess of Speech, Mīmāṁsā, eager for fighting, appearing like another Pārvatī with her face beautiful like the Moon of Dharma, and the three Vedas her three eyes, surrounded by the Sāṁkhya, Nyāya, Vaiśeṣika (the work of Kaṇāda), Mahābhāṣya and other Śāstras and pointing out towards the directions with her thousand hands in the form of exploding Nyāya. (7).

Peace : But how came to effect such a union of the Śāstras, which are by nature opposed to each other and logic ?

Faith : Daughter,

When those (schools) who have a common origin though mutually opposed join together when attacked by a (common) enemy good comes out of that union. (8).

They (the Śāstras) born from the Vedas, though they are opposed to each other internally, unite together to over-throw the non-believers (in the Vedas) and protect the Vedas. Those who reflect on the truth of the Śāstras do not really contradict each other.

For—

The tranquil, endless, invisible, unborn Light is variously praised as Brahmā, Acyuta (Viṣṇu), Umāpati (Śiva) according to the predominance of qualities. Thus, the Lord of the Universe can be attained through various good systems which are based on the Vedas and have taken diverse paths, just as the ocean is reached by streams of water. (9).

विष्णुभक्तिः : ततस्ततः ।

श्रद्धा : ततो देवि, परस्परं करितुरगपदातीनां निरन्तरशरनिकरधारा-संपातोपदर्शितदुर्दिनानां तेषामस्माकं च योधानां सङ्ग्रामस्तुमुल-संप्रहारः प्रावर्तत । तथाहि—

बहुलरुधिरतोयास्तत्र सस्रुः स्रवन्त्यो
निबिडपिशितपङ्काः कङ्करङ्कावकीर्णाः ।
शरदलितविदीर्णोत्तुङ्गमातङ्गशैल-
स्खलितरयविशीर्णच्छत्रहंसावतंसाः ॥ १० ॥

तस्मिन्नेवातिमहति महादारुणे सङ्ग्रामे परापरपक्ष-विरोधितया पाषण्डागमैरग्रेसरीकृतं लोकायतं तन्त्रमन्योन्य-सैन्यविमर्दनैर्नष्टम् । अन्ये तु पाषण्डागमा मूलनिर्मूलतया सदागमार्णवप्रवाहेण पर्यस्ताः । सौगतास्तावत्सिन्धुगान्धार-पारसिकमागधान्ध्रहूणवङ्गकलिङ्गादीन्म्लेच्छप्रायान्प्रविष्टाः । पाषण्डदिगम्बरकापालिकादयस्तु पामरबहुलेषु पाञ्चालमालवा-भीरावर्तभूमिषु सागरोपान्तनिगूढं संचरन्ति । न्यायाद्यनु-गतमीमांसयावगाढप्रहारजर्जरीकृता नास्तिकतर्कास्तेषामेवागमा-नामनुपथं प्रयाताः ?

विष्णुभक्तिः : ततस्ततः ?

श्रद्धा : ततो वस्तुविचारेण कामो हतः, क्षमया क्रोधपारुष्यहिंसादयो निपातिताः, सन्तोषेण लोभतृष्णादैन्यानृतपैशुन्यवाक्स्तेयासत्प्रति-ग्रहादयो निगृहीताः, अनसूयया मात्सर्यं जितम्, परोत्कर्ष-संभावनया मदो निषूदितः, परगुणाधिक्येन मानः खण्डितः ।

D. Viṣṇu : Then.

Faith : Then, Goddess, there began the battle of dreadful encounters between our soldiers and theirs, who created the appearance of a rainy day with elephants, horses and foot-soldiers by the incessant shower of the host of arrows. For—

There the rivers of abundant blood as their waters flew, whose mud was pieces of flesh (lying) in plenty, were covered with wretched birds; the huge elephants which were shattered by the arrows and were scattered (here and there) formed the rocks, and stopped their speed, whose ear-ornaments were the umbrellas fallen here and there that looked like haṁsa birds. (10).

In that great and fierce battle, the materialist who is opposed to both the parties (the Vaidika and Advaitika) was placed in the front by the heretics and was killed in the conflict (between two armies). The other anti-Vedic schools were destroyed by the flow of the ocean of Vedic thoughts. The Buddhists entered the almost barbarous countries of Sindhus, Gāndhāras, Pārasīkas, Māgadhas, Āndhras, Hūṇas, Vaṅgas, Kaliṅgas etc. The heretic Digambaras (Jaina), Kāpālikas and others live hidden in the Pāñcālas, Mālavas, Ābhīras and Āvarta near the ocean, which (countries) abound in illiterates. The logic of the anti-Vedic schools shattered by the Mīmāṁsā accompanied by Nyāya had the same fate of the (heretic) śāstras.

D. Viṣṇu : What happened then?

Faith : Concupiscence was defeated by Investigation into Truth. Anger, Harshness, Injury etc. were defeated by Patience, Contentment subdued Greed, Desire Helplessness, Falsehood, Slander, Theft, Acceptance of a Bad Path etc; Spite has been defeated by Non-spite, Arrogance was killed by Respect for others' virtues and Conceit was put an end to by excess of Superior qualities.

विष्णुभक्तिः : (सहर्षम्) साधु साधु संपन्नम् । अथ महामोहस्य को वृत्तान्तः ?

श्रद्धा : देवि, महामोहोऽपि योगोपसर्गैः सह न ज्ञायते क्वापि निलीनस्तिष्ठतीति ।

विष्णुभक्ति : अस्ति तर्हि महाननर्थशेषः । प्रहरणीयश्चासौ । यतः—

अनादरपरो विद्वानीहमानः स्थिरां श्रियम् ।
अग्नेः शेषमृणाच्छेषं शत्रोः शेषं न शेषयेत् ।।११।।

अथ मनसः को वृत्तान्तः ?

श्रद्धा : देवि, तेनापि पुत्रपौत्रादिव्यसनजनितशोकावेशेन जीवोत्सर्गाय व्यवसितम् ।

विष्णुभक्तिः : (स्मितं कृत्वा।) यद्येवं स्यात्सर्व एव वयं कृतकृत्या भवामः । पुरुषश्च परां निर्वृतिमापत्स्यते । किंतु कुतस्तस्य दुरात्मनो जीवत्यागः ?

श्रद्धा : एवं देव्यां प्रबोधोदयाय गृहीतसंकल्पायामचिरं शरीरेण सह नैव भविष्यति ।

विष्णुभक्तिः : तद्भवतु । अस्य वैराग्योत्पत्तये वैयासिकीं सरस्वतीं प्रेषयामः ।

(इति निष्क्रान्तौ ।)

प्रवेशकः ।

(ततः प्रविशति मनः संकल्पश्च ।)

मनः : (सास्रम् ।) हा पुत्रकाः, क्व गताः स्थ । दत्त मे प्रियदर्शनम् । भो भोः कुमारकाः रागद्वेषमदमात्सर्यादयः, परिष्वजध्वं माम् । सीदन्ति ममाङ्गानि। हा न कश्चिन्मां वृद्धमनाथं संभावयति ! क्व गता असूयादयः कन्यकाः ? आशातृष्णाहिंसादयो वा स्नुषाः ? कथं ता अपि मन्दभाग्यस्य मे समकालमेव दैवहतकेनापहृताः ?

D. Viṣṇu : (*Joyfully*). Well done. What news of Great Delusion ?

Faith : Goddess, it is not known where Great Delusion has hidden himself along with the Obstacles of Yoga.

D. Viṣṇu : If so the great danger is still there. He should be destroyed.

A wise person desiring lasting good will not be careless and leave behind remnants of fire, debt and enemy. (11).

But what news of Mind?

Faith : Oh Goddess! he too overcome with grief for the loss of his sons and grand-children, has made up his mind to put an end to his life.

D. Viṣṇu : (*Smiling*). If it is so, our work is accomplished. Man also shall attain supreme bliss. But where is that wicked one going to end his life ?

Faith : When the goddess is thus determined to bring about the rise of awakening, he will not remain with his body (alive) for long.

D. Viṣṇu : Well, we shall send Sarasvatī, daughter of Vyāsa to arouse Dispassionateness in him.

(*Exit*)

Interlude.

(*Then enter Mind and Determination*)

Mind : (*Weeping*) Alas, my sons! where have you gone? Let me look at your beloved faces Embrace me my sons, Passion, Hatred, Arrogance, Spite and others. My limbs are affected. Ha! nobody cares for me who am old and destitute! Where are my daughters Spite and others? And where are my daughters-in-law Hope, Desire, Injury and others ? What, have they been all slain at the same time by the wretched person because of my bad luck!

विसर्पति विषाग्निवद्दहति सर्वमर्माविध-
स्तनोति भृशवेदनाः कषति सर्वकार्श्यं वपुः ।
विलुम्पति विवेकितां हृदि च मोहमुन्मूलय-
त्यहो ग्रसति जीवितं प्रसभमेव शोकज्वरः ॥१२॥

(इति मूर्च्छितं पतति ।)

संकल्पः : (सास्रम् ।) राजन्, समाश्वसिहि समाश्वसिहि ।

मनः : (समाश्वस्य ।) कथं देवी प्रवृत्तिरपि न मामेवमवस्थं समाश्वासयति ।

संकल्पः : (सास्रम्) देव, कुतोऽद्यापि प्रवृत्तिः । यतः श्रुतकुटुम्बव्यसनसंजातशोकानलदग्धहृदया हृदयास्फोटं विनष्टा ।

मनः : हा प्रिये, क्वासि देहि मे प्रतिवचनम् । ननु देवि,

स्वप्नेऽपि देवि रमसे न विना मया त्वं
स्वापे त्वया विरहितो मृतवद्भवामि ।
दूरीकृतासि विधिदुर्ललितैस्तथापि
जीवत्यवेहि मन इत्यसवो दुरन्ताः ॥ १३ ॥

(पुनर्मूर्च्छति ।)

संकल्पः : राजन्, समाश्वसिहि समाश्वसिहि ।

मनः : (समाश्वस्य ।) अलमस्माकमतः परं जीवितेन । संकल्प, चितामारचय । यावदनलप्रवेशेन शोकानलं निर्वापयामि ।

(ततः प्रविशति वैयासिकी सरस्वती ।)

सरस्वती : प्रेषितास्मि भगवत्या विष्णुभक्त्या । यथा 'सखि सरस्वति, गच्छापत्यव्यसनखिन्नस्य मनसः प्रबोधनाय । यथा च तस्य वैराग्योत्पत्तिर्भवति तथा यतस्वेति' । तद्भवतु । तत्संनिधिमेवोपसर्पामि : (उपसृत्य) वत्स किमेवमतिविक्लवोऽसि ? ननु विदितपूर्वैव भवता भावानामनित्यता, अधीतानि च त्वयैतिहासिकान्युपाख्यानानि । तथाहि—

Oh! This fever of grief spreads (all over the body) like the fire of poison, it pierces all my vital parts, causes great pain and wounds my body which is already wounded, destroys my reasoning power and produces delusion in the heart. Thus it forcibly devours my life. (12).

(*Falls unconscious*).

Deter. : (*With tears*) Oh King! be comforted.

Mind : (*Reviving*) What! Even Lady Activity does not console me who am in this condition?

Deter. : (*Tearfully*) My Lord, where is Activity now? She died of broken heart, her heart already burnt by the fire of grief born out of hearing the loss of her family.

Mind : My dear, where are you? Reply to me! Well dear, you, who even in dream did not enjoy without me, without you whom in deep sleep I become like dead, you are separated from me by bad luck, yet mind continues to live. Life does not depart so easily. (13).

(*Again faints*)

Deter. : Oh King! be comforted.

Mind : (*Consoled*) Enough of my living hereafter. Determination, get the pyre ready so that I can put an end to the fire of grief by entering fire.

(*Then enters Sarasvatī daughter of Vyāsa*)

Sarasvatī : I am sent by Goddess Devotion to Viṣṇu thus "Friend Sarasvatī, go to enlighten Mind who is miserable because of the death of his children and try to arouse dispassion in him". Well, let me go near him (*going near*) Son, why are you so upset? It is known to you that all the beings

भूत्वा कल्पशतायुषोऽम्बुजभवः सेन्द्राश्च देवासुरा
मन्वाद्या मुनयो मही जलधयो नष्टाः परं कोटयः ।
मोहः कोऽयमहो महानुदयते लोकस्य शोकावहः
सिन्धोः फेनसमे गते वपुषि यत्पञ्चात्मके पञ्चताम् ॥१४॥

तद्भावय भावानामनित्यताम् । नित्यमनित्यवस्तुदर्शनो न पश्यति शोकावेगम् । यतः--

एकमेव सदा ब्रह्म सत्यमन्यद्विकल्पितम् ।
को मोहस्तत्र कः शोक एकत्वमनुपश्यतः ॥१५॥

मनः : भगवति, शोकवेगदूषिते मनसि विवेक एवमनवकाशं लभते ।

सरस्वती : वत्स, स्नेहदोष एषः । प्रसिद्ध एवायमर्थः स्नेहः सर्वानर्थप्रभव इति ।

तथाहि--

उप्यन्ते विषवल्लिबीजविषमाः क्लेशाः प्रियाख्या नरै-
स्तेभ्यः स्नेहमया भवन्ति नचिराद्वज्राग्निगर्भाङ्कुराः ।
येभ्योऽमी शतशः कुकूलहुतभुग्दाहं दहन्तः शनै-
र्देहं दीप्तशिखासहस्रशिखरा रोहन्ति शोकद्रुमाः ॥१६॥

मनः : देवि, यद्यप्येवं तथापि न शक्नोमि शोकानलदग्धः प्राणान्धारयितुम् । संपन्नं यदन्तकाले त्वं तावद्दृष्टासि ।

सरस्वती : इदं च परमकृत्यं यदात्महत्याव्यवसाय इति । अपि च । अमीषामपकारिणामर्थे कोऽयमत्यावेशो भवतः । पश्य तावत्--

are transitory, you have studied traditional accounts and tales. Brahmā (the Lotus born), gods along with Indra and demons, Manu and others, sages, Earth, Ocean and other crores of people having been born and having lived for hundreds of Kalpas perish. Then why is this Great Delusion causing grief to the people born when the body which is like the foam on the sea dissolves into those five elements of which it is composed. (14).

Therefore reflect upon the non-eternal nature of things. He who sees the eternal does not see the flurry of grief. For—

Brahman is one, eternal and is truth. All else is imaginary. What delusion or what grief can there be for him who sees the Oneness ? (15).

Mind : Goddess, Discrimination cannot find a place in the mind which is corrupted by the flurry of grief. (15).

Sarasvati : Child, this is the fault of attachment. This fact is well known that 'attachment is the source of all evils.' For—

Men sow troubles in the form of the so-called fondness, which are as dangerous as the seeds of a poisonous creeper. From which then quickly spring up shoots in the form of affection which are full of fire as dangerous as lightning. From that grow the trees of sorrow in hundreds, with the thousand branches burning with flames, which slowly burn the body like the burning of the fire in the husk (of grains). (16).

Mind : Goddess, still it is impossible for me to carry on my life which is already burnt by the fire of grief. It is my good fortune that I have seen you at the time of my death.

Sarasvati: This attempt of suicide by you is a great crime. And also, this great devotion of yours towards those who do harm to you. See.

क्वचिदुपकृतिः कर्तामीभिः कृता क्रियतेऽथवा
तव न च भवन्त्येते पुंसां सुखाय परिग्रहाः ।
दधति विरहे मर्मच्छेदं तदर्थमपार्थकं
तदपि विपुलायासाः सीदन्त्यहो बत जन्तवः ॥ १७ ॥

अपि च,

तीर्णाः पूर्णाः कति न सरितो लङ्घिताः के न शैला
नाक्रान्ता वा कति वनभुवः क्रूरसंचारघोराः ।
पापैरेतैः किमिव दुरितं कारितो नासि कष्टं
यद्दृष्टास्ते धनमदमषोम्लानवक्त्रा दुरीशाः ॥ १८ ॥

मनः : देवि, एवमेतत् । तथापि—

लालितानां स्वजातानां हृदि संचरतां चिरम् ।
प्राणानामिव विच्छेदो मर्मच्छेदादरुंतुदः ॥ १९ ॥

सरस्वती : वत्स, ममतावासनानिबन्धनोऽयं व्यामोहः ।
उक्तं च—

मार्जारभक्षिते दुःखं यादृशं गृहकुक्कुटे ।
न तादृङ्ममताशून्ये कलविङ्केऽथ मूषके ॥२०॥

तत्सर्वानर्थबीजस्य ममत्वस्योच्छेदे यत्नः कर्तव्यः । पश्य—

प्रादुर्भवन्ति वपुषः कति वा न कीटा
यान्यत्नतः खलु तनोरपसारयन्ति ।
मोहः स एष जगतो यदपत्यसंज्ञां
तेषां विधाय परिशोषयति स्वदेहम् ॥ २१ ॥

मनः : देवि, भवत्वेवम् । तथापि दुरुच्छेद्यस्तु ममत्वग्रन्थिः । (विचिन्त्य । सोच्छ्वासम् ।) सर्वथा त्रातोऽस्मि भवत्या । (इति पादयोः पतति ।)

Wives, children and other relations are never for the happiness of men. This has never happened before, it shall not happen and it does not happen. In their absence they cause extreme pain. It is astonishing that even then people suffer making great effort for their sake in vain. (17).

Moreover—

How many flooded rivers are not crossed, how many mountains are not ascended and how many forests which are fierce with the movements of wild animals are not travelled through. What difficult task is there which you were not made to do by these sinners ? You were made to face wicked masters whose faces were polluted by the soot of the arrogance caused by wealth. (18).

Mind : Goddess, It is so. Even then.

To part with one's own offspring who were fondled and who remain in the heart is as painful as to give up one's own life. (19).

Sarasvatī : Child, this delusion is caused by the feeling of mine. It is said.

The grief caused when the demestic fowl is eaten by the cat is not the same as when the sparrow or mouse is eaten, where there is no feeling of mine. (20).

Therefore, you should try to remove the feeling of mineness, which is the seed of all evils. See. How many insects are born on the body and yet people by hand remove them from the body. So it is an illusion to give the name of "Children" to them and afflict one's body. (21).

Mind : Goddess, let it be so. Even then the knot of mineness cannot be cut asunder (*Thinking and taking a breath*). In all respects I am saved by you (*Falls at her feet*).

सरस्वती : वत्स, उपदेशसहिष्णु ते हृदयं जातम् । अत एतदपरमुच्यते--

वशं प्राप्ते मृत्योः पितरि तनये वा सुहृदि वा
शुचा संतप्यन्ते भृशमुदरताडं जडधियः ।
असारे संसारे विरसपरिणामे तु विदुषां
वियोगो वैराग्यं द्रढयति वितन्वञ्शमसुखम् ॥२२॥

(ततः प्रविशति वैराग्यम् ।)

वैराग्यम् : (विचिन्त्य ।)

अस्राक्षीन्नवनीलनीरदजलोपान्तातिसूक्ष्मायत-
त्वङ्मात्रान्तरितामिषं यदि वपुर्नैतत्प्रजानां पतिः ।
प्रत्यग्रक्षरदस्रविस्रपिशितग्रासग्रहं गृध्नतो
गृध्रध्वाङ्क्षवृकास्तनौ निपतिताः को वा कथं वारयेत् ॥२३॥

अपि च,

श्रियो ज्वालालोला विषयजरसाः प्रान्तविरसा
विपद्गेहं देहं महदपि धनं भूरि निधनम् ।
बृहच्छोको लोकः सततमबलानर्थबहुला
तथाप्यस्मिन्घोरे पथि बत रता नात्मनि रताः ॥२४॥

सरस्वती : वत्स, एतद्वैराग्यं त्वामुपस्थितम् । तदेतत्संभावय ।

मनः : क्वासि पुत्रक ?

वैराग्यम् : (उपसृत्य) अहं भो अभिवादये ।

मनः : वत्स, जातमात्रेण त्वया त्यक्तोऽस्मि । परिष्वजस्व माम् ।

वैराग्यम् : (तथा करोति ।)

मनः : वत्स, त्वद्दर्शनात्प्रशान्तो मे शोकावेशः ।

वैराग्यम् : तात, कोऽत्र शोकावेशः ? यतः--

Sarasvati : My child, your heart has become now willing to take advice. Therefore, I shall tell you more. Fools beat their belly and are afflicted by grief when their father, son or friend become subject to death. For the wise in this world which is essenceless and which is miserable in the end, separation strengthens their dispassionateness and gives the happiness of calmness. (22).

(*Then enters Dispassionateness*).

Dispassion: (*Thinking*) If Prajapati (the Creator) had not created the body with the flesh covered merely with the skin big and delicate like the edge of a fresh blue lotus, how could have any one stopped the vultures, crows and wolves falling on the body with the object of seizing the mouthfuls of raw smelling flesh with blood flowing fresh (23). Moreover,

Prosperity is fickle like the flames of fire, the pleasures born out of sense-objects result in disgust, the body is the abode of miseries, even great wealth is very perilous, the world is a great misery, woman is perpetually harmful, but inspite of all these people are interested in this terrible path but no one is interested in the (knowledge of) Self. (24).

Sarasvatī : Child, Dispassionateness has come to you. Receive him with respect.

Mind : My son! where are you ?

Dispas. : (*Going near*) Sir, I salute you.

Mind : You left me as soon as you were born. Embrace me.

Dispas. : (*Does so*).

Mind : Child, seeing you, the flurry of my grief has been calmed down.

Dispas. : Father, what is this flurry of grief ? For, when the

पान्थानामिव वर्त्मनि क्षितिरुहां नद्यामिव भ्रश्यतां
मेघानामिव पुष्करे जलनिधौ सांयात्रिकाणामिव ।
संयोगः पितृमातृबन्धुतनयभ्रातृप्रियाणां यदा
सिद्धो दूरवियोग एव विदुषां शोकोदयः कस्तदा ॥२५॥

मनः : (सानन्दम् ।) देवि, एवमेतद् यदाह वत्सः। तथाहि तावदवधारयतु भवती ।

निरन्तराभ्यासदृढीकृतस्य
सस्नेहसूत्रग्रथितस्य जन्तोः ।
जानासि किंचिद्भगवत्युपायं
ममत्वपाशस्य यतो विमोक्षः ॥२६॥

सरस्वती : वत्स, भावानामनित्यताभावनमेव तावन्ममतोच्छेदस्य प्रथमोऽभ्युपायः । तथाहि--

न कति पितरो दाराः पुत्राः पितृव्यपितामहा
महति वितते संसारेऽस्मिन्गतास्तव कोटयः ।
तदिह सुहृदां विद्युत्पातोज्ज्वलान्क्षणसंगमान्
सपदि हृदये भूयो भूयो निवेश्य सुखी भव ॥२७॥

मनः : भगवति, तव प्रसादादपास्त एव व्यामोहः । किन्तु—

भगवति तव मुखशशधरगलितैर्विमलोपदेशपीयूषैः ।
क्षालितमपि मे हृदयं मलिनं शोकोर्मिभिः क्रियते ॥२८॥

तदस्यार्द्रस्य शोकप्रहारस्य भेषजमाज्ञापयतु भगवती ।

सरस्वती : वत्स, नूनमुपदिष्टमेवात्र मुनिभिः ।

अकाण्डपातजातानामार्द्राणां मर्मभेदिनाम्
गाढशोकप्रहाराणामचिन्तैव महौषधम् ॥२९॥

मनः : एवमेव भगवत्येतद्दुर्वारं नु चेतः । यतः—

अप्येतद्वारितं चिन्तासन्तानैरभिभूयते ।
मुहुर्वाताहतैर्बिम्बभ्रमच्छेदैरिवैन्दवम् ॥३०॥

coming together of father, mother, relations, sons brothers and dear ones definitely ends in their separation, like the coming together of travellers on the road, like the fallen trees on the river, like the clouds in the sky and like the co-passengers in a ship, where is the cause of misery for the wise ? (25).

Mind : (*With joy*). Goddess, what my son says is true. For let the Goddess ascertain for herself. Do you know of any device to free the person, who is bound with the thread of attachment and whose bondage is tightened by constant practice, from the bondage of 'Mineness'? (26).

Sarasvatī: Child, the first device to get rid of 'Mineness' is meditation on the transitoriness of beings. For— In this well-spread great Universe how many crores of your fathers, wives, sons, uncles and grandfathers have gone. Therefore resolving in your heart again and again that the meeting of friends is as short-lived as the lightning, be happy. (27).

Mind : Goddess, by your blessing my delusion is removed. But, Goddess, my heart even though washed by the nectar of the pure advice flowing from your face-moon is made impure by the waves of grief. Therefore will the Goddess prescribe a medicine for this fresh attack of grief? (28).

Sarasvatī: Child, well, has it been prescribed by the sages. 'Absence of anxiety' is the great medicine for the violent attacks of fresh grief which come unexpectedly, which pierce the vitals. (29).

Mind : Yes, my Goddess, this mind is uncontrollable. Even when it is controlled it is overpowered by the trains of thought as the disc of the moon is over powered by the layers of clouds brought about by the wind again and again. (30).

सरस्वती : वत्स, श्रूयताम् । चित्तस्यायं विकारः । ततः कस्मिंश्चिच्छान्ते विषये चित्तं निवेश्यताम् ।

मनः : तत्प्रसीदतु भगवती । कोऽसौ शान्तो विषयः ?

सरस्वती : वत्स, गुह्यमेतत् तथाप्यार्तानामुपदेशे न दोषः ।

नित्यं स्मरञ्जलदनीलमुदारहार-
केयूरकुण्डलकिरीटधरं हरिं वा ।
ग्रीष्मे सुशीतमिव वा ह्रदमस्तशोकं
ब्रह्म प्रविश्य भज निर्वृतिमात्मनीनाम् ॥३१॥

मनः : एवमेतत् । संप्रति हि—

नार्यस्ता नवयौवना मधुकरव्याहारिणस्ते द्रुमाः
प्रोन्मीलन्नवमल्लिकासुरभयो मन्दास्त एवानिलाः ।
अद्योदात्तविवेकमार्जिततमःस्तोमव्यलीकान्पुन-
स्तानेतान्मृगतृष्णिकार्णवपयःप्रायान्मनः पश्यति ॥३२॥

सरस्वती : वत्स, यद्यप्येवं तथापि गृहिणा मुहूर्तमप्यनाश्रमधर्मिणा न भवितव्यम् । तदद्यप्रभृति निवृत्तिरेव ते सधर्मचारिणी ।

मनः : (सलज्जम् ।) यदादिशति देवी ।

सरस्वती : शमदमसंतोषादयश्च पुत्रास्त्वामनुचरन्तु । यमनियमादयश्चामात्याः । विवेकोऽपि त्वदनुग्रहादुपनिषद्देव्या सह यौवराज्यमनुभवतु । एताश्च मैत्र्यादयश्चतस्रो भगिन्यो भगवत्या विष्णुभक्त्या तव प्रसादनाय प्रहितास्ताः सप्रसादमनुमानय ।

मनः : यदादिशति देवी । मूर्ध्नि निवेशिताः सर्वा एवाज्ञाः ।
(इति सहर्षं पादयोः पतति ।)

Sarasvatī : Child, listen. This is only a perversion of the mind. Therefore concentrate your mind on a peaceful object.

Mind : My Goddess, be pleased. What is this peaceful object ?

Sarasvatī : Child, this is a secret. Even then there is no harm in giving advice to those who are really miserable. Think perpetually of Hari, who is dark blue as a cloud and who wears a splendid necklace, bracelets, ear-rings and a diadem, or be one with the Brahman which is free from grief and is like a cool pond in summer and enjoy the bliss belonging to your self. (31).

Mind : It is so. Now.

The women are the same possessing fresh youth, the same trees full of bees, the same soft breeze fragrant with the newly opening Mallikās, but the mind today sees these as appearances like the water of the ocean of mirage as the form of darkness which is washed by discrimination. (32).

Sarasvatī : Child, even if it is so, a house-holder should not give up the house-holder's duty even for a moment. Therefore, Resignation will be your spouse from now onwards.

Mind : (*Bashfully*) As the Goddess commands.

Sarasvatī : Let the sons, Tranquillity, Self Restraint and Content accompany you. Morality and Observance shall be thy Ministers. Discrimination shall through your blessings have the post of heir-apparent with sacred Lore as his consort. Receive the four sisters, Friendliness, Joy, Compassion and Reason sent by Devotion to Viṣṇu to please you.

Mind : As the Goddess commands. All your commands are laid on my head (*prostrates at her feet happily*).

सरस्वती : साम्राज्यमनुतिष्ठस्व । एते च यमनियमादयः सादरमायुष्मता द्रष्टव्याः । एतैरेव सहायुष्मान्यौवराज्यमधितिष्ठतु । त्वयि च स्वास्थ्यमापन्ने क्षेत्रज्ञोऽपि स्वां प्रकृतिमापत्स्यते । यतः—

त्वत्सङ्गाच्छाश्वतोऽपि प्रणयजलधरोपप्लुतो बुद्धिवृत्ति-
ष्वेको नानेव देवो रविरिव जलधेर्वीचिषु व्यक्तमूर्तिः ।
तूष्णीमालम्बसे चेत्कथमपि वितता वत्स संहृत्य वृत्ती-
र्भात्यादर्शे प्रसन्ने रविरिव सहजानन्दसान्द्रस्तदात्मा ॥३३॥

तद्भवतु । ज्ञातीनामुदकदानाय नदीमवतरामः ।

मनः : यदाज्ञापयति देवी ।

(इति निष्क्रान्ताः सर्वे ।)

इति प्रबोधचन्द्रोदये वैराग्यप्रादुर्भावो नाम पञ्चमोऽङ्कः ।

Sarasvatī: Enjoy sovereignty now. Let these Morality, Observance and others be treated by you with respect. Along with these be you the Crown Prince when you recover your health (Natural state), the Jīva also will attain his natural state. For—

It is due to the association with you that the one eternal God (i. e. Puruṣa) is overwhelmed by the clouds of affection and appears in a manifested form (as if he were many) in the functions of the intellect, as the (one) Sun (appears as many) in the waves of the ocean. If you my dear, remainest quiet, somehow withdrawing your extended functions, then his self will shine forth with his innate intense bliss like the Sun (reflected) in a clear mirror. (33).

Let it be so. Let us get into the river to pay homage to our relatives.

Mind : As the Goddesss commands.

(*Exeunt omnes*)

षष्ठोऽङ्कः

(ततः प्रविशति शान्तिः ।)

शान्तिः : आदिष्टास्मि महाराजविवेकेन । तथा वत्से, विदितमेव भवत्या किल ।

अस्तं गतेषु तनयेषु विलीनमोहे
वैराग्यभाजि मनसि प्रशमं प्रपन्ने ।
क्लेशेषु पञ्चसु गतेषु समं समीहां
तत्त्वावबोधमभितः पुरुषस्तनोति ॥ १ ॥

तद्भवती त्वरिततरं देवीमुपनिषदमनुनीय मत्सकाशमानयत्विति ।

(विलोक्य) ममाम्बा सहर्षं किमपि मन्त्रयन्ती इत एवागच्छति ।

(ततः प्रविशति श्रद्धा ।)

श्रद्धा : अये, अद्य खलु राजकुलमारोग्ययुक्तमालोक्य चिरेण मे पीयूषेणेव लोचने पूर्णे ।

असतां निग्रहो यत्र सन्तः पूज्या यमादयः ।
आराध्यते जगत्स्वामी वश्यैर्देवानुजीविभिः ॥ २ ॥

शान्तिः : (उपसृत्य) अम्ब, किं मन्त्रयन्ती प्रस्थिता ?

श्रद्धा : (अये, अद्येत्यादि पठति ।)

शान्तिः : अथ मनसि कीदृशी स्वामिनः पुरुषस्य प्रवृत्तिः ?

श्रद्धा : यादृशी वध्यस्य ग्राह्यस्य भवति ।

शान्तिः : तत्किं स्वाम्येव साम्राज्यमलंकरिष्यति ?

श्रद्धा : एवमेतत् यथात्मानमनुसंधत्ते ततो देव एव स्वाराट् सम्राट् च भवति ।

ACT VI

(Then enters Śānti)

Peace : I am commanded by king Discrimination thus:— Child, it is known to you (that)

After the sons (of Mind) have perished, after Delusion has vanished, after Mind associated with Dispassionateness has become tranquil and the five troubles (Kleśas) have disappeared simultaneously, Man's desire towards the awakening of Truth is born. (1).

Therefore go quickly and bring Goddess Upaniṣad to me after pacifying her. (*Looking*). My mother is coming this side murmuring something.

(Then enters Faith.)

Faith : Well, seeing the Royal family free from (illness) troubles, today my eyes are filled with nectar (of happiness).

Where the wicked are destroyed, the good Self-restraint etc. are revered and the Lord of the Universe is worshipped by the dependents of the Lord (Jivas) who are under His control. (2).

Peace : (*Going near*) Mother, Murmuring what, are you coming?

Faith : (*Repeats* Well, etc.)

Peace : Well, what is the attitude of the Supreme Man towards Mind ?

Faith : Just as it would be towards a captive who deserved to be killed.

Peace : What then, is the Lord himself going to assume Sovereignty ?

Faith : It is so. When he inquires into himself then He himself becomes one who shines in himself, shines well in everything (as non-distinct from the Supreme Self).

शान्तिः : अथ देवस्य मायायां कीदृशोऽनुग्रहः ?

श्रद्धा : ननु निग्रह इति वक्तव्ये कथमनुग्रहः शक्यते वक्तुम् ? देवोऽपि हि सर्वानर्थबीजमियं माया सर्वथा निग्राह्येति मन्यते।

शान्तिः : यद्येवं का तर्हीदानीं राजकुलस्य स्थितिः ?

श्रद्धा : शृणु,

नित्यानित्यविचारणाप्रणयिनी वैराग्यमेकं सुहृ-
त्सन्मित्राणि यमादयः शमदमप्रायाः सहाया मताः ।
मत्र्याद्याः परिचारिकाः सहचरी नित्यं मुमुक्षा बला-
दुच्छेद्या रिपवश्च मोहममतासङ्कल्पसङ्गादयः ॥३॥

शान्तिः : अथ धर्मे स्वामिनः कीदृशः प्रणयः ?

श्रद्धा : पुत्रि, वैराग्यसंनिकर्षात्प्रभृति नितान्तमिहामुत्रफलभोगविरस एव स्वामी । तेन,

स नरकादिव पापफलाद्भयं भजति पुण्यफलादपि नाशिनः ।
इति समुज्झितकामसमन्वयं सुकृतकर्म कथञ्चन मन्यते ॥४॥

किंत्वसौ प्रत्यक्प्रवणतां स्वामिनो विचिन्त्य कृतकर्तव्यमिवात्मानं मत्वा स्वयमेव धर्मः शून्यव्यापारोऽभूत् ।

शान्तिः : अथ तानुपसर्गान् गृहीत्वा, महामोहो निलीय स्थितस्तेषां को वृत्तान्तः ?

श्रद्धा : पुत्रि, तथा दुरवस्थागतेनापि महामोहहतकेन स्वामिनः प्ररोचनाय मधुमत्या विद्यया सहोपसर्गाः प्रेषिताः । अयमभिप्रायः । यद्येतेष्वासक्तः स्वामी विवेक उपनिषच्चिन्तामपि न करिष्यतीति ।

Peace : Then, what is his favour towards Illusion ?

Faith : How can you say favour when you should say disfavour ? The Lord believes that this Illusion who is the source of all troubles should be destroyed by all means.

Peace : If it is so what now is the condition of the Royal family?

Faith : Listen.

His beloved is Inquiry into eternal and non-eternal things, his only friend is Dispassionateness, his truthful allies are Morality etc., Tranquillity, Self-restraint etc. are his attendants, Friendliness and others his servants, Desire for liberation is always his companion. The enemies like Delusion, Feeling of Mineness, Volition, Attachment etc. are to be forcibly uprooted. (3).

Peace : Then what is his feeling towards Dharma?

Faith : Daughter, since he has been associated with Dispassionateness he is very much disinterested in the enjoyments of fruits in this or the other world.

He is afraid of the perishing fruits of meritorious actions in asmuch as he is afraid of hell, which is the fruit of sin. Thus having given up mental concern with objects desired, he observes holy rites to some extent. (4).

But Dharma considering the master's inclination towards the inner self, has himself become void of actions, thinking that he has done his duty.

Peace : Delusion took away the magic faculties with him and hid himself. What news of them ?

Faith : Daughter, Grand Delusion even in that miserable plight (hiding himself) sent forth Honey-Wisdom with the magic faculties to divert Man. (This was the purpose). The idea was that King Discrimination would be attracted by these and he would not even think of Upaniṣad.

शान्तिः : ततस्ततः ?

श्रद्धा : ततस्तैर्गत्वा क्वापि स्वामिन्यैन्द्रजालिकी विद्योपदर्शिता ।
तथा हि,

शब्दानेष शृणोति योजनशतादाविर्भवन्ति स्वत-
स्तास्ता वेदपुराणभारतकथास्तर्कादयो वाङ्मयाः ।
ग्रथ्नाति स्वयमिच्छया शुचिपदैः शास्त्राणि काव्यानि वा
लोकान्भ्राम्यति पश्यति स्फुटरुचो रत्नस्थलीर्मेरवीः ॥५॥

मधुमतीं च भूमिमापन्नः स्थानाभिमानिनीभिर्देवताभिरुपच्छन्द्यते भो इहोपविश्यताम् । नात्र जन्ममृत्यू । अनुपाधिरमणीयो देशः । एष त्वामुपस्थितो विविधविलासलावण्यपुण्यमयो मङ्गलार्थ-व्यग्रपाणिः प्रणयपेशलो विद्याधरीजनः ।

तदेहि, यतोऽत्र—

कनकसिकतिलस्थलाः स्रवन्तीः
पृथुजघनाः कमलानना वरोरूः ।
मरकतदलकोमला वनाली-
र्भज निजपुण्यचितांश्च सर्वभोगान् ॥६॥

शान्तिः : ततस्ततः ?

श्रद्धा : पुत्रि, तदाकर्ण्य मायया श्लाघ्यमेतदित्युक्तम् । मनसा चानुमोदितम् । सङ्कल्पेन प्रोत्साहितम् । स्वामी संप्रति सन्मित्रपथमिवापन्नः ।

शान्तिः : (सखेदम्) हा धिक् हा धिक् पुनरपि तामेव संसारवागुरामपि पतितः स्वामी ।

श्रद्धा : न खलु न खलु ।

शान्तिः : ततस्ततः ?

Peace : And, then ?

Faith : Then they went and performed some magic (on him). For—

He listens to sound at a distance of hundred Yojanas on his own. Passages from Vedas, Purāṇas, Bhārata stories, Tarka etc. manifest themselves to him, he composes works of science and poetry in pure words at his will and roams about the world and sees the shining region of Mount Meru full of gems. (5).

Subjected to Honey-Wisdom, he is being deceived by the presiding deities of places thus: 'Sir, please sit here'. Here there is no birth or death. This place is beautiful by nature. These Vidyādhara ladies who are tender with love, charmingly pleasing with various kinds of amorous gestures are at your service with auspicious objects (like curds, mirror etc.) in their hands. Therefore, come, because here

There are rivers with their banks of golden sand, women with lotus-like faces, heavy hips and big thighs, and rows of trees soft as petals made of emeralds. Enjoy all these pleasures acquired through your own virtues. (6).

Peace : And then ?

Faith : Daughter, hearing this Illusion said 'this is praiseworthy'. And Mind also applauded. Volition encouraged this. Now the Master is as if he has come in the company of good friends.

Peace : (*Sorrowfully*) What a shame, what a shame, again the master has fallen into the snare of mundane existence.

Faith : It must not be, it must not be!

Peace : And then ?

श्रद्धा : ततः परिपार्श्ववर्तिना तर्केण तान्सर्वान्क्रोधावेशकषायितनयनमालोक्याभिहितः । स्वामिन्, किमेवमेभिर्विषयामिषग्रासगृध्नुभिरास्थानिकैः पुनरपि तेष्वेव तथैव विषमविषयाङ्गारेषु निपात्यमानमात्मानं नावबुध्यसे । ननु भोः,

भवसागरतारणाय यासौ नचिराद्योगतरिस्त्वयाश्रिता ।
अधुना परिमुच्य तां मदात्कथमङ्गारनदीं विगाहसे ॥७॥

शान्तिः : ततस्ततः ?

श्रद्धा : ततस्तद्वचनमाकर्ण्य स्वस्ति विषयेभ्य इत्यभिधायावधीरिता मधुमती ।

शान्तिः : साधु साधु । अथ क्व प्रस्थितास्ति भवती ।

श्रद्धा : आदिष्टाहं स्वामिना यथा विवेकं द्रष्टुमिच्छामि ।

शान्तिः : तत्त्वरतां भगवतीति ।

श्रद्धा : तदहं राजसन्निधिं प्रस्थिता ।

शान्तिः : अहमपि महाराजेनोपनिषदमानेतुमादिष्टा । तद्भवतु स्वनियोगं संपादयावः ।

(इति निष्क्रान्ते ।)

प्रवेशकः ।

(ततः प्रविशति पुरुषः ।)

पुरुषः : (विचिन्त्य । सहर्षम्) अहो माहात्म्यं देव्या विष्णुभक्तेः । यत्प्रसादान्मया,

तीर्णाः क्लेशमहोर्मयः परिहृता भीमा ममत्वभ्रमाः
शान्ता मित्रकलत्रबन्धुमकरग्राहग्रहग्रन्थयः ।
क्रोधौर्वाग्निरपाकृतो विघटितास्तृष्णालताविस्तराः
पारेतीरमवाप्तकल्पमधुना संसारवारांनिधेः ॥८॥

(ततः प्रविशत्युपनिषच्छान्तिश्च ।)

उपनिषत् : सखि, कथं तथा निरनुक्रोशस्य स्वामिनो मुखमालोकयिष्यामि । येनाहमितरजनयोषेव सुचिरमेकाकिनी परित्यक्ता ?

Faith : Then, Reasoning who was near him looked at them with his eyes red with anger and told him 'My Lord how is it, you do not realise that you are again being thrown into the same fierce fire of sense objects in the same (old) way by these courtiers of yours who are there (like vultures) to grasp the mouthfuls of flesh i.e. sense objects!'.

Well sir, you who have recently boarded the boat of Yoga, to cross the ocean of worldly illusion, how can you be now so mad as to give up that (boat) and plunge into the river of fire? (7).

Peace : And then?

Faith : Then hearing those words (the king) bidding good-bye to the senses ignored the Honey-Wisdom.

Peace : Well done, well done. Where are you going?

Faith : I have been commanded by the Lord "I wish to see Discrimination".

Peace : Then, you be quick.

Faith : I am also commanded by the king to bring the Sacred Lore. Let us therefore fulfil our respective duties. (*Exeunt*).

INTERLUDE

(*Enters Man*)

Man : (*Musing with Joy*) See, the greatness of Goddess Devotion to Viṣṇu! by whose favour I have crossed the billows of misery, avoided the whirlpools of the feeling of "This is mine", loosened the clutches of the sharks and crocodiles in the form of friends, wife and relatives, removed the submarine fire of anger, torn asunder the spreading creepers of desire, and have almost reached the other shore of the ocean of Saṁsāra. (8).

(*Then enter Upaniṣad and Peace*)

Upaniṣad: Friend, how can I look at the face of the unkind Lord who had left me alone for such a long time as if I was the wife of another.

शान्तिः : देवि, कथं तथाविधविपत्पतितो देव उपालभ्यते ?

उपनिषत् : सखि, न दृष्टा त्वया मे तादृशी दशा। येनैवं ब्रवीषि।

शृणु—

बाह्वोर्भग्ना दलितमणयः श्रेणयः कङ्कणानां
चूडारत्नग्रहनिकृतिभिर्दूषितः केशपाशः।
कैः कैर्नाहं हतविधिबलादोहिता दुर्विदग्धै-
र्दासीकर्तुं सपदि दुरितैर्दूरसंस्थेऽविवेके ॥६॥

शान्तिः : सर्वमेतन्महामोहस्य दुर्विलसितम्। नात्र देवस्यापराधः। तेन मोहेन मनः कामादिद्वारेण प्रबोधयता त्वत्तो दूरीकृतो विवेकः। एतदेव कुलस्त्रीणां नैसर्गिकं शीलं यद्विपन्मग्नस्य स्वामिनः समयप्रतीक्षणमिति। तदेहि दर्शनप्रियालापेन संभावय देवम्। संप्रत्यपहता विद्विषः। संपूर्णास्ते मनोरथाः।

उपनिषत् : सखि, संप्रत्यागच्छन्ती वत्सया गीतयाऽहं रहस्युक्ता यथा भर्ता स्वामी च पुरुषस्त्वया यथाप्रश्नमुत्तरेण संभावयितव्यः। तथा प्रबोधोत्पत्तिर्भविष्यतीति तत्कथं गुरूणामध्यक्षं धार्ष्ट्यमवलम्बिष्ये।

शान्तिः : देवि, अविचारणीयमेतद्वाक्यं भगवत्या गीतायाः, अयमेव चार्थो भगवत्या विष्णुभक्त्या विवेकस्वामिनो निरुक्तः। तदेहि। संभावय दर्शनेन भर्तारमादिपुरुषं च।

उपनिषत् : यथा वदति प्रियसखी। (इति परिक्रामति।)

(ततः प्रविशति राजा श्रद्धा च।)

राजा : अयि वत्से, द्रक्ष्यति शान्तिः प्रियामुपनिषदम्।

श्रद्धा : देव, गृहीतोपदेशैव शान्तिर्गता कथं तां न द्रक्ष्यति ?

Peace : Goddess, how can you blame the Lord who had fallen into such misery?

Upaniṣad: Friend, you did not see my plight that is why you speak like this. Listen.

(When I was being dragged) the rows of bangles with their gems fallen had been broken, and (my) hair was dishevelled by the humiliation caused by the catching hold of my head-ornament. Thus which wicked one (who was there and then) did not desire to make me his slave, such being the strength of my misfortune? (9)

Peace : This is all the evil doing of Delusion. Here my Lord is not in fault. Delusion removed Discrimination from you by instructing the Mind through Concupiscence. etc. But it is the natural disposition of respectable women that they wait for the success of their husbands who are drowned in misery. Therefore come and please my Lord with your appearance and pleasing words. Now the enemies are destroyed. All your desires are fulfilled.

Upaniṣad: Friend, just now while coming I was told in secret by my daughter Gītā that I should please my husband and Man by giving suitable answers to their questions. Then Rise of Awakening will come. But how can I be so confident in the presence of elders?

Peace : Goddess, the saying of Gītā need not be questioned. The same idea was already given to Discrimination by the Goddess Devotion to Viṣṇu. Therefore, come, honour your husband and the Primeaval Man by your appearance.

Upaniṣad: As my dear friend says (*They walk round*)

(*Then enter King and Faith*)

King : My dear, will Peace meet my dear Upaniṣad?

Faith : My Lord, Peace left only after she had received instruction (to do so). Then how will she not meet (her)?

राजा : कथमिव ?

श्रद्धा : देव, प्रागेव कथितमेतद्देव्या विष्णुभक्त्याऽऽसीत्, यथा मन्दराभिधाने शैले विष्णोरायतने देव्यां गीतायां तर्कविद्याभयादनुप्रविष्टेति ।

राजा : कथं पुनस्तर्कविद्याया भयम् ?

श्रद्धा : देव, इममर्थं सैव प्रस्तोष्यति । तदागच्छतु देवः । एष स्वामी त्वदागमनमेव ध्यायन्विविक्ते वर्तते ।

राजा : (उपसृत्य ।) स्वामिन्, अभिवादये ।

पुरुषः : वत्स, प्रक्रमविरुद्धोऽयं समुदाचारः । यतो ज्ञानवृद्धतया भवानेवास्माकमुपदेशदानेन पितृभावमापन्नः । कुतः—

पुरा हि धर्माध्वनि नष्टसंज्ञा
देवास्तमर्थं तनयानपृच्छन् ।
ज्ञानेन सम्यक्परिगृह्य चैतान्
हे पुत्रकाः संशृणुतेत्यवोचन् ॥१०॥

तद्भवान्पितृत्वेनास्मासु वर्ततामित्येष एव धर्मः ।

शान्तिः : एष देवि, देवेन सह स्वामी विविक्तो वर्तते । तदुपसर्पतु देवी ।

उपनिषत् : (उपसर्पति ।)

शान्तिः : स्वामिन्, एषोपनिषद्देवी पादवन्दनायागता ।

पुरुषः : न खलु न खलु । यतो मातेयमस्माकं तत्त्वावबोधोदयेन । तदेषैवास्माकं नमस्या । अथवा

अनुग्रहविधौ देव्या मातुश्च महदन्तरम् ।
माता गाढं निबध्नाति बन्धं देवी निकृन्तति ॥११॥

उपनिषत् : (विवेकमालोक्य नमस्कृत्य दूरे समुपविशति ।)

पुरुषः : अम्ब, कथ्यताम् । क्व भवत्या नीता एते दिवसाः ।

King : How is that ?

Faith : My Lord, Goddess Devotion to Viṣṇu has already told that she (Upaniṣad) out of fear of Logic has entered Goddess Gītā in the temple of Viṣṇu in the mountain called Mandara.

King : Whence is then the fear of Logic ?

Faith : This she herself will explain to you. So, come, my Lord. Here is the Master (Man) sitting alone awaiting your arrival.

King : (*Going near*) Sir, I greet thee.

Man : Son, this formality is opposed to the (usual) order for, as you have greater knowledge you have attained my fatherhood through giving advice to me. For—

In ancient days the gods forgot the path of Dharma and then asked their sons about it. They (the Sons) having grasped them thoroughly through knowledge addressed them thus "Oh Sons! listen well". (10).

Therefore you be towards me like a father. This is the right attitude.

Peace : Goddess, here the master is sitting alone with my Lord. Therefore, go near.

Upaniṣad: (*Goes near.*)

Peace : Master, Goddess Upaniṣad has come to prostrate at your feet.

Man : No. No. She is my mother because of the Rise of the Knowledge of Reality. Therefore she should be respected by us. Or else,

There is a great difference between the way a mother blesses and the way Upaniṣad does. The mother tightens the bondage, while the Goddess cuts it asunder. (11.)

Upaniṣad: (*Seeing, Discrimination salutes him and sits at a distance.*)

Man : Mother, tell us where you spent all these days.

उपनिषत् : स्वामिन्,

नीतान्यमूनि मठचत्वरशून्यदेवा-
गारेषु मूर्खमुखरैः सह वासराणि ।

पुरुषः : अथ ते जानन्ति किमपि भवत्यास्तत्त्वम् ?

उपनिषत् : न खलु । किन्तु

ते स्वेच्छया मम गिरां द्रविडाङ्गनोक्त-
वाचामिवार्थमविचार्य विकल्पयन्ति ॥१२॥

तेन केवलं तेषां परार्थग्रहणप्रयोजनमेव मद्विचारणम् ।

पुरुषः : ततस्ततः ?

उपनिषत् : ततः कदाचित्

कृष्णाजिनाग्निसमिदाज्यजुहूस्रुवादि-
पात्रैस्तथेष्टिपशुसोममुखैर्मखैश्च ।
दृष्टा मया परिवृताखिलकर्मकाण्ड-
व्यादिष्टपद्धतिरथाध्वनि यज्ञविद्या ॥१३॥

पुरुषः : ततस्ततः ?

उपनिषत् : ततो मया चिन्तितम् । अपि नामैषा पुस्तकभारवाहिनी मे ज्ञास्यति तत्त्वम् ? अत एवास्याः सन्निधौ कानिचिद्वासराणि नयामि ।

पुरुषः : ततस्ततः ?

उपनिषत् : ततस्तामहमुपस्थिता । तया चाहमुक्तास्मि । भद्रे, किं ते समीहितमिति । ततो मयोक्तम् । आर्ये अनाथास्मि त्वयि निवस्तुमिच्छामीति ।

पुरुषः : ततस्ततः ?

उपनिषत् : ततो मयोक्तम् ।

यस्माद्विश्वमुदेति यत्र रमते यस्मिन्पुनर्लीयते
भासा यस्य जगद्विभाति सहजानन्दोज्ज्वलं यन्महः ।
शान्तं शाश्वतमक्रियं यमपुनर्भावाय भूतेश्वरं
द्वैतध्वान्तमपास्य यान्ति कृतिनः प्रस्तौमि तं पूरुषम् ॥१४॥

Upaniṣad: Lord,

I spent these days of mine in the retreats of Sannyasins, in public places and empty temples in the company of talkative fools.

Man : Do they know anything of your philosophy ?

Upaniṣad: No, but,

They interpret my word by arbitrary conjuctures without understanding their meaning, as if they were spoken by the Dravida woman. (12).

The purpose of their discussion is only to get some other meaning which suits their own philosophy.

Man : Then ?

Upaniṣad: Then, once,

I came across Yajñavidyā on the way, surrounded by deer skins, fire, sacrificial fuel, clarified butter, sacrificial vessels like the ladies called Juhu, Sruva etc., and with sacrifices, among which oblations, animal sacrifices and Soma sacrifices are prominent and the performance of which is described in all ritual texts. (13).

Man : Then ?

Upaniṣad: I thought : 'May she that carries the burden of books know me. I shall therefore stay with her for a few days.'

Man : Then ?

Upaniṣad: Then I went near her. She then told me, 'My dear, what do you want ?' Then I told her: Revered one, having no shelter I would like to stay with you.

Man : Then?

Upaniṣad: Then I said:

I adore that Puruṣa out of whom the Universe arises, in whom it exists with joy, and into whom it is absorbed again, by whose lustre the world shines (i. e. becomes manifest), the light that is effulgent with its natural bliss; the Lord of all beings who is tranquil, eternal and without actions, to whom holy men go after having dispelled the darkness of duality, not to come back again. (14).

ततस्तयोक्तम्—

पुमानकर्ता कथमीश्वरो भवेत्
क्रिया भवोच्छेदकरी न वस्तुधीः ।
कुर्वन्क्रिया एव नरो भवच्छिदः
शतं समाः शान्तमना जिजीविषेत् ॥१५॥

तन्मे नातिप्रयोजनं भवत्याः परिग्रहेण तथापि यदि कर्तारं भोक्तारं पुरुषं स्तुवन्ती भवती कियन्तं कालमत्र वस्तुमिच्छति को दोषः ?

राजा : (सोपहासम् ।) अहो धूमान्धकारश्यामलितदृशो वृष्प्रज्ञत्वं यज्ञविद्याया येनैवं कुतर्कोपहता ।

अयः स्वभावादचलं बलाच्चल-
त्यचेतनं चुम्बकसन्निधाविव ।
तनोति विश्वेक्षितुरीक्षितेरिता
जगन्ति मायेश्वरतेयमीशितुः ॥१६॥

तस्मात्तमोन्धानामियमनीश्वरदृष्टिः । अबोधप्रभवं संसारं कर्मभिः शमयन्ती यज्ञविद्या नूनमन्धतमसमन्धकारेणापि निनीषति ।

स्वभावलोनानि तमोमयानि
प्रकाशयेद्यो भुवनानि सप्त ।
तमेव विद्वानतिमृत्युमेति
नान्योऽस्ति पन्था भवमुक्तिहेतुः ॥१७॥

पुरुषः : ततस्ततः ।

उपनिषत् : ततो यज्ञविद्यया विमृश्योक्तम् । सखि, त्वत्संनिकर्षात् दुर्वासनोपहतैरस्मदन्तेवासिभिः कर्मसु श्लथादरैर्भवितव्यम् । तत्प्रसीदतु भवती स्वाभिलषितदेशगमनाय ।

Then she said,

How can a Puruṣa who is not an agent be the Supreme Lord ? Action alone destroys Saṁsāra, not the Knowledge of truth. Only a man destroying Saṁsāra by performing actions can desire to live for a hundred years with tranquil mind. (15).

So I do not benefit much by accepting you. Even then, what is the harm if you stay here sometime, praising that Puruṣa, who is an agent and enjoyer ?

King : (*In derision*) Oh! How corrupt is the Knowledge of Yajñavidyā whose vision is darkened by the darkness of the smoke, and hence she is deluded by heretic logic.

As iron, though motionless by nature and non-sentient, is forced to move in the proximity of a magnet, in the same way Illusion is prompted to spread out the worlds by the (mere) looking-on of the spectator of the Universe. This is what constitutes the Lord's quality of being the Lord. (16).

Therefore the view that there is no Supreme Lord is that of those who are blinded by ignorance. Yajñavidyā desiring to annihilate the Saṁsāra which is caused by ignorance through actions (which are themselves a result of ignorance) is definitely desiring to remove pitch darkness through darkness.

Knowing him who illumines the seven worlds which are of perishable nature and full of darkness, the wise man transcends death. There is no other path leading to freedom from existence. (17).

Man : Then ?

Upaniṣad: Then Yajñavidyā said after some reflection : My friend, in your company our disciples will be influenced by bad tendencies and they will not respect Karma. Therefore be pleased to go to the place of your liking.

पुरुषः : ततस्ततः ?

उपनिषत् : ततोऽहं तामतिक्रम्य प्रस्थिता ।

पुरुषः : ततस्ततः ?

उपनिषत् : ततः कर्मकाण्डसहचरी मीमांसा मया दृष्टा—

विभिद्य कर्माण्यधिकारभाञ्जि
श्रुत्यादिभिश्चानुगता प्रमाणैः ।
अङ्गैर्विचित्रै रभियोजयन्ती
प्राप्तोपदेशैरतिदेशकैश्च ॥१८॥

पुरुषः : ततस्ततः ?

उपनिषत् । ततोऽहं तामपि तथैवाश्रयमभ्यर्थितवती । अथ तयाप्युक्तास्मि भद्रे, किंकर्मासीति । ततो मया तदेवोक्तम् । यस्माद्विश्वमित्यादि पठितम् ।

पुरुषः : ततस्ततः ?

उपनिषत् : ततो मीमांसया पार्श्ववर्तिनां मुखमालोक्याभिहितम् । अस्त्येवास्माकमस्याः लोकान्तरफलोपभोगयोग्यपुरुषोपनयनेनोपयोगः । तत्क्रियतामेषां कर्मोपयुक्तम् । तत्र तेषामन्तेवासिनां मध्ये केनाप्यन्तेवासिनैतदनुमोदितमेव । अपरेण तु प्रसिद्धप्रतिष्ठेन मीमांसाहृदयाधिदैवतेन कुमारिलस्वामिनैवं प्रोक्तम्—देवि, नेयं कर्मोपयुक्तं पुरुषमुपनयति, किन्तु अकर्तारमभोक्तारमीश्वरम् । न चासावीश्वरः कर्मसूपयुज्यते । ततोऽपरेणोक्तम् । अथ किं लौकिकात्पुरुषादन्य ईश्वरो नामास्ति ? ततस्तेन विहस्य पुनरुक्तम् । अस्ति । तथा हि—

एकः पश्यति चेष्टितानि जगतामन्यस्तु मोहान्धधी-
रेकः कर्मफलानि वाञ्छति ददात्यन्यस्तु तान्यर्थिने ।
एकः कर्मसु शिष्यते तनुभृतां शास्तेव देवोऽपरो
निःसङ्गः पुरुषः क्रियासु स कथं कर्तेति संभाव्यते ॥१९॥

राजा : (सहर्षम्) साधु कुमारिलस्वामिन्, साधुप्रज्ञोऽस्यायुष्मन्,

Man : Then ?

Upaniṣad: Then I left her and proceeded.

Man : And then ?

Upaniṣad: Then I met Mīmāṁsā, the friend of Karma-Kāṇḍa,

Attended by the means of Knowledge like Śruti etc., dividing the rituals according to qualifications, and joining them with various auxiliaries according to the available injunctions and rules for extended application. (18).

Man : Then ?

Upaniṣad: Then I entreated her too for shelter. She too asked me, What do you want ? I then repeated, "From whence the Universe, etc."

Man : And then ?

Upaniṣad: Then Mīmāṁsā looked at the face of the people sitting around and said: 'The Puruṣa (1) who is capable of enjoyment in the other world (who is other than the body) whom she (Upaniṣad) has brought will serve our purpose. Therefore make her to accept ritual action (as means of salvation). One of the disciples then approved this. But another well renowned one Kumarila who is the presiding disciple deity of the heart of Mīmāṁsā said: "Goddess, she does not bring a Puruṣa fit for action but a Lord who is neither a doer nor an enjoyer. This Lord cannot be used for action." Then some-one else queried, 'Is there a Lord who is other than the Puruṣa living in the world ?' Then he smiled and said again. Yes. It is thus:

There is one who beholds the actions of the Creatures, while the other's intellect is blinded by delusion; one desires the fruits of actions while the other gives them to the seeker; one engages himself in actions while the other is a deity, the protector, as it were, of the embodied ones; how can this Puruṣa, who is not attached to actions, be considered to be an agent? (19).

King : (With joy) Well said Kumārila, your understanding is correct.

द्वौ तौ सुपर्णौ सयुजौ सखायौ
समानवृक्षं परिषस्वजाते ।
एकस्तयोः पिप्पलमत्ति पक्व-
मन्यस्त्वनश्नन्नभिचाकशीति ।।२०।।

पुरुषः : ततस्ततः ?

उपनिषत् : ततोऽहं मीमांसामभिमन्त्र्य प्रस्थिता ।

पुरुषः : ततस्ततः ?

उपनिषत् : ततो मया बहुभिः शिष्यैरुपास्यमानास्तर्कविद्या अवलोकिताः ।

काचिद्विश्वविशेषकल्पनपरा न्यायैः परा तन्वती
वादं सच्छलजातिनिग्रहमयैर्जल्पं वितण्डामपि ।
अन्या तु प्रकृतेर्विभज्य पुरुषस्योदाहरन्तो भिदां
तत्त्वानां गणनापरा महदहंकारादिसर्गक्रमैः ।।२१।।

पुरुषः : ततस्ततः ?

उपनिषत् : तथैवाहं ताः समुपस्थिता । ताभिश्चानुयुक्तया मया तदेव कर्मोदाहृतम् । यस्माद्विश्वमित्यादि । ततस्ताभिः सप्रकाशोपहासमुक्तम्——आः वाचाले, परमाणुभ्यो विश्वमुत्पद्यते । निमित्तकारणमीश्वरः । अन्यया तु सक्रोधमुक्तम्——आः पापे, कथमीश्वरमेव विकारिणं कृत्वा विनाशधर्मिणमुपपादयसि । ननु रे प्रधानाद्विश्वोत्पत्तिः ।

राजा : अहो तर्कमतयस्तर्कविद्या एतदपि न जानन्ति । सर्वं प्रमेयजातं घटादिवत्कार्यमिति परमाणुप्रधानोपादानकारणमप्युपेक्षणीयमेवेति । तथा हि——

Two birds with beautiful feathers, inseparable friends, cling to one and the same tree; one of them eats the ripe fruit while the other looks on without eating. (20).

Man : Then ?

Upaniṣad: Then I took leave of Mīmāṁsā and proceeded.

Man : And then ?

Upaniṣad: Then I met Rational Philosophies accompanied by many disciples.

One of the schools of Tarkavidyā viz. Vaiśeṣika, is engaged in establishing the differential (Viśeṣa) of the Universe; another (viz. Nyāya) deals with disputation (Jalpa), discussion (Vāda) and polemics (Vitaṇḍā) by arguments containing good tricks (chala), futile answers (Jāti) and faulty syllogisms (nigraha); yet another (viz. Sāṁkhya) stating the difference between matter and soul after separating them is engaged in enumerating the principles Mahat, Ahaṁkāra etc., in the order of cosmogony. (21).

Man : Then ?

Upaniṣad: Then I went near them. When asked by them I told the same thing "From whence the Universe etc." Then they openly ridiculed me and said, "Oh talkative one, the universe originates from actions. God is only an efficient cause." Another one said with anger, "Oh ! sinful one ! how can you make the Lord subject to change and hence attribute to him perishable properties ? Oh, you, the world arises from Primary Matter."

King : Well, the logic-minded schools of Logic do not even know this. Every thing which is an act of knowledge is an effect like a pot. (Therefore the ideas of) the atoms or primary matter being the material cause of the world are to be discarded.

अम्भःशीतकरान्तरिक्षनगरस्वप्नेन्द्रजालादिवत्
कार्यं मेयमसत्यमेतदुदयध्वंसादियुक्तं जगत् ।
शुक्तौ रूप्यमिव स्रजीव भुजगः स्वात्मावबोधे हरा-
वज्ञाते प्रभवत्यथास्तमयते तत्त्वावबोधोदयात् ॥२२॥

विकारशङ्का तु मुग्धवधूविकल्पविलसितमिव । तथा हि—

शान्तं ज्योतिः कथमनुदितानन्दनित्यप्रकाशं
विश्वोत्पत्तौ व्रजति विकृतिं निष्कलं निर्मलं च ।
तद्वन्नीलोत्पलदलरुचामम्बुवाहावलीनां
प्रादुर्भावे भवति नभसः कीदृशो वा विकारः ॥२३॥

पुरुषः : साधु साधु, प्रीणयति मानसं ममायं प्रज्ञावतो विमर्शः । (उपनिषदं प्रति) ततस्ततः ?

उपनिषत् : ततस्ताभिः सर्वाभिरेव क्रुद्धाभिरुक्तम्—अहो, विश्वविलयेन मुक्तिमेषां वदन्ती नास्तिकपथं प्रस्थिता निगृह्यतामिति । ततः ससंरम्भं मां निग्रहीतुं प्रधाविताः सर्वाः ।

पुरुषः : (सत्रासम्) ततस्ततः ?

उपनिषत् : ततोऽहं सत्वरतरं परिक्रम्य दण्डकारण्यं प्रविष्टा । ततो मन्दार-शैलोपकल्पितस्य मधुसूदनायतनस्य नातिदूरे—

बाह्वोर्भग्ना दलितमणयः श्रेणयः कङ्कणानां
चूडारत्नग्रहनिकृतिभिर्दूषितः केशपाशः ।

इत्याद्यवस्था मम संजाता ।

पुरुषः : ततस्ततः ?

उपनिषत् : यतो देवायतनान्निर्गत्य गदापाणिभिः पुरुषैरतिनिर्दयं ताड्य-मानास्ता दिगन्तमतिक्रान्ताः सर्वाः ।

For—

Just as the moon seen in water, just as a city in the sky, just as dreams and magic, so also the Universe is an effect, an object of knowledge, unreal, subject to origin, destruction etc. It arises when Viṣṇu, who is self awakening is unknown, like silver in a shell and a serpent in a garland, but disappears when the knowledge of truth has arisen. (22).

The apprehension of mutability (of the Absolute) is like the behaviour of a mentally deluded woman.

How can that tranquil Light, which is beginningless bliss, eternally luminous, partless and stainless, be subject to changes when the Universe originates ? In the same way, what kind of change happens to the sky when rows of clouds shining like the petals of a blue lotus appear ? (23).

Man : Well done, well done, this discourse of an intelligent one pleases my mind. (Towards Upaniṣad). Then ?

Upaniṣad: Then I was told by all of them who were angry: "Kill her who has become an atheist by saying that liberation is attained by the annihilation of the Universe." Then all of them rushed to kill me.

Man : (*In fear*) Then ?

Upaniṣad: Then I ran fast and entered the Daṇḍaka forest. Then not far from the temple of Madhusūdana built by the stones of Mandara mountain, I whose rows of bangles with their gems had fallen and broken etc., was subjected to this plight.

Man : Then ?

Upaniṣad: Then some people with clubs in their hands came out of the temple and beat them mercilessly.

Then they who were all beaten mercilessly by some people with clubs in their hands who came out of the temple, crossed the borders and fled away.

राजा : (सहर्षम् ।) न खलु भवतीमतिक्रामतो भगवान् विश्वसाक्षी क्षमते ।

पुरुषः : ततस्ततः ?

उपनिषत् :

छिन्ना मुक्तावलिरपहृतं स्रस्तमङ्गाद्दुकूलं
भीता गीताश्रममथ गलन्नूपुराहं प्रविष्टा ॥२४॥

तत्र वत्सया गीतया मां तत्रागतामालोक्य ससंभ्रमं मातर्मातरिति परिरभ्योपवेशितास्मि । विदितवृत्तान्तया तया चोक्तम् । अम्ब, नात्र खेदयितव्यं मनः । ये खलु त्वामप्रमाणीकृत्य यथेष्टमसुरसत्त्वाः प्रचरिष्यन्ति तेषामीश्वर एव शास्ता । उक्तं च तेन भगवता तानधिकृत्य । तथा च गीतायाम्—'तानहं द्विषतः क्रूरान्संसारेषु नराधमान् । क्षिपाम्यजस्रमशुभानासुरीष्वेव योनिषु' इति ।

पुरुषः : (सकौतुकम् ।) देवि, त्वत्प्रसादाज्ज्ञातुमिच्छामि कोऽयमीश्वरो नामेति ।

उपनिषत् : (सकोपमिव ।) को नामात्मानमजानन्तमन्धमिव प्रत्युत्तरं दास्यति ।

पुरुषः : (सहर्षम् ।) कथमहमात्मा पुरुषः परमेश्वरः ।

उपनिषत् : एवमेतत् । तथाहि—

असौ त्वदन्यो न सनातनः पुमान्
भवान्न देवात्पुरुषोत्तमात्परः ।
स एष भिन्नस्त्वदनादिमायया
द्विधेव बिम्बं सलिले विवस्वतः ॥२५॥

पुरुषः : (विवेकं प्रति ।) भगवन्, उक्तमप्यर्थं भगवत्या न सम्यगवधारयामि ।

अवच्छिन्नस्य भिन्नस्य जरामरणधर्मिणः ।
मम ब्रवीति देवीयं सत्यानन्दचिदात्मताम् ॥२६॥

King : (*With joy*) The Lord who is the witness of everything does not endure anybody who violates you.

Man : Then?

Upaniṣad: Then with my pearl necklace shattered to pieces and the upper garment which slipped from my person taken away, and with my anklets slipping I entered the hermitage of Gītā full of terror. (24).

There my daughter Gītā who saw me coming hurriedly came to me calling "Mother, Mother," embraced me and made me sit. After coming to know what had happened, she said: "Mother, do not be mentally distressed. God will take care of those demoniac people who disregarding you preach (their own philosophy) freely. Concerning them the Lord himself said "I will cast down these malicious cruel abject wretches in the demoniac wombs".

Man : (*With curiosity*) Goddess, by your grace I wish to know who this God is ?

Upaniṣad: (*As if with Anger*) Who can give a reply to one who like a blind man does not know his own self?

Man : (*With delight*) What ! Am I the man, the self, the Supreme Lord?

Upaniṣad: It is so. For—

The eternal Puruṣa is no other than you, and you are not different from that Lord, the Supreme Puruṣa. Through beginningless Illusion, he is separate from you, like the reflection of the Sun in water. (25)

Man : (*To Discrimination*) Sir, I do not fully comprehend what this Goddess has said.

This Goddess says that I am different from God, am limited and am subject to old age and death; am identical with Reality, Bliss and Intelligence. ! (26).

विवेकः : पदार्थानवज्ञानाद्वाक्यार्थो नावगम्यते । आर्येणोक्तं यत्सत्यमेव ।

पुरुषः : तदवबोधाय भगवानुपायमाज्ञापयतु ।

विवेकः : अयमुच्यते —

एषोऽस्मीति विविच्य नेतिपदतश्चित्तेन साधँ कृते
तत्त्वानां विलये चिदात्मनि परिज्ञाते त्वमर्थे पुनः ।
श्रुत्वा तत्त्वमसीति बाधितभवध्वान्तं तदात्मप्रभं
शान्तं ज्योतिरनन्तमन्तरुदितानन्दः समुद्द्योतते ॥२७॥

पुरुषः : (सानन्दम् ।) श्रुतमर्थं परिभावयति ।

(ततः प्रविशति निदिध्यासनम् ।)

निदिध्यासनम् : आदिष्टोऽस्मि भगवत्या विष्णुभक्त्या । यथा निगूढमस्मदभिप्रायमुपनिषद्विवेकेन सह बोधयितव्या । त्वया च पुरुषे वस्तव्यमिति । (विलोक्य ।) एषा देवी विवेकपुरुषाभ्यां नातिदूरे वर्तते । यावदुपसर्पामि (उपसृत्य उपनिषदं प्रति जनान्तिकम् ।) देव्या विष्णुभक्त्या समादिष्टं यथा संकल्पयोनयो देवता भवन्ति । मया च समाधानेन विदितं तथा आपन्नसत्त्वा भवतीति । तत्र च क्रूरसत्त्वा विद्या नाम कन्या त्वदुदरे वर्तते प्रबोधोदयश्च । तत्र विद्यां सङ्कर्षविद्यया मनसि संक्रामयिष्यसि । प्रबोधचन्द्रं पुरुषे समर्प्य वत्सविवेकेन सह मत्समीपमागमिष्यसीति ।

Discri. : The meaning of the sentence is not comprehended because the meanings of the words are not understood. So what you said is true.

Man : Please inform me the means by which one gets that understanding.

Discri. : It is thus:

"This I am" the idea of the pure spiritual essence of the self is mixed up with the mind. When the purely spiritual self has been discriminated with the aid of "not this", when the gross elements have been dissolved by thinking that they are in reality nothing but this state, then the meaning of "thou" is known to be the spiritual self. Then, on hearing "Thou Art That", (the self) becomes effulgent with bliss internally abounding the self luminous, tranquil, infinite light, from which the darkness of Saṁsāra has been removed. (27).

Man : (*Blissfully*) He contemplates on the meaning of all that has been heard.

(*Then enters Contemplation*).

Contemp : I have been commanded by the Goddess Devotion to Viṣṇu : "You should make Upaniṣad along with Discrimination, understand my view-point. You should remain in the man. (*Looking*) Here is the Goddess not far from Discrimination and Man. I shall go near her (*Going near Upaniṣad and aside*). Goddess Devotion to Viṣṇu has said that the divine beings conceive by volition (will). I have understood through meditation that you are pregnant. There is in your womb a daughter of cruel nature called Knowledge, and also the Rise of Awakening. There through the science of Attraction transfer Knowledge to Mind. Handing over Rise of Spiritual Awakening to Man come to me along with dear Discrimination".

उपनिषत् : यदादिशति देवी। (इति विवेकमादाय निष्क्रान्ता।)

(निदिध्यासनं पुरुषो विशति।)

पुरुषः : (ध्यानं नाटयति।)

(नेपथ्ये आश्चर्यमाश्चर्यम्।)

उद्दामद्युतिदामभिस्तडिदिव प्रद्योतयन्ती दिशः
प्रत्यग्रस्फुटदुत्कटास्थि मनसो निर्भिद्य वक्षःस्थलम्।
कन्येयं सहसा समं परिकरैर्मोहं ग्रसन्ती भज-
त्यन्तर्धानमुपैति चैकपुरुषं श्रीमान्प्रबोधोदयः ॥२८॥

(ततः प्रविशति प्रबोधोदयः।)

प्रबोधोदयः

किं वाप्तं किमपोहितं किमुदितं किं वा समुत्सारितं
स्यूतं किं नु विलायितं नु किमिदं किंचिन्न वा किंचन।
यस्मिन्नभ्युदिते वितर्कपदवीं नैवं समारोहति
त्रैलोक्यं सहजप्रकाशदलितं सोऽहं प्रबोधोदयः ॥२९॥

(परिक्रम्य।) एष पुरुषः। यावदुपसर्पामि। (उपसृत्य।)

भगवन्, प्रबोधचन्द्रोदयोऽहमभिवादये।

पुरुषः (साह्लादम्।) एहि पुत्र, परिष्वजस्व माम्।

(प्रबोधोदयस्तथा करोति।)

पुरुषः : (सानन्दम्।) अहो, विघटिततिमिरपटलं प्रभातं संजातम्।

तथा हि—

मोहान्धकारमवधूय विकल्पनिद्रा-
मुन्मथ्य कोऽप्यजनि बोधतुषाररश्मिः।
श्रद्धाविवेकमतिशान्तियमादिकेन
विश्वात्मकः स्फुरति विष्णुरहं स एषः ॥३०॥

सर्वथा कृतकृत्योऽस्मि भगवत्या विष्णुभक्तेः प्रसादात्।

सोऽहमिदानीम्—

सङ्गं न केनचिदुपेत्य किमप्यपृच्छन्
गच्छन्नतर्कितफलं विदिशं दिशं वा।
शान्तो व्यपेतभयशोककषायमोहः
स्वायंभुवो मुनिरहं भवितास्मि सद्यः ॥३१॥

Upaniṣad: As the Goddess commands. (*Goes away taking Discrimination*) (*Contemplation enters Man*)

Man : (*Meditates*)

(*Behind the Curtain— Wonderful, Wonderful*)

This girl (Knowledge) suddenly comes out freshly breaking the hard chest of Mind and disappears suddenly devouring Delusion along with his followers. And Rise of Spiritual Awakening goes to the One Puruṣa. (28).

Rise of S. A. : I am the Rise of Spiritual Awakening by whose rising the three worlds, destroyed by (my) natural splendour, cease to be the object of arguments such as whether they are attained or lost, born or destroyed, woven together or dissolved or whether they are something or nothing. (29).

(*Turning round*)—Here is Man, let me go near (*Going near*) Sir, I, Rise of the Moon of (Spiritual) Awakening, salute you.

Man : (*Joyfully*) Come son, embrace me.

(*Rise of the Moon of Spiritual Awakening does so*)

Man : (*Blissfully*) Dawn has come destroying the layers of darkness. For—

After shaking off the darkness of delusion, after throwing off the sleep of error, a cool ray of Awakening has been born. I am that Viṣṇu who becomes manifest as the Universal Self through faith, discrimination, reason, peace, self-restraint etc. (30).

By all means by the grace of Devotion to Viṣṇu, I have attained what is to be attained.

Now I shall be a sage who is in a house only at night, who is not attached to anything, who does not ask for anything, who wanders in any direction without aiming at any fruit, tranquil, free from fear, sorrow, impurities and delusion. (31).

(ततः प्रविशति विष्णुभक्तिः ।)

विष्णुभक्तिः : (सहर्षमुपसृत्य ।) चिरेण खल्वस्माकं संपन्नाः सर्वे मनोरथा येन प्रशान्तारातिं भवन्तमवलोकयामि ।

पुरुषः : देव्या विष्णुभक्तेः प्रसादात्किं नाम दुष्करम् ? (इति पादयोः पतति ।)

विष्णुभक्तिः : (पुरुषमुत्थापयति ।) उत्तिष्ठ वत्स, किं ते भूयः प्रियमुपकरोमि ।

पुरुषः : अतः परमपि किं प्रियमस्ति ? यतः—

प्रशान्तारातिरगमद्विवेकः कृतकृत्यताम् ।
नीरजस्के सदानन्दे पदे चाहं निवेशितः ॥३२॥

तथाप्येतदस्तु (भरतवाक्यम् ।)

पर्जन्योऽस्मिन् जगति महतीं वृष्टिमिष्टां विधत्तां
राजानः क्ष्मां गलितविविधोपप्लवाः पालयन्तु ।
हत्वोन्मेषोपहततमसस्त्वत्प्रसादान्महान्तः
संसाराब्धिं विषयममतातङ्कपङ्कं तरन्तु ॥३३॥

(इति निष्क्रान्ताः सर्वे ।)

इति श्रीकृष्णमिश्रविरचिते प्रबोधचन्द्रोदयनाम्नि नाटके
जीवन्मुक्तिर्नाम षष्ठोऽङ्कः ॥६॥

समाप्तमिदं नाटकम् ।

(*Then enters Devotion to Viṣṇu*)

D. Viṣṇu : (*Approaching joyfully*) All my wishes have been speedily accomplished. I now behold you who have vanquished all the enemies.

Man : When there is the grace of Devotion to Viṣṇu what thing is difficult to be achieved ? (*Flls at her feet*).

D. Viṣṇu : (*Raising him up*) Rise up son. What more pleasure can I give to you ?

Man : What can be more pleasant than this. For—

Discrimination whose enemies are vanquished has done his duty, and I am placed in the (Supreme Lord) who is always Bliss and Stainless. (32).

Even then let this be there:

Let the raining clouds shower plenty of rain on the earth; may the kings with all calamities overcome rule the earth, may the great men cross the ocean of Saṁasāra full of the mire of mineness, by your grace, after removing the darkness (of ignorance) through awakening (of knowledge). (33).

(*Exeunt omnes*)

Index of Verses occurring in the Play